FUN –draiser for UCC

Sell Cookie Dough

Talent Show sign up for the talent show, (with an entry fee)

Jail —

Short Story essay —

Pictionary —

SECRETS OF
SUCCESSFUL
FUNDRAISING

The Best From The
Non-Profit Pros

COMPILED AND EDITED BY
CAROL WEISMAN

This Book is a Gift

From:

_____

To:

_____

SECRETS OF
SUCCESSFUL
FUNDRAISING
The Best From The
Non-Profit Pros

COMPILED AND EDITED BY
CAROL WEISMAN

Published by
F. E. Robbins & Sons Press
St. Louis, Missouri

Copyright © 2000 by Board Builders
Second printing 2002, revised

48 Granada Way
St. Louis, MO 63124
1-888-500-1777
Fax: 314-991-0202
E-mail: carol@boardbuilders.com
www.boardbuilders.com

Illustration by Sandy Sineff

Cover and text layout by Ad Graphics, Inc., Tulsa, OK • 918-252-1103

Printed in the United States of America.

ISBN 0-9666168-2-0

SECRETS OF
SUCCESSFUL
FUNDRAISING

The Best From The
Non-Profit Pros

COMPILED AND EDITED BY

CAROL WEISMAN

Preface

As competition for the charitable dollar continues to heat up, nonprofits are asking some very fundamental questions about new ways to raise funds to support their missions. This book is about choices and options. It is about getting past "We've always done it this way, we've tried that before, and it's not my job." This is not an "everything you've always wanted to know" book. It is not a book about one way of doing things. In fact, we can't even agree on the spelling of fundraising. You'll see it as one word, two words, and hyphenated!

Many of the authors, such as Peter Brinckerhoff, Elaine Floyd and myself have other books out on their topics which describe the "how to" of social entrepreneurism, writing newsletters and governance in far greater detail.

You might want to contact some of the authors directly for additional information or specific project help, which is why we've included their contact information. Steve Epner, Jeane Vogel, Peter Brinckerhoff, Davis Allen, David LaGreca, Terrie Temkin, Mark Mersmann and Art Seltzer, Larry Checco and I have full time consulting practices. Steve Epner, Terrie Temkin, Peter Brinckerhoff, David LaGreca and I are also on the speaking circuit. If you have a crowd and a check, we love to speak. (This is not to say that all of us don't do some pro-bono work.)

Folks ask me how I put the team of authors together. Some are old friends, like Stan Corfman who I've known for a million years from Star Island, a Unitarian retreat center we go to in the summer. Peter Brinckerhoff and Steve Epner have been my mentors since I began my business. David LaGreca and I met when we were both bidding for the same work. (He got the job!) Jill Osur was in an audience I spoke to, asking fabulous questions. David Campbell and I met because we are on the faculty of the Learning Institute for Nonprofit Organizations together.

Some folks, like Jeane Vogel and Davis Allen, I've met because they have done a great job for my clients. Terrie Temkin wrote a marvelous article years ago which I forwarded to a client. I wrote her a fan letter and we became friends. Elaine Floyd was one of the many gifts I've received from my membership in the National Speaker's Association. The first time I met Larry Checco, he was in a tuxedo at a black tie dinner in D.C., the next time in a bathing suit, poolside in Miami. I can't wait to see what he has on when we next meet! I heard Eleanor Cicerchi at a workshop and was awed by her knowledge of direct mail. Mary Ann Blank, Mike Schroeder and Kathleen Rae King began as clients and have become friends. Kathleen particularly wanted to thank her development team for their input and words of wisdom for her chapter. Mark Mersmann and Art Seltzer work with my pal Steve Epner. And finally, I have yet to meet Cele Garrett in person. We met over the phone when she called me about an article she was writing.

The team at Ad Graphics who designed the cover and set the pages are an absolute joy to work with. They are either saints or have incredible medication bills. I think it's probably the former.

Thanks to Dr. Sandy Sineff for his wonderful cartoon and to Babette Morgan for her excellent copy editing. Speaking of editing, I want to thank the authors for their incredible patience. I'm dyslexic. When they would get rough drafts of materials, I would manage to spell their names differently every time. It was never disrespectful, but rather a genetically predetermined bent towards highly creative spelling.

I must be living under a lucky star to have Maureen Gelzer as my assistant. She is totally responsible for updating this revised addition. Thank you. Thank you. Thank you.

And as always, a special thank you to my husband Frank Robbins who shares my delight when a particularly marvelous chapter comes in and listens to my rantings when things don't go as planned.

Because of this incredible team, I think we have produced a book that will help you find more money for your mission.

Carol Weisman

Dedication

For all those who have the courage to ask,
And to all who have the heart to say "YES!"

Table of Contents

THE CUTTING EDGE

TOOLS AND TECHNIQUES TO MAKE IT WORK

"If you have some extra money, we have a building on its way, but we have nothing to put in it like chairs. So if you have extra money in your pocket and it's making you feel bulky and unsightly, please give us lots of money and you will get a much better chair in heaven. Maybe closer to the dessert table."

— Anne Lamott

WHERE TO START

CHAPTER 1

Getting Comfortable with the F Word: Fund-raising and the Nonprofit Board Member

Carol Weisman

Many of us grew up with the philosophy that it is not polite to discuss money, that there is perhaps something even obscene about the topic. I contend that the real obscenity is to tolerate poverty, disease, hunger, or a world without the arts. Money can make a big difference in attacking these fronts, which is an excellent reason to talk about it, and how to get more of it for your nonprofit organization.

Some surprises are great: winning the lottery, finding out you have a large tax refund on the way, getting a raise. Some surprises are not so great. Like joining a nonprofit board and finding out after you're in the boardroom that there are major financial expectations, both to give and get money.

While few people join boards because they just love to raise money, the sooner they get comfortable with the concept and how critical it is, the better. Here goes.

Where to start:

Fundraising must begin at home. If board members expect the community to support their organization, the first thing they need to do is to write checks of their own. Granted, the size of the donations may vary greatly, but each member needs to write a check.

There are several reasons for this. A donation should be viewed as an investment rather than a gift. The difference between an investment and a gift is that with an investment, there is an expectation of a future relationship that includes dividends. When you buy stock, you follow the market to chart its progress. An investment in a nonprofit implies the same kind of involvement and vigilance.

Many of us who buy stock also make a concerted effort to purchase the products in which we have invested. It is the same with investing in a nonprofit. Sometimes you will be the direct user of the service such as becoming a season subscriber with an arts group. Sometimes you will refer others if it is a service that you don't currently need, such as services from a food pantry or from a disease-specific group.

Another reason for board members to financially support their organizations is that this is an expectation of funders. The question of 100 percent board giving is frequently one of the first questions asked by funders. Why should they give their institutional dollars if the group closest to the organization doesn't personally support the cause?

A third reason is to avoid hypocrisy. How can board members ask someone else to do something they won't do? Granted, all of us can't write a seven-figure check, but all of us can write a check, even if it's only for $5.00.

We have a development staff. Why should we have to get involved?

Still, many boards are reluctant to get involved with fundraising. Some will go to great lengths to avoid it. One board asked me to help it hire a development director so that it wouldn't have to deal with fund raising anymore.

Development staff and boards have to work together like truffle hound and master. One has to point out the treasure and the other has to dig it up. The roles may vary, but it has to be a team effort. If you're not going to get involved, I said, don't waste your money on hiring someone. The board assured me I was wrong.

One year and three development directors later, we met again. Board members were still in avoidance. "Couldn't we form a development board to raise the money?" they asked. I suggested they bite the bullet, get some training and try it themselves. They cried uncle and got to work.

Once they started to raise money on their own, working with a development professional proved a whole lot easier.

It takes some effort for board and staff to work well together. Board members frequently don't understand the development process, and staff members may overlook some complicating factors.

The most common aspect of the giving process that staff members overlook is that every time a board member asks for a donation, he or she incurs debt.

I remember one development director asking me to ask ten friends for $10 apiece. I told her that I wouldn't get on the phone for $10, knowing that I would be asked by each of my contacts to support their charities in return, and that their requests wouldn't be in the $10 range.

My best friend is not a wealthy woman, but she has wealthy friends. When she asks for a large donation, her friends rarely turn her down. When they ask her to work at their golf tournament for a day or to organize a dinner dance, she also rarely turns them down. There is often a quid pro quo when it comes to giving and friends.

Frank discussions of where board members can fit into the fund-raising process will help to ensure success. Many board members choose not to be directly involved for sound reasons, but even then they can take the truffle hound role and point out the money.

Take, for example, a professional who has clients who are wealthy. Say—a doctor who is on the board of a nonprofit that specializes in the disease she treats. Obviously, there is a very special doctor-patient relationship that precludes asking for money or turning over names. But it is certainly in the best interest of the patient to get involved in funding a cure. What to do?

The doctor can ask the patient to call the organization personally. The conversation would go something like this: "You might want to get more involved with the X, Y or Z Foundation. Obviously, I wouldn't give them your name, but here is the card of their executive director. I think you'd have a lot to offer this group."

Then the physician gets out of the middle of the process. It's up to the patient or his or her family then to take the initiative.

With other professional relationships, the code of confidentiality may be less strict and a client can be asked directly whether a call from the nonprofit organization would be welcome.

The bottom line is that board and staff have to work together for maximum effectiveness.

Can't we just get a group to raise the money and turn it over to us?

Board members often decide that they want to look for a group of people who will raise buckets of money and then turn it over to them to spend. It is a marvelous fantasy. Granted, there are a few organizations where this works, especially when the people raising the money have the same cultural and religious values as the people spending it. Groups such as the Jewish Federation or Catholic Charities have members who raise money and others who decide how it is going to be spent. But these members may well be on the fund-raising committee one year and the appropriations committee the next.

For some large organizations, such as hospitals or symphonies, foundations or friends groups are willing to raise money. The funds raised are sometimes significant and usually revolve around social activities and special events.

For the most part, though, people who raise money don't want to turn it over to others with no say in how it is used.

Once again, the people who are closest to the organization, namely the board members, have to get involved in the process.

Years ago, I volunteered at a store whose proceeds went to charity. It was run by a sorority. After I had worked there for six years

I asked if I could propose a charity for a donation. I was reminded that only sorority members could propose charities. I had raised more money than any other volunteer but could not have a say in where the money went.

It took two years to get the rule changed. Even then, a volunteer could only recommend one charity once. After eight years of volunteering, I left. The simple fact is that many people who do the work want a say in expenditure of funds.

How do you let board candidates know what you expect?

From time to time, I meet board and staff leaders who are shocked that their board members didn't know what would be expected of them. When asked what they had done to let them know, many respond, "but everyone knows that board members are supposed to be involved in fund-raising."

The truth is, many people are clueless about what board service entails. The franker your pre-membership meetings are, the less the chance that either the organization or the board member will be disappointed.

To prevent misunderstandings, I recommend a letter of commitment that is signed by the board member. Two copies are sent. One for the board member to keep and one to be returned to the office.

The nominating committee should write the specifics of the board commitment letter and then present it to the entire board for approval. This is an opportunity to get issues in the open for board members who aren't participating fully in the governance process.

The letter should be revised annually, as the needs of the nonprofit vary from year to year. Fundraising expectations will be much higher in the midst of a capital or endowment campaign. Other years, community education may take priority, requiring a different sort of board activity. A letter of commitment looks something like this:

Sample Board Commitment Letter

Dear _____

Thank you for agreeing to serve on the board of _____

_____

As I'm sure you know, our mission is _____

_____

Our vision of the future of our agency is _____

_____

We expect the following of our board members:

Attendance policy: Our meetings are (list times, date and place)

_____

We have the following financial expectations of our members:

_____

Your participation in the following events is expected (List special events and the level of participation expected; for example, bring a foursome to the golf tournament, buy and bring a table to the dinner dance.)

_____

_____

The length of your term is _____

We anticipate that you will need to devote at least _____ (hours a week, month or year) to serve on this board.

All board members are asked to serve on at least one committee. As we discussed, you will be on the _____

_____ committee.

To help with the orientation process and to welcome you, your board mentor (or sponsor) is _____

_____(include phone number).

Should you have any questions about being able to fulfill your duties, please call _____

_____(include phone number).

What can you expect from us? We will not waste your time. We will give you material regarding the programs and financial status of our nonprofit in a timely manner. We will not keep secrets. If there is a problem, we will let you know as soon as possible. We do (or don't) have board insurance. Please call if you would like a copy of the policy.

Please sign the enclosed two copies. Keep one and send the other in.

Welcome aboard. We look forward to working with you to

_____

_____

(refer once again to the mission)

_____   _____
Board candidate   Chair of nominating
                                                committee or board
                                                president or chair

Date_____

How do you change your board's giving philosophy?

Even established boards need to change their philosophy of giving from time to time. For instance, if you have always had generous United Way support and your community has not filled their coffers to the usual level, your board might have to be far more aggressive to meet its budget.

What do you do when your board members have never believed that raising funds was their job? You hear "but we have a development person, don't we?" or (hear highly virtuous tone) "I give my time and time is money."

The only way to answer these statements is to come back to the mission. The question for the board is "Can we serve our clients with the funds we have, or do we have to reduce services as a result of the shortfall?" There are really only two options when there is not enough money: raise more or reduce services. Ask "If we reduce services, which programs are we going to cut?"

I remember being in a boardroom where just such a scenario was discussed. It went something like this:

Executive director: "We didn't receive a large grant we had expected. We either have to raise additional funds with the board's help or reduce services."

Dead silence. The director went on to discuss which of their services to abused children would have to be cut. Do we drop our group for adolescent rape victims or shorten the hours of our preschool for abused toddlers? (notice the use of the word "we")

The board began to see that money was tied to mission and asked questions about the shortfall, such as how much had to be raised and by when. One marvelous diva looked at the executive director and proclaimed in flouncing tones, "Well, it's obvious I'm going to have to do this myself." She then looked at the board and asked who was going to help. Several members agreed to ensure the funding shortfall was met, formed an ad hoc committee and got to work.

This was the first time that members of this particular board had seen that if they didn't get involved, children would suffer. Up until that point, ensuring adequate financial resources had always been the responsibility of the executive director and the development staff.

The earth moved and the board began to step up to the plate. Once they began to raise funds, the attendance at meetings increased. They wanted to make sure that the funds they raised were spent wisely.

The fact is, people don't like it when you change the rules. Boards basically have three choices: train board members in fund raising, reduce the scope of services or get new board members.

When board members are unwilling to make the transition and take responsibility for the fiscal health of the agency, the board can assess what the board member brings to the table and decide whether the value of intellectual resources, insight or contacts makes it worthwhile for the board to keep this member.

We're going to talk about training later, and we've touched on the pain involved in reducing services. Getting rid of board members, while at times incredibly difficult, can be easier than one might think.

First of all, you need a solid board rotation system and you have to have active, enforced bylaws. If board members are uninvolved or are disconnected and don't come to meetings, maybe they don't have the time or interest to continue to serve.

I've been amazed when I've called people and asked "is this really a good time for you to be involved?" and they've said, "Actually, no." They are relieved and you are relieved. You have a slot on your board for someone who has what it takes to serve.

The trick to getting a board member to step down is to have them leave as a friend. This can be a real challenge. Always go back to mission, and always look for another opportunity for that board member to serve within your organization.

A conversation might go something like this: "You are up for reelection to the board. We've noticed that you haven't been able to attend many meetings in the last year. We need all the help we can to (state mission). We don't want to lose your expertise. We are hoping that you will agree to serve on the (name committee or advisory board). That way we won't be losing the unique gifts you bring to the table and you won't be burdened by so many meetings."

You then write a glowing article in your newsletter about what this person has accomplished while serving on the board and what future activities he or she plans to be involved in. Sometime these articles take a great deal of creativity to write!

At times, asking members to step down is not so easy. Remember, mission comes first.

Do we want a board of all "heavy hitters?"

Sometimes we sit in a boardroom and think, "Wouldn't it be great if we had a roomful of people who could just write checks to get this done."

Board members of affluence and influence are marvelous, but there is a downside. Without diversity at some level, you might make poor decisions.

One board built a soup kitchen to serve the poor and homeless, but it wasn't on a bus line. No one who worked directly with clients and knew their needs was involved in the decision making.

If you do decide to have a board of only "movers and shakers," make sure you tap into their minds as well as their wallets. One group with major heavy hitters on the board was asking $50,000 per board member and getting it. The board held only one meeting a year, which lasted three hours. When a new development director was hired, he made it a point to get to know the board members and was astounded at the talent on the board. He said that asking only for money was like buying a huge mainframe computer and using it only to play solitaire. The more he got to know them, the easier his job became and the more money they raised.

Who should solicit your board?

Asking board members to give is the job of the board, specifically, the board president. At the end of the year, a letter from the president should be sent to every board member. The is no reason why staff cannot draft this letter. It could read something like this:

Dear Ralph,

Your help on the strategic plan was invaluable. Your merger experience in the corporate world certainly saved us from some common pitfalls.

You have been generous with your time and knowledge, and now I'm going to once again ask you to be generous with your pocketbook.

As you know, there are x, y, and z things we cannot do without additional revenue.

Thanks to your work in the planning process, you of all people know that your gift will be used to get the most mission for the money. Thanks for digging deep.

It is an honor to serve with you.

Sincerely,

Sally
Board President

How else can board members financially support the mission?

There are as many ways to support a mission financially as there are board members. Frequently, members just don't know how many ways they can affect the bottom line. For a board retreat or a longer meeting, try this exercise:

Ask board members to break into groups of three. Take a large piece of paper and have them write the alphabet down one side and then ask what they can do to affect the bottom line, starting with each letter of the alphabet. Sometimes the effect is hilarious, sometimes thought provoking, but it gets the brain thinking.

Members who can't personally write big checks need to understand that they are integral members of the fund-raising team. I've seen board members who have neither influence nor affluence raise vast sums. One board member asked his boss for their old computer system for his nonprofit when his company was moving. "Old" in corporate terms was two years. His employer donated the system and also asked the hardware company to donate its time to install and network the system at 72 work sites. Later, his employer went to the nonprofit to receive an award and gave even more— a large check and five laptop computers for field staff.

Another board member, who owned an asphalt company, redid a playground at a shelter for battered women. He asked his buddies and their kids to help as a Mother's day project to honor everything their moms did for them. The kids got their scouting troops involved and brought new tricycles for the children who lived at the shelter.

Also, never underestimate the power of a board member who can tell a personal story. I was once on a board with a woman named Judy who was one of the greatest fund-raisers I've ever met. She was a battered woman who had overcome many obstacles. She left school in eighth grade and got her G.E.D. at 35. When she went into corporations to tell her story, she always left with a significant check.

Judy, like most board members, needed some training in public speaking. Groups like Toastmasters and the National Speakers Association can help train your board and staff on how to deliver a powerful message.

(Hint: Never, never, never leave a speech without getting the home addresses of those in the audience for your database.) Raffles or other giveaways by the host are one way to collect the information, or simply ask for the names and addresses of those who would like to receive your newsletter or hear more about volunteer opportunities.

Board members can also get donations of time from their friends and colleagues. One board member called a friend who was a labor lawyer and asked for a donation of two hours of time. He agreed and eventually grew so interested in the group that he became both a contributor and a board member.

Holidays and special occasions are a great time for board members to solicit their friends and colleagues. When my cousin Cynthia Frohlichstein, a breast cancer survivor, threw a huge bash for her 70th birthday, she made it known that she had everything she needed, but that she would appreciate donations in memory of her mother, who had also had breast cancer, to a research program. We gladly wrote the checks.

Don't forget Mother's Day and Valentine's Day. For certain causes, the Fourth of July might make sense.

Ask board members to get a list of friends and colleagues and to write a letter with a stamped envelope enclosed. Here's an example from the divorce recovery program at Valentine's Day:

My dear friends,

You have helped me through a really bad time in my life, and I'm asking for your help once again. As Valentine's Day approaches, think about those who are without someone who loves them and whom they love.

Just as you gave generously to me, with personal support when I needed it, I hope that you will give generously to Second Chapter, a divorce recovery program. This program helped me, as it has many others, complete the healing process.

Training and the nonprofit board member.

Many board members don't want to raise money because they don't know how. Counter that reluctance by asking: "Would you be willing to try with support and training?" It's amazing how many board members are willing to get involved if assured that they aren't going to be embarrassed.

There are many ways and places to get fund-raising training. Your local chapter of the National Society for Fundraising Executives (NSFRE) may have training available or the names of experts in your area. To find a chapter near you, you can check their Web site at www.nsfre.com.

If you are in an area without a chapter, you may want to call your United Way or Junior League to ask whether they know someone who could work with your group.

Training should be consistent with your strategic plan. If your strategy for raising funds is a capital campaign, don't hire someone to teach you to put on special events.

When setting up a training program for board members, build in a sense of safety, warmth and encouragement, especially through those first few fund-raising calls.

I remember the first time I made a major donor call. I chose someone I thought would be perfect, a friend of my mother's since childhood. Not only did she not give me a donation, she told me that I needed a haircut and that I shouldn't wear pale colors! She may have been right about the haircut and the choice of colors, but her comments put me back a year.

In retrospect, I showed up unprepared and alone. Had I brought the executive director with me and some solid information on the program I was promoting, the interview would have gone quite differently, I'm sure.

Your board member's first experience should be a positive one. Whenever possible, structure an initial success.

Also, let folks know that rejection is part of the process, that it hurts but is by no means deadly. I tend to rely on Nietzsche's words: "That which does not kill you shall make you strong." I'm quite sure he was talking about fundraising.

The best fund-raisers I've found are those who are comfortable with rejection and bounce back. A friend who was an abused child and is a phenomenal fund-raiser once said, "They may say no, but they never hit me."

Being prepared for rejection helps tremendously.

Does this sound like sales training? Well, it really is. You have to know and understand "the product" which in this case is your mission and the programs you have established to meet those ends.

Consider using your board retreat when people are relaxed and away from their day-to-day grind, as a time for training.

Start by establishing why the mission is important. Some groups emphasize this by having the retreat in the venue where they deliver services. If you are a theater company, have your retreat on the stage. If you are a scouting group, consider a meeting with a cookout at one of your campgrounds. Don't forget to make the s'mores. They taste as good when you're 60 as they did at 6.

Another way to bring the mission into the retreat is to have clients tell their story. Obviously, this has to be an empowering experience rather than an invasion of privacy. As part of one of the best retreats I've ever facilitated, a woman came in to tell how, thanks to this nonprofit, she had regained her dignity and taken control of her life 30 years after having been the victim of incest. There wasn't a dry eye in the house. Telling her story, she said, was a small down payment on the debt she owed this agency.

If it's impossible to bring in a client, ask a social worker or teacher or other line worker to present a case study. Make sure the story is about a person and not about numbers.

Experience the mission. If you are a school for special needs children, spend the day in a wheelchair, try to learn Braille.

Summary:

Board members who truly understand the needs of the people they serve will understand the critical need for money to serve them. For those who make the connection, fund-raising will become an integral part of their service to the mission they value.

Carol Weisman

Carol Weisman, president of Board Builders, is a speaker, author, trainer and consultant who specializes in volunteerism, fund raising and governance. Ms. Weisman has a Master's Degree is Social Work and a Masters Degree in Education from Washington University in St. Louis. She has served on 25 boards and has been president of 7.

Carol has worked as a medical social worker in pediatric oncology, hematology and neurology and neurosurgery at St. Louis Children's Hospital and Children's Hospital National Medical Center. She has published extensively on governance and volunteerism and is the author of "Build a Better Board in 30 Days: A Practical Guide for Busy Trustees" published by the F. E. Robbins and Sons Press. She is also featured in the PBS/Learning Institute Program on "Building a Board with a Passion for Mission."

In addition to traveling the world giving keynotes, training and doing board retreats, Carol is a member of the board of the Gateway Chapter of the National Speaker's Association. She serves on the Board of the Sequoia National Park Foundation.

Carol lives with her sweet, long suffering husband of 26 years. Their oldest son Frank Robbins V lives in New York where he is an actor by night and an aspiring real estate mogul during the day. Their other son Jono Robbins just finished art school with a major in ceramics and glass blowing and is starting to look for a teaching position. The dog and cat are long gone, and Carol is thinking of letting the plants die.

Carol Weisman MSW, CSP
Board Builders, Inc.
48 Granada Way, St. Louis, MO 63124
phone: 888-500-1777 (toll free) • FAX: 314-991-0202
E-MAIL: carol@boardbuilders.com
www.boardbuilders.com

CHAPTER 2

Feasibility Studies: Ready, Get Set . . .

Davis Allen, CFRE

Are We Ready?

Before we run a race, we learn the route. Before we jump into a pool, we test the water. Before we make a pie, we look at the recipe. Before we launch a capital campaign, we conduct a study.

A nonprofit's board of trustees is the group responsible for the organization's well-being. Before venturing into bold or risky enterprises, the board should first test the organization's ability to pull it off. Before undertaking a capital-funds drive to expand or stabilize the nonprofit's operations, it's wise to take a good, hard look at the marketplace. A feasibility study serves this purpose.

What are the factors you'll need to take into account before launching a study? Who should do it? Whom should you interview? How much will it cost? When is the best time to do it? What information should you discover from it? In this chapter, we will look at these questions and many related ones as well.

What Is A Feasibility Study?

James Greenfield, the veteran fund-raising consultant and editor of *The Nonprofit Handbook*, describes the feasibility study as *a proven market research technique to verify everything necessary to design a campaign for maximum success.*[1] It is sometimes called a

---

[1] James M. Greenfield, ed.; <u>The Nonprofit Handbook: Fund Raising</u> (New York: John Wiley & Sons, Inc., 1997) p. 116.

precampaign investigation, or fund-raising planning study. But "feasibility study" is still the term frequently used by campaign planners.[2] It sounds less like jargon, and it captures the heart of the matter—Let's find out if we can do this!

In simple terms, the feasibility study is a thorough examination of your institution's readiness to ask and the community's willingness to give. In looking at what is feasible, the study will test many things: the long-range plan and each of its projects and priorities, the costs, and the timetable for getting started. How prepared is your organization to undertake such a challenge? Do your supporters agree with the urgency of your plans?

You must be prepared for a campaign that will challenge all of your organization's resources. It may require several years to accomplish. You may be attempting to secure resources that exceed the budget size by four or five times, while sustaining a balanced annual operating budget.

The study will begin to assess questions that are vital to the success of your campaign:

- Who might make the largest gifts to our project?
- How can we evaluate our board and staff's potential for securing these gifts?
- What is the image of our organization?
- What leaders are available and interested?
- What are the potential problems that we should anticipate?

The study will also be your first opportunity to renew relationships with your organization's long-lost friends, including past board members, grateful clients, and lapsed donors. The final study report

---

[2] Some organizations do not like the term "feasibility study." Their concern is that if the study should determine that the project and the campaign are not feasible, then their donors will lose confidence in the organization's ability to complete large-scale plans. Later, this chapter will demonstrate how this logic is misguided, but you can avoid similar concerns completely if you substitute the comparable term "planning study."

will include many valuable indicators about the performance of your organization and the structure of a campaign, such as a campaign goal, a timetable, leadership, and a list of potential donors.

Can We Do A Campaign Without A Study?

When the board and staff of nonprofit organizations first consider whether to conduct a feasibility study, their concerns are generally "How much will it cost?" or "How much time will it take to complete?" or "Who's going to do it?"

Studies should be considered tasks that are revitalizing rather than onerous. It is valuable to everyone, both inside and outside the organization, to enter into and engage in this venture. Studies should be considered investments rather than expenditures. Even if your organization ultimately chooses to postpone or scrap the proposed campaign, your study will reveal a great deal about your operation and its position in the community. The study will always pay for itself, and then some. (See Budgeting for the Study on p. 42.)

Nonetheless, because studies are large undertakings, many board members of your organization will ask whether the feasibility study can be eliminated. Perhaps it can be, if your organization has a local, loyal constituency with extraordinary leadership and resources. But for a vast majority of organizations facing a capital campaign, the study is a necessary procedure for determining which approaches will lead to a successful outcome.

There are five common criteria for measuring an organization's readiness for a campaign. A deficit in any one of these areas could sink your campaign.

- Demonstrated leadership.
- Sufficient cultivation of potential and actual donors
- Realism in assessing situations and in setting objectives.
- A tradition of giving.
- Visibility in the community.

If your organization suffers from a shortage in any of these areas, and most do, this could present grave challenges for the organization when it seeks major funding support. Therefore, these challenges should be addressed before a campaign starts. Avoiding them may mean a major course-correction midstream and a resulting loss of confidence and support.

The study will also prevent you from underestimating or overestimating your organization's value in the eyes of your constituents. Without a study, you may set out to raise what you suspect is a tolerable level of funds, only to learn during the campaign that you could have achieved even greater goals. Worse, you may fail in the end to meet your capital goals and incur a serious loss of confidence, along with the public's resistance to provide support for years into the future. Worse still, in your eagerness to get the money you need, you may fail to achieve even your annual income goal. Avoid these traps, and conduct a feasibility study that will ensure strong support for your campaign.

Objectives Of A Study

Whether your organization is large or small, your campaign must be prepared to withstand tests of credibility, relevance, urgency, and practicality. In order to develop a campaign that rises to these standards, the study process should include the following objectives:

- **To determine the organization's campaign GOAL:** How much money can you raise?

A study should help determine the potential for giving that might be expected for your organization's capital campaign. The feedback from supporters and a critical analysis of the marketplace should assist in making an informed judgment regarding the potential scope of your program.

The findings should be examined in relation to similar campaigns by organizations that have used proven fund-raising concepts and principles, taking into account any elements that may be unique to your organization or its prospective donor markets.

Is the proposed goal realistic for this community? This region? If it's not realistic, why not? What are the problems? Is there a favorable economic climate within your constituencies or the community, as indicated by a sound economic outlook and the reasonable absence of conflicting campaigns and competing enterprises?

- **To evaluate the strength of THE CASE of the proposed capital program:** What are we trying to accomplish? How will the initiative improve upon our ability to fulfill our mission?

The organization's case is a very brief written summary that explains the need, scope and objectives of the proposed capital project. The case statement summary will be explained in fuller detail later in the chapter, but its essential purpose is to help the interviewees understand the strengths, weaknesses and priorities of your appeal. The study should air any negative factors and potential remedies. Positive factors should be described also—and suggestions made to develop them to their fullest advantage.

Is the case or argument for a capital campaign well-defined? Does it reflect the institution's mission, goals and objectives? Is it compelling? Will it be understood by the organization's constituencies? Will it motivate potential donors to give? Have the needs been studied and accepted by the governing board? Are the needs verified and documented? Do they reflect a sense of urgency?

- **To identify potential major CONTRIBUTORS to the campaign:** Who are the contributors who will make or break the campaign?

An axiom of major-gift fundraising is that 90 percent of the funds raised will come from 10 percent of the donors. A small percentage of the donors to your campaign—whether they are individuals, corporations, foundations, or public agencies—will contribute a large percentage of the campaign's income. (Refer to the Capital Gift-Range Chart on p. 46.)

During the study, it is *essential* to identify an ample number of major contributors and to ask them to consider gifts that represent their true capacity and inclination. The study will help you to discover these people and the level of funding they should be asked to consider.

- **To identify POTENTIAL LEADERS:** Who will lead the campaign?

If the campaign is to succeed, leaders must be able to give and to solicit at the upper levels suggested by the gift-range chart below. They must hold the respect of the community. They must lend their name to the campaign and be willing to give the necessary time to the institution and its causes.

Can this quality leadership be enlisted from the board, the constituency, or from the larger community? Who can be the chairperson? What about the campaign so excites this person that he or she would agree to take charge?

- **To assess the IMAGE of the organization:** What public relations or promotional activity will be required to motivate the community to support this program?

The study should examine how your organization and its work are perceived by those who have the capacity to make a major gift or are prospects for campaign leadership. Furthermore, if your campaign is large enough to affect the entire community, your institution must enjoy a positive image within business, social, and political circles. Are there public relations problems that will have to be resolved before any campaign can start or endure?

- **To recommend a TIME LINE that will move the organization through a campaign in the shortest time span with maximum results:** What is the best timing and schedule for your campaign?

Given the scope of your program, the probable size of the top-level prospect list, and the special characteristics of the appeal, the study's recommendations should include the timing for key phases of the campaign. Are there conflicting campaigns in progress or contemplated in the near future? What impact will they have on yours? How much time is needed to ensure the success of this campaign: nine, twelve, eighteen, or more months, or two, five, or ten years?

Additional Benefits Of A Study

The following intangible benefits could be just as valuable as the benefits listed above. For the potential contributor or leader, participation in the planning process can be pivotal to "buy-in." People appreciate being asked for their opinions on a one-to-one basis. If you wait to get in touch with your key supporters until the moment when they are being asked to consider a "stretch" or "sacrificial" gift to your campaign, they may feel that they are appreciated merely for their money. This is the important difference between "development" and "fund-raising"; if you make the mistake of asking for merely the gift, you have given too much emphasis to the means rather than the ends. Once the donors understand your program (the case) and what their gift will help you accomplish, the gifts should come.

Here's a list of some intangible benefits of a study, compliments of Alan Young. The study:

- *Helps presell the campaign*—it informs those being interviewed about an organization's plans.

- *Helps strengthen relationships*—especially in the event someone being interviewed has not been a particularly strong booster of the organization.

- *Makes new friends*—if for no other reason than individuals like being asked for their opinions.

- *Helps raise the sights*—underscores the fact that this will not be a "business as usual" kind of campaign, particularly in terms of the size of gifts that will be required.

- *Serves as a process for change*—helps people adjust to new ideas and, at the very least, feel that they had a chance to give meaningful input into key decisions.[3]

---

[3] Alan M. Young, National Society of Fundraising Executives' (Arlington, Va.) International Conference presentation, Philadelphia, 1998.

Methods And Steps

Ideally, planning should be started at least a year in advance of the start of the campaign in order to achieve the following tasks:

- Allow ample time to conduct an assessment of the organization's needs.

- Develop the strategic plan.

- Recruit, organize and train the necessary volunteer force.

- Get the technical-support systems in place (gift-tracking, recognition, fund accounting).

- Create a favorable campaign climate.

Once you have a clear idea of what capital needs exist (your board and staff have completed a thorough assessment of the organization's needs and established through a strategic-planning process that a campaign *is* a priority), it is time to begin the feasibility study process.

Personnel:

To launch a precampaign study, you will want to form an ad-hoc planning committee of board members to provide oversight and advice about the study process. This group, in tandem with the staff, will guide the precampaign planning and design.

In essence, the feasibility study is about interviewing your constituency. Easy, right? Conducting interviews may seem an elementary procedure, but, except for small, local projects, the study process requires the assistance of a professional with strong interpersonal skills, unimpeachable integrity, and an investigator's sixth-sense about finding the "whole truth." For these reasons, and to ensure interviewees that their responses will be taken accurately, impartially, and confidentially, it is absolutely essential that precampaign interviews be done by outside counsel. You should not trust this process to an amateur or even a competent staff person.

To conduct the study, analyze the findings, and prepare a recommendation, the study leader must have a lot of experience in conducting studies and running campaigns. With impartial inquirers, interviewees will be more open in expressing their opinions about the organization and their potential support of your campaign.

Nearly every professional fund-raising consulting firm or seasoned fund-raising executive is experienced in leading a study. And during a 20-60 minute interview, the experienced interviewer can see familiar patterns. At the end of each meeting with a stranger, he or she can fairly predict the interviewee's interest, giving potential, and leadership potential—and usually predict these things more reliably than the nonprofit CEO who may have known the prospect for years.

How should professional counsel for the study be identified, interviewed, and hired? The board committee on fund development should conduct the search and bring back to the board a list of prospective study leaders. The board can ask members of the executive staff—the chief financial officer, the development director, or the executive director—for a list of candidates they have researched. The board should give preference to the recommendations of the staff person who will be working most closely with the study leader.

The organization should mail a Request for Proposal (RFP) or Request for Quote (RFQ) to all candidates on the list. (A sample RFP is included as Exhibit A. in the chapter's Appendix.) The RFP asks when the study-leader candidates can begin, the budget and fees required, and the timetable to completion. Candidates are then asked to respond with a proposal within 30 or 45 days. The proposal should include the cost of their services and the time required to deliver the final report. Board members and staff should be available during this period to answer any other questions that candidates may have.

The development committee should invite two or three of those who submit proposals for personal interviews to verify their ability to secure answers to the questions in the study. Reference checks on each firm and its staff are mandatory before final selection.

There should be clarity about who is hiring the study leader and to whom the study team reports throughout the contract period. The answer can be any of the following (and everyone on this list must agree with the decision): chairman of the board, chairman of the development committee, president or executive director, development director, or chief development officer.

The development committee should review the written agreement for services and understand all of its details, including payment dates and amounts, what expenses will be included, which study team members will be assigned, and similar arrangements.[4]

One word about a common assumption: the board's selection of the study leader is a decision that is distinct from the selection of the counsel who will conduct the campaign. Although the person or firm selected to lead the study is often selected to be the campaign counsel, this should never be assumed or, even worse, negotiated as part of the study leader's agreement.

If the study leader is interested in becoming the consultant for the campaign, then certainly his or her performance during the study process will influence the board's choice for the campaign. In doing the study, the organizational team members and the study leader learn how they work together. Furthermore, the study leader could have another advantage in qualifying for the campaign position because he or she will become intimately familiar with the organization, its cause, and its key stakeholders. Nonetheless, during the period when the study is first arranged and then conducted, both parties must remain impartial about the future choice of the campaign counsel.

Budgeting for the Study:

A study consists of three phases: the design of the study methods, the interviews, and the evaluation. The costs associated with each stage will vary depending upon the scope of your study—on

---

[4] Greenfield, <u>The Nonprofit Handbook</u>, pp. 114-115.

the prestudy planning required, the presentation materials required, the number of people to be interviewed, the distances to be covered, and areas of the country. The interviews require the most time and, therefore, the greatest expenditure. In some instances, the interviewees may be close enough to include several in one day, in which case out-of-pocket expenses, such as air fares, accommodations, and meals, will be marginal.[5]

Your study leader's fee will be your largest expense. Check with a national organization, such as the National Society of Fund Raising Executives in Alexandria, Va., for guidance about market rates for consultants and feasibility studies (703-684-0410; http://www.nsfre.org). To compare rates, you will need the consultants' hourly or daily rates and their estimate of how much time the job will require. Some consultants may prefer to give you a quote for the entire job, but you still need to ask for a detailed description of their services during the study, so that you can be certain that you have comparable proposals.

Here is a chart that includes possible tasks and related expenses. The organizational representatives and the study leader must be clear about the party responsible for each task. Notice that many of the tasks can be managed or directed by the organization's professional staff, such as drafting the case summary. Similarly, some of the tasks are administrative, such as scheduling appointments and sending letters to interviewees; many organizations will perform these tasks with in-house staff. If this is the case, the time that the study leader invests in the study will be reduced accordingly, and, therefore, his or her fee should be reduced in kind.

The chart indicates with symbols (o) those parties that could be involved in each task. When an individual is in the best position to manage a task, the symbol in the appropriate box is darker.

---

[5] Jack Kerber; senior consultant, St. Louis office for Staley/Robeson/Ryan/St. Lawrence, Inc.

Feasibility Study Task Chart

Description of Tasks	Tasks which can be managed by:			
	Organizational Director	Organizational Manager	Study Leader	Study Leader's Administrator
PREPARATION				
Develop case summary	●		O	
Develop study questions	O		●	
Develop interviewee list (30-40)	●	O	O	
Draft interviewee invitation letter	●		O	
Send letters to interviewees	O	●		
Calls to set interviews		●		O
Send confirmations to interviewees		O	O	●
Send thank-yous to interviewees		O	O	●
INTERVIEWS				
Conduct 15 interviews			●	
EVALUATION				
Compile and analyze results			●	O
Prepare evaluation report			●	O
Present written and oral report to steering comm	O	O	●	
Present reports to Board	O	O	●	

The study leader's expenses might also cover out-of-pocket items such as meals, travel and transportation, mailings (interview requests, thank-you letters, report summaries), and telephone charges.

The expenses for the entire campaign, including the precampaign study, should not exceed 10 to 20 percent of the total raised.[6] Therefore, the amount you will spend for a study will be a tiny portion of the percentage that you raise. Small and mid-sized organizations often pale at the expense required to conduct a feasibility study. This is one of the first true tests of campaign's feasibility. While it's true that a study may determine that you are not ready for a campaign, in the course of the study you will have gathered many valuable opinions, which will help you serve your constituents more effectively on an annual basis. You will have not sacrificed anything.

If an organization believes that it cannot afford a feasibility study, it simply cannot afford a campaign. And if it chooses to compromise the feasibility study, then the campaign will be compromised. It will be destined to solicit its best prospects for gifts that are too small and to recruit leaders who are inadequate for the enormous task at hand. If the campaign is to be successful, the organization should—*must*—invest in a feasibility study.

Materials:

The board and staff should work with the study leader to prepare a number of key documents. At a minimum, these materials should include:

- *QUESTIONNAIRE,* or set of interview questions. No two questionnaires are the same. The study leader can provide stock questions for the campaign at hand (See Exhibit B. in the chapter's Appendix), but they should be customized to your organization and the objectives of your campaign. Refer to the beginning of this chapter for a list of traditional objectives.

---

[6] Bobbie Strand, Bentz Whaley Flessner, American Prospect Research Association conference presentation, 1995.

- *A Case Summary Statement*, which articulates the need, scope and objectives of the proposed capital project. This case summary will be the primary attachment mailed to your interviewees. This one- or two-page document must be so enticing that those who read it will be excited about your mission and agree to be interviewed, even if they do not agree with some points made in the case. It must demonstrate that this campaign will fulfill a defined need in the community once the campaign is successfully completed. Also it must affirm the organization's long-range and strategic plans.

- *A Preliminary Gift-Range Table*, which illustrates the gifts required to meet the desired goals in an ideal campaign. This table suggests how many gifts should be raised at each funding level to quickly achieve the campaign goal. For simplicity sake, this illustration is for a $1 million campaign, but, for campaigns of $10 million or $100 million, the proportional figures can be extrapolated. Samples of tables for campaigns of various magnitudes are readily available in texts about capital campaigns or through consultants.

Capital Gift-Range Table: $1,000,000 Goal

Gift Range ($)	No. Gifts Required	No. Prospects Required	Subtotal ($)	Cumulative Total ($)
200,000	1	3	200,000	200,000
100,000	1	3	100,000	300,000
75,000	1	3	75,000	375,000
50,000	3	10	150,000	525,000
25,000	4	15	100,000	625,000
10,000	8	25	80,000	705,000
7,500	12	35	90,000	795,000
5,000	15	45	75,000	870,000
2,500	15	45	37,500	907,500
Less than 2,500	100+	300+	92,500	1,000,000
TOTALS:	160+	480+		1,000,000

It's important to notice several proportions and relationships in this table. In an ideal campaign at least one gift should achieve 10 percent of the goal, the top 10 gifts should exceed one-half of the goal, and the next 50 gifts should achieve 90 per cent of the goal. Also, it is a generally accepted rule of thumb that there should be three prospects for each gift.[7]

This table will become an important discussion item during the interview. If the interviewee says that he or she will consider a campaign contribution, the interviewer should take out the preliminary gift table and say, for example, "I'm not soliciting your gift, but you understand the purpose of the feasibility study, which is to tell us whether we can successfully complete this campaign. Where would you put yourself on this table based on a 3-5 year pledge? Of course, your response will be kept confidential and will not be attributed to you."

If these top prospects cannot be identified during the feasibility process, then the campaign will be weakened, but not jeopardized. If a top gift of 10 percent of your goal gives your top prospects "sticker shock," then before the campaign begins redistribute the top gifts at a lower level. For instance, in this example, the top of the table might include three gifts of $100,000. In any case, the feasibility study must identify a critical mass of leadership gifts in order to ensure a healthy range of gifts and a successful campaign.

After the interviewer has completed the interviews, he or she will refine the preliminary table, incorporating the interviewers' reactions to it. In time, this table will be used to determine the campaign goal and to set solicitation strategies. The table, in its various forms, will become a valuable planning and implementation tool for the campaign.

---

[7] Goettler Associates, *The Feasibility Study: Foundation for a Successful Campaign*, The Goettler Series (Columbus, Oh., Goettler Associates, 1995).

- *A Diagram Of The Organizational Structure*, which illustrates the individuals in the team responsible for completing the campaign. Volunteers, staff and counsel should be represented in their hierarchical and functional positions, including the organization's professional program staff. This diagram will demonstrate to the interviewee that the campaign has leadership, credibility, and team strength.

The following materials are not essential for the feasibility study, but they may prove to be handy for interviewees who require assurances about the sound planning of your campaign:

- *An Overall Program Planning Chart,* which will identify each major step in the development process and the time frame expected to carry them forth. The board and staff determines the timetable of the organization's program, such as completing the renovation of their main building in time to celebrate the 250th anniversary. Depending upon this program timetable, the campaign plan should include enough time to raise leadership gifts, major gifts, broad-based gifts and wrap-up gifts. Has the organization projected a time when it hopes to secure a minimum level of leadership pledges (usually 50 percent of the total goal) before it announces the campaign to the general public? Has the agency coordinated its projected campaign with other agencies who have initiated or intend to initiate similar campaigns?

- *Program Growth Projections* that are likely to result from new or expanded facilities.[8] Given the changes proposed in your campaign, the organization's expenses will shift. This long-term budgeting must estimate the fundamental changes that will occur as a result of this campaign. For instance, if you are erecting and furnishing a building, you will be have higher utility bills, expanded staff, more programs, more marketing, etc.

- *A Project Budget* identifying the funds necessary to support the campaign initiative, including direct and indirect costs. The

---

[8] Young.

campaign costs should not exceed 10-20 percent of the amount of money you expect to raise. If you exceed this level, your constituency will object, and so should your board.

To help develop and maintain a favorable climate for the campaign, the organization should prepare the necessary campaign publications and materials, such as campaign brochures, estate-giving pamphlets, web sites, videos, hand-carried prospectus kits, and standard forms for reporting, recording, and acknowledging gifts and pledges. The marketing and public relations departments should begin to plan their materials as well—their own web sites, press releases, articles in newsletters, billboards or other publicity that will raise the community's awareness about your organization and its campaign.

- **Selecting interviewees:**

To complete 30-40 interviews, the organization's list of prospective interviewees can range from as few as forty names to as many as 150. The organization should mail invitation letters to all prospective interviewees, including self-addressed return cards to improve the response rate. Then the study leader might send letters to the interviewees to introduce him or her and to indicate the days during which interviews will be scheduled. This paves the way for an administrator to make calls and schedule the interviews.

The list of prospective interviewees should be as inclusive as possible. The organization can never be certain where big-gift donors or campaign leaders will emerge. Consider including representatives of each of the organization's constituent groups, including program participants and their parents or grandparents, past donors (as measured by size of gifts and consistency of giving), and active volunteers (starting with board members). Community leaders should also be interviewed, including businesspeople, foundation officers, government officials and politicians. And don't forget people who participate in or support programs sponsored by organizations that are similar to yours.

- **Interviews:**

All interviews are in-depth, generally lasting anywhere from 20 to 60 minutes. The interviewer, in setting up the appointment, should shoot for as much as an hour, but many community leaders have busy schedules. If the appointment is for only 20 minutes, the interviewer should prepare for a short interview and select the essential questions. If the interview is supposed to be only 20 minutes, then only the interviewee can extend this time period.

The interviewers should ask hard, straightforward questions and request candid, direct answers, because these are important matters. The organization cannot wait until it is actually asking for gifts before tackling the tough questions.

Interviewers should assure their interviewees that, while all feedback gathered during the interview may be included in the study, the specific source of the information will never be attributed to an individual. The participant's names will be listed in an appendix attached to the study. Only in this manner can sensitive information critical to the progress of the campaign be elicited from interviewees.[9]

- **Research:**

Prospective capital-gift donors are the primary targets for your campaign and, therefore, the primary interviewees. How do you identify them? Your organization should have in place an information base regarding existing and prospective donors. The staff should be able to assemble giving histories for major donors and for current and former board members. Don't overlook the $100 annual donors who have given loyally for many years; these may turn out to be good candidates for major outright gifts or planned gifts.

Other questions: Does the organization have a sound base of donors? Has the agency identified a potential donor base that it has not cultivated? Can the agency identify an anchor gift or two that

---

[9] Henry R. Rosso Associates, <u>Achieving Excellence in Fund Raising</u> (San Francisco: Jossey-Bass Publishers, 1991), p. 83.

will provide immediate credibility and draw community attention to the campaign?

• **Leadership:**

Internally, the board and staff should be asking themselves several questions about their readiness to lead. For instance, what are the experiences of the agency's chief executive with capital fund-raising efforts? What proportion of the chief executive's time can realistically be dedicated to fund-raising without adversely affecting the day-to-day activities of the agency? How much have members of the agency's professional staff worked previously with fund-raising? Would their efforts demand new hires and expanded staff? Has the chief executive of the agency, along with the board chair, determined the availability of internal expertise among board and staff members in areas of law, fund-raising, financing and construction?

• **Findings and recommendations from the study:**

The written report of the study should contain at least these elements: a statement of the purpose of the study, the study findings (the patterns of views expressed by the interviewees), an analysis of the findings (the study leader's evaluation of the participants' views), the study leader's recommendations, and (if a campaign is feasible) a recommended campaign plan, timetable and budget.

Usually, the first copies of the study report are reviewed by the organization's development director, development committee chair and executive director. The final report is then distributed to the full development committee or the board. Often the study leader makes an oral presentation to interested individuals or groups.

The organization ordinarily has no reason to be concerned about any unfavorable findings and every reason to be responsive to the participants' justifiable interest in the results. Indeed, this sharing of problems usually serves to strengthen a board.

The board should be given ample opportunity to meet and discuss the report and ask questions about its contents before being requested to vote on its recommendations. This process can be vitally important for instilling a sense of ownership among the volunteer stakeholders.

Has the board determined the capital campaign to be its No.1 priority, and is it prepared to commit the necessary time to achieve the campaign goal? The vote on a recommended capital campaign is an opportunity for the board to express its enthusiastic approval and support.[10] If the vote is unanimously in favor of the campaign, then it should be reported as such in the solicitation materials.

- **Setting a campaign goal:**

The goal that you set for the campaign is often less than the total amount the organization requires to fund its capital project. Rarely are all of the required funds secured through fund-raising alone, especially for "bricks and mortar" projects. To complete a construction project, the board and staff must consider all income and expense factors. Your organization may also need to issue a bond or take out a loan. Contractors don't accept pledges when they need to be paid!

Feasibility studies are not—and probably cannot be—exercises in scientific precision; and prospective donors' initial giving intentions can change, particularly in response to inspiring leadership. Consequently, there are many variables to consider in setting the campaign goal.

In determining campaign goals, the board should carefully consider the feasibility study's recommendations, as they reflect the giving intentions of its potential donors. It is a common practice to set a preliminary goal and refine it—after the leadership gifts have been solicited and before the campaign "goes public." This adjustment normally takes place when you feel that you have reached at least half of your goal.

Some organizations have adopted campaign goals in excess of what studies found to be feasible—and they have succeeded in

---

[10] Maurice G. Gurin, <u>What Volunteers Should Know for Successful Fund Raising</u> (New York: Stein and Day, 1982), pp. 75-76.

achieving them. If the funds needed are far beyond what could be raised in the traditional campaign period of two to three years, the consultant could recommend a capital development program that extends longer, raising the total funds in several years, beginning with the most urgent needs in the first phase.

Conclusion

The feasibility study is an in-depth evaluation of your organization and its future prospects. It is an investment in an important venture during a period in your organization's growth or survival. You can't afford to risk the expense and effort of a capital campaign without exploring your chances and giving your constituents a chance to buy into the process. Even if you decide to postpone or scrap the capital campaign, the interaction with constituents that the study provides will strengthen your relations with donors and generate short-term gifts. Follow these principles and methods, and your study will stimulate successful development activities for years to come.

APPENDIX

Exhibit A. Request for Proposal for Feasibility Study Leaders

Objective

Our objective is to conduct a capital campaign in the time-frame of *[time-frame]* for the purpose of making all needed repairs to the physical plant, retiring the current debt and establishing an endowment fund to serve as a capital cushion for the future.

Background

[Organization's name] serves as a community center, a neighborhood anchor, and is an historic landmark. *[Description of the organization, including its mission, location and major programs.]*

Membership and Constituency

[Be as specific as possible]

Assessed Need

[Explain what the Organization hopes to accomplish through the proposed campaign.]

1.

2.

Scope of Work

[Organization name] is seeking a fundraising consultant to do a feasibility study to see if the goal can be met by soliciting organizational members, friends, area businesses, corporations and foundations.

The feasibility study will entail personal interviews with __ persons who will be selected by the committee and consultant.

The consultant will work with the organization's committee in preparing a case statement and letter to be sent to those to be interviewed.

In the proposal, the committee would like to know:

— The definition of the consultants' scope of work, and how they would go about performing the feasibility study.

— The hourly rate used in figuring your bid.

— What type of interim reports would be made to the committee.

— What is a reasonable schedule, including start and finish date.

— Who would be doing the feasibility study, as well as arrangements for an alternate.

Three references of business conducted in the last two years are requested. Please submit your proposal to the Committee at *[organization and address]*. Bids will be accepted until *[date]*.

If you have questions, please contact _____ at _____ days, _____ evenings.

Exhibit B. Sample Feasibility Interview Questions

1. When did you become affiliated with *[the organization]*? Why?

2. How have you been involved with *[the organization]* since then?

3. Describe the attributes (skills, talents, leadership, orientation) of the Board . . . of the staff. How could they be strengthened?

4. Please comment on the quality of the programs and services that *[the organization]* provides.

5. Do you understand what the Board proposes to do? Have you read the case summary?

6. If so, do you agree that a campaign is necessary?

7. Do you think *[the organization]* can implement and be successful in a campaign of $____?

8. What do you feel is the level of support of the community? Among which groups?

9. Who would you recommend as volunteer leadership for the campaign?

10. Would you be willing to work in such a campaign? To what extent?

11. Who might have the capacity for a significant gift to this campaign?

12. Will you (and/or your company) support such a campaign financially? (Where on the gift-range table?)

Davis Allen, CFRE

For a quarter-century Davis Allen, CFRE (Certified Fund Raising Executive), has done what we all desire: he has managed to combine his passion with his work. He has always loved education and the arts. In his first job after college, he managed the cultural-events box office at Duke University.

Davis has worked for a variety of educational and cultural institutions including Opera Theatre of Saint Louis, where he was the Director of Development, Webster University, where he was the Director of Major Gifts, and The Alliance Theatre in Atlanta Georgia, The St. Paul Chamber Orchestra in Minnesota and the Houston Symphony Orchestra in Texas. He even gave money away (another fund-raiser's desire) when he was the program director for the Gateway Foundation in St. Louis.

Davis now runs his own consulting firm. Recent clients include Campbell House Museum, Craft Alliance, Laumeier Sculpture Park, and LOOP Theatre. His clients appreciate his practical, action-oriented approach to fund-raising initiatives.

In addition to consulting, Davis is in demand as a speaker and instructor. His most requested presentations include "Major Gifts for Organization of All Sizes," "Feasibility Studies: Who Needs 'em," and "Board-Staff Fundraising: It Takes You to Tango."

Davis has a B.A. from Vassar College and a M.A. in Human Resource Development from Webster University. Since 1986, he has been certified by the Association of Fund Raising Professionals.

Davis lives with his wife Penny who is a consultant in arts-education programs. Their children, James and Daniel, are big fans of theater. In fact, the whole family has performed together in several of their church's summer musicals. Davis is a people-person and he enjoys creative projects.

Davis Allen, CFRE
Development Counsel
621 Clark Avenue, St. Louis, MO 63119
314-962-9733 • Fax: 314-962-4074
allenwg@att.net

Mama Said, Never Put All Your Eggs in One Basket: Boards, Strategic Thinking and the Need for Diversified Revenue

Terrie Temkin, Ph.D.

Theee poet Arthur Guiterman once said, "Keep out of ruts; a rut is something which if traveled in too much, becomes a ditch." As stewards of an organization, board members are responsible for keeping the organization running smoothly and in the right direction. Because most people prefer to take a road with which they are familiar, far too many retrace their steps again and again, wearing the road down to the point where their organizations end up in Guiterman's ditch. This is especially true when it comes to fund-raising. So many board members are afraid of this responsibility that they take what they perceive as the path of least resistance. Then they are shocked when their organization stalls, miles from its destination.

Your organization can avoid wearing a rut in the road by venturing off the beaten track. Sometimes even a small detour will make a rewarding difference. The key to a successful journey is to keep your final destination clear in your mind and your map handy so that you can make the best choice from your options. Ready to travel? Let's go.

The Responsibility For Navigating

When mapping out your organization's journey, it is imperative to consult both your professional staff and your board. The information and insight possessed by each group is different, yet equally critical to the organization's ultimate ability to reach its destination. Staff members tend to have control of the details necessary for driving the organization day-to-day. They are usually the ones with the long-term perspective and the nitty-gritty knowledge of that strange entity we call the nonprofit world. It is board members who have the potential to plot unique routes by building on the diversity of their experience and viewpoints.

Most current books on governance suggest that the board of directors should set the organization's final destination, or mission, and determine—at a macro level—how the organization might best achieve that mission. This means setting goals, strategies and policies that are in line with the mission, vision and values. Strategic thinking with a long-range perspective becomes the defining responsibility of boards.

Strategic thinking is fun. It challenges boards to think creatively and to envision the "what ifs . . . ." But it requires more than merely dreaming dreams. All plans have associated costs that must be covered; and, as one unknown pop philosopher reminds us: He who wants milk should not set his stool in the middle of the field in the hopes that the cow will back into him. If your board wishes to see its vision come to fruition, it must also tackle the issue of how that vision is to be funded—a process that in itself involves a great deal of strategic thinking.

Mapping Out The Trip

A board should consider many factors when deciding how best to fund its plan. The first is to decide how much money it needs— and when it needs it. The staff should be able to supply board members with program budgets and timelines geared to objectives previously defined by the board. Neither document needs to be studied line by line. But the organization can only benefit if each board member puts his or her business hat on. Board members must be realistic and plan for contingencies as they consider the strategic implications of the suggested allocations of both money and time.

Review timelines carefully. They are critical in several ways to developing a good fund-raising plan. First, by helping your board visualize its needs for resources, they ensure that the organization does not take on more projects than it can handle. Second, some fund-raisers lend themselves better than others to certain times of year. A timeline will red-flag, for instance, the fact that, given the current date of the major fund-raiser, all the planning will have to be done over the summer when most of the volunteer and paid staff are away on vacation. A timeline will also point up situations where the board is relying on funds such as grant money that can't possibly come in within the desired time frame.

Once your board has decided how much money it needs and by when, it can begin to look at funding-raising options. And options abound. Among them:

Personal contributions
- Face-to-face solicitation
- Direct mail
- Telemarketing
- Door-to-door solicitation
- Online solicitation
- Matching gifts
- Planned giving

Grants
- Foundation grants
- Government grants
- Corporate sponsorship

Earned income
- Special events
- Neighborhood fund-raising (for example, bake sales, car washes and garage sales)

- Cause-related marketing
- Affinity marketing (such as the promotion of credit cards that sport the organization's logo in return for a percentage of the credit card companies' profits)
- Joint ventures
- Fees for services
- Unrelated business

Thinking Multiple Revenue Streams

The key is to pick several of these methods to guarantee a steady stream of revenue. Mama always said: Never put all your eggs in one basket—you may drop or lose the basket.

Fund-raising techniques go through cycles. For about 15 years special events were hot, hot, hot. Now they are losing their luster. Affinity marketing was all the rage until it began to seem as if every nonprofit organization was offering its own credit card and the Internal Revenue Service stepped in to collect unrelated business income tax (UBIT) on the percentage retained by the nonprofit. Fund-raising on the Internet appears to be the next major trend. But it may be short-lived if the issue of state-by-state registration cannot be worked out. The point is, while revenue prospects can seem rosy if your organization hits a cycle on its upswing, an organization can lose big if it employs a practice that is on its downswing—especially if the board was counting too heavily on that source of cash.

The organization may also lose big if the board fails to face the fact that the appeal of its mission can go in cycles as well. For years, AIDS organizations, overlooked by mainstream funding sources, went begging. Then, suddenly, it seemed that everyone was throwing money in their direction. Today, with the new drug treatments that allow people living with AIDS to lead longer, healthier lives, the mission has lost its sense of urgency, and AIDS organizations are once again scrounging for funds.

For these reasons, it is important for organizations to develop balanced fund-development programs. A balanced program will show income from each of the general categories of personal contributions, grants, and earned income.

Diversity within each of these categories is also important. An organization that counts on getting 25 percent or more of its income from any one source is crossing into a danger zone. And while the zone may be cautionary yellow at 25 percent, it is definitely red at 33 percent. What would your organization give up if a third of its expected income did not come in? Many organizations had to face this when, in 1992, the United Way went through a credibility crisis that affected its fund-raising ability and, consequently, its gifting ability. They faced it again when the federal government changed its funding process to block grants in the mid 1990's. Organizations that relied heavily at the time on one or both of these funding sources found themselves scrambling to stay alive.

One way to encourage diversity within the category of personal contributions is to be sure that the board has designed a fund-raising plan that targets those within the organization as well as those without. Traditionally, many organizations functioned under the belief system that the sweat equity board members and volunteers contributed to their organization was sufficient. They looked only outside the organization for cash donations. Today most realize that those closest to the organization have a responsibility to support it financially as well.

Thinking Strategically about Funding

There's an old saying that applies well to fund-raising: Dig where the gold is unless you just need the exercise. As part of deciding where to "dig," boards must evaluate the **potential** of each fund-raising strategy to meet their needs. While a car wash may bring in enough dollars for a high school band looking to buy a new drum set, it won't bring in enough dollars for a university to fund its endowment. Looking for the gold also means being realistic about whose deep pockets the organization will attempt to tap. A local bank may be extremely philanthropic. But if your organization is a health-related charity and the bank funds the arts, it is a waste of time and effort to approach the bank.

It might be far easier and more productive to approach for funds the local gangster who wants to buy respectability. There are organizations that state, there is no money so dirty that it can't be made clean with the tears of widows and orphans. Is that your organization? Or do you find that idea distasteful? Deciding your **philosophy** of fund-raising is critical.

Related to philosophy is **image**. While you may not be taking money from gangsters, every day your board has to look beyond the dollar signs and decide whether it wants its organization known as the bingo group or the organization that sells burial plots. Development efforts always have a public relations component. The question you must constantly ask is, what kind of an image are we projecting if we go ahead with this idea?

Sensibilities may easily be ruffled if the avenues pursued by the board are not **mission-appropriate**. Some people were very uncomfortable, for example, when they learned that the founder of Mothers Against Drunk Driving (MADD) accepted money from liquor companies.

This brings us to **stakeholders' needs and desires**. How will your contributors, clients, staff, board members and the public feel if, for instance, your board decides to implement a fee for services that have traditionally been free, or to incorporate affinity marketing into your fund-raising mix? You had better feel confident that clients will see the inherent value in your services and be willing to pay or that enough people will view the affinity offering as a benefit and opt to take advantage of it. If people react negatively, they will share their displeasure with the world and your organization's image will suffer. A minimal benchmark against which any development idea should be measured is the commitment level of your board. If the board fails to enthusiastically back an idea, it is probably not an idea to implement.

Fund-raising plans should fit the **board's worldview**. Some boards are more comfortable with traditional fund-raising methods such as grants, special events and direct solicitation. Others are motivated only by entrepreneurial approaches—for example, establishing a for-profit business to generate income for the nonprofit. (See Figure 1.) Because the worldview may shift with any changes in

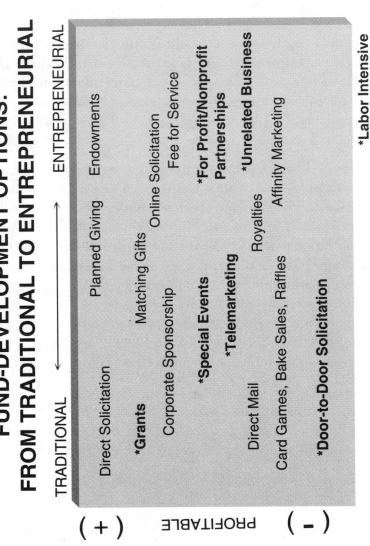

FUND-DEVELOPMENT OPTIONS: FROM TRADITIONAL TO ENTREPRENEURIAL

TRADITIONAL → ENTREPRENEURIAL

PROFITABLE (+) (−)

Direct Solicitation

Planned Giving   Endowments

*Grants   Matching Gifts

Corporate Sponsorship   Online Solicitation

Fee for Service

*Special Events

*Telemarketing

*For Profit/Nonprofit Partnerships

*Unrelated Business

Direct Mail   Royalties   Affinity Marketing

Card Games, Bake Sales, Raffles

*Door-to-Door Solicitation

*Labor Intensive

Figure 1

your board roster, this should not be a defining issue. At the same time, board members must be committed to whatever fund-raising efforts are undertaken, so their preferences should carry some weight.

My facetious example earlier of a university looking to fund its endowment by holding a car wash raises another issue for board consideration. Whatever fund-development strategy the board selects should make sense for the **sophistication level** of the organization. In the example above, one could assume that the major contributors so essential to a university's viability might have limited confidence in an administration that supported operations at this rudimentary level. After all, university development offices typically function at the cutting edge.

A related issue is your organization's stage of existence. Organizations have **life cycles** just as people do. When an organization is in its infancy, it is consumed with the basics. Capital campaigns and endowment funds are probably years down the road when, as the organization grows to maturity, a permanent home and security become important. In the early years, unless an organization's mission is truly unique and topical, a board's ability to promote a new organization to a for-profit partner is probably limited. Businesses looking for nonprofit partners are generally looking to associate with a well-recognized organization so as to bask in its reflected goodness.

Another important fund-raising issue is the **availability of sufficient staffing**—paid or volunteer—with the appropriate skills. For example, your organization may need only one or two people to operate a planned giving program, but they must be highly skilled individuals with a great deal of specialized knowledge.

The need for specialized knowledge is not as much of a concern if your organization is putting together an auction, but a need for bodies—a lot of bodies—is. People are needed to solicit items, put together a catalog, sell tickets, serve as auctioneer, man the checkout counter, arrange for food and entertainment, and encourage sales. If the organization's staffing numbers fluctuate during the year—perhaps it is located in the Snow Belt and your volunteer core migrates to the sun cities in the winter—this should be taken into consideration as well.

The **risk** that your organization is assuming by choosing a particular fund-raising course must be considered, too. Some of the most treasured fund-raising techniques of nonprofits are filled with risk. Raffles, for example, are illegal in almost every state. True a nonprofit only rarely is busted for running a raffle, but it does happen. The board can either take the chance that some agency will choose to make an example of your organization, or it can meticulously work the loopholes that often exist in state law. Still, your board must be aware of where the potential for problems exists.

Board members should look carefully at the following:

- Down payments, such as those incurred in special event planning (for example, the organization must cancel the event)

- Situations or events that could lead to personal injury or property damage (for example, someone gets food poisoning at the bake sale)

- Investment decisions

- Maintenance of inventory (for example, storage costs eat up the projected profits from a cookbook)

- Reporting and registration requirements (for example, Florida has begun to fine organizations in other states that have not registered with the state of Florida to solicit funds if those organizations receive any money from Florida. This is true *even if there was no effort to solicit in Florida*—say, someone stumbled over a Web page, thought the organization was interesting, and decided to send a check.)

- The reputations of for-profit partners

- Potential backlash from organization members who resent a particular course of action

- Constraints imposed by funding agencies (for example, reporting requirements that demand administrative oversight not paid for by the grant)

- Unexpected tax liability

- Government sanctions, including the loss of 501(c)3 status

The potential for **tax liability** is often overlooked when organizations consider their fund-raising options. Yet several fine options, such as the sale of goods and services not directly related to the mission of the organization are taxable. Many organization stakeholders recoil from the idea of paying taxes, but nonprofits raise a lot of money pursuing unrelated business income. The key, once again, is to think strategically about the benefits versus the costs.

Unfortunately, **cost** is one more obvious factor that is all too often overlooked. Another of my favorite sayings is: Sometimes money just costs too much. The most blatant example of this is the board that opts for a special event because it wants to avoid direct solicitation. It invests months of preparation and many dollars in direct and indirect costs to raise a couple thousand dollars. And it still has to solicit. Soliciting for ticket sales, underwriting, and giveaways, by the way, is more time-consuming than asking for a major gift and the potential for significant return is far less. The lesson here is that no decision about how your organization's funds will be raised should be made without first looking at the total costs. Your board should remember that despite the importance of each of the factors listed above, the ultimate goal is still to generate enough funds to facilitate the achievement of the organization's mission. Even nonprofits have to be able to make a profit—"nonprofit" is a tax code, not a goal!

Finally, with just under 1.6 million nonprofit organizations in this country—a figure that grows by approximately 40,000 a year—your board must consider its **competition**. What are others in the community doing to raise money? Does the board feel compelled, for instance, to offer frequent flyer points for contributions either because everyone else is doing it or to set the organization apart? How can your board ensure that its organization wins its share of the market?

Spending the time to analyze these issues and the potential ramifications of any decisions your board makes is one way to ensure that the organization will effectively compete. The process does not have to be difficult. Your board must talk about the issues above—always framing its responses in relation to the mission of the organization. Its conclusions should be written down. Some of the conclusions, such as the degree of risk that the organization is comfortable in assuming, should probably be codified as policy. Then, the board should ask how well each of the fund-raising techniques it is considering stacks up when measured against its conclusions.

One easy way for your board to visualize the comparisons is if it creates a grid with the decisions about the issues on the vertical axis and the fund-development options on the horizontal axis (See Figure 2.). If the board puts a check mark in any box where the fund raising methodology meets the set standard, a quick look at the completed grid will show which methods are most appropriate.

Thinking Contingencies

Earlier, I asked what your organization would do if a large portion of its expected income did not come in. Regardless of how hard your board tries to generate realistic numbers in the budgeting process, it is likely to find itself short in some area sometime during the year.

Organizations that include legacy money in their budget projections often face this as income from legacies is impossible to accurately predict. There may be little money that comes in one year even though it has been coming in fairly consistently in the past. I have heard board members from more than one organization jest about taking out a contract on contributors who have indicated that a sizable amount of money is being left to the organization in their wills. However, hiring a hit man is probably out of your price range, and it does push the ethics envelope.

As you travel the funding road there is always the possibility of becoming involved in a serious crash through no fault of your own. Those who lost millions of dollars in 1995 in the Foundation for New Era Philanthropy pyramid scheme undoubtedly felt the shock of finding the world as they knew it turned upside down in a matter of moments. Unfortunately, you face this risk whenever your plans

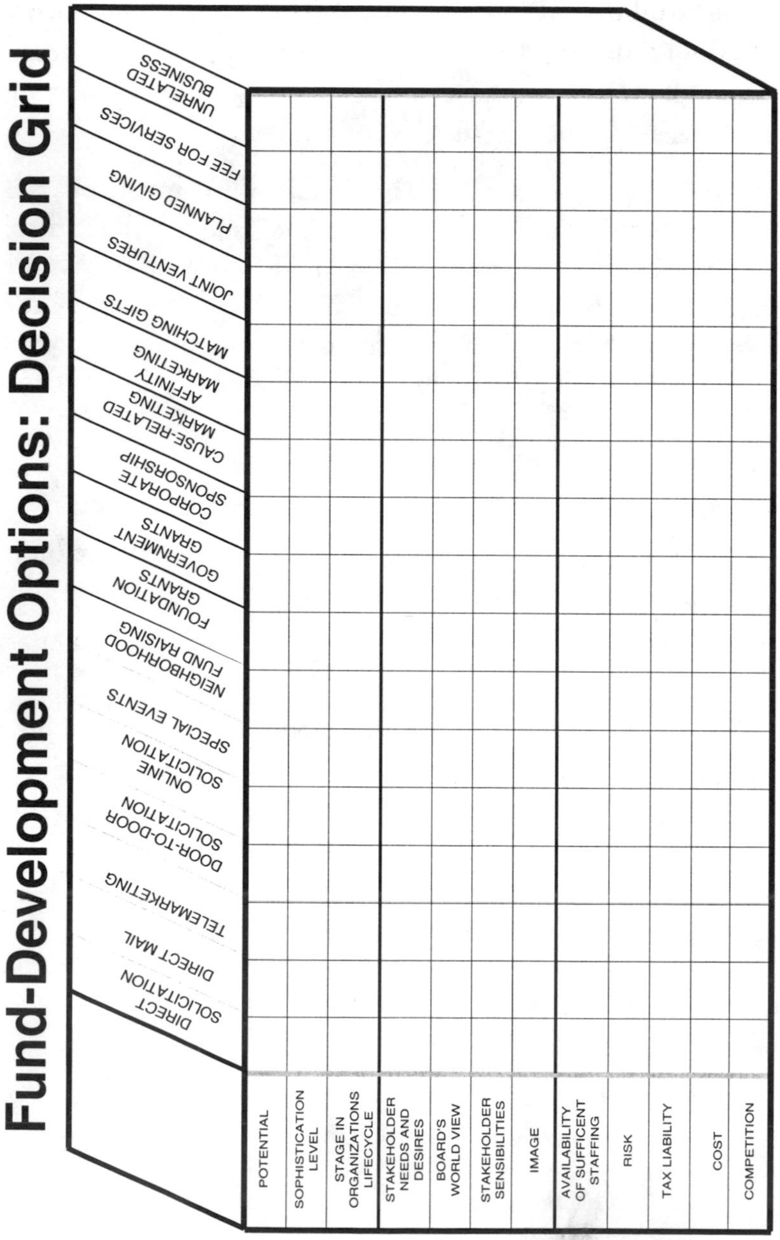
Fund-Development Options: Decision Grid
DIRECT SOLICITATION
DIRECT MAIL
TELEMARKETING
DOOR-TO-DOOR SOLICITATION
ONLINE SOLICITATION
SPECIAL EVENTS
NEIGHBORHOOD FUND RAISING
FOUNDATION GRANTS
GOVERNMENT GRANTS
CORPORATE SPONSORSHIP
CAUSE-RELATED MARKETING
AFFINITY MARKETING
MATCHING GIFTS
JOINT VENTURES
PLANNED GIVING
FEE FOR SERVICES
UNRELATED BUSINESS
POTENTIAL
SOPHISTICATION LEVEL
STAGE IN ORGANIZATIONS LIFECYCLE
STAKEHOLDER NEEDS AND DESIRES
BOARD'S WORLD VIEW
STAKEHOLDER SENSIBILITIES
IMAGE
AVAILABILITY OF SUFFICENT STAFFING
RISK
TAX LIABILITY
COST
COMPETITION

Figure 2

are dependent upon others, including corporate sponsors or joint venture partners, who may decide to put their money elsewhere this year or who suddenly file bankruptcy. Therefore, it is critical that your board plan for contingencies, with back up fund-raising ideas beyond those specified in the original plan.

The Journey

So, the board has identified your organization's destination, unfolded the map and spent several hours talking among traveling companions about where everyone wants to go and why. The pros and cons about making certain stops over others have been debated. The costs have been discussed and the options narrowed to those that are both affordable and appealing. You are ready to pull out of the drive.

As with any other journey, the planning you have done should make for a memorable trip. Just a few final hints:

Share the driving. It will increase the pleasure for everyone as work teams coalesce, friendships emerge, and people feel they are truly helping the organization make an impact on the community.

Seek adventure. There is no reason to follow last year's fund-raising plan. The less traveled roads will not only keep you out of the ditches, but also provide you with some of your best board experiences—as long as you always keep sight of your final destination.

Terrie Temkin, Ph.D.

Terrie Temkin is a perfectionist. It's apparent in everything she touches, from her elegant style of dress to tweaking a time line for a strategic plan. An award-winning speaker and an engaging group facilitator, she brings over 30 years of nonprofit management and adult education experience to her work as a consultant specializing in board, staff, and organizational development.

For five years she wrote a biweekly column in the *Miami Herald* entitled "On the Board." Her articles are found in such publications as *Advancing Philanthropy, Board Member, Community Jobs, Nonprofit World* and many more. She is frequently asked to present to chapters of the National Society of Fund-Raising Executives, Directors of Volunteer Services, and various support centers. She provides facilitated roundtables for executive directors and board chairmen, as well as coaching for individuals wishing to transition from for-profits into nonprofits. She also teaches graduate-level courses in nonprofit management.

Besides owning and managing her own international consulting firm, Nonprofit Management Solutions, Inc., Terrie is a principal in Integrated Strategies for Nonprofits, a consortium of consultants transforming organizations to better impact their communities. For 9 years, she served as executive director of the largest, most creative and financially productive district of Women's American ORT, a national organization that supports a worldwide network of vocational schools. Prior to that she served as a special events fund-raiser for the American Heart Association, a program director for the Wisconsin Region of the B'nai B'rith Youth Organization, and a nationally recognized trainer for the Hospital Learning Centers.

Terrie was selected as Woman of the Year in Nonprofit Communication (2002) by the Association of Women in Communication, Atlantic-Florida Chapter.

Terrie Temkin, Ph.D.
NonProfit Management Solutions, Inc.
P.O. Box 7536, Hollywood, Florida 33081
phone: 866-985-9489 (toll free) • FAX: 954-989-3442
terriet@nonprofitmanagementsolutions.com
www.nonprofitmanagementsolutions.com

CHAPTER 4

The Client/Consultant Relationship – Succeeding as Partners

Kathleen Rae King and Larry Checco

To be successful, the relationship between client and consultant must be considered a partnership, one built on mutual respect, trust, and an understanding of each other's needs. Yet, far too often the expectations of one party or the other are either unrealistic, misdirected or go unmet. This can lead not only to a disastrous relationship, but also to a development project that does not meet its goals, or worse!

Small nonprofits, in particular, may lack the time and personnel needed to build these partnerships. Also, the type of consulting work being performed and the personalities involved will dictate how client and consultant relate to each other.

Whatever your organization's circumstances, some basic principles and insights will help you to lay a solid foundation for your partnership.

> **TIP:** *Because our focus is on development, it may be helpful for you to view a prospective consultant almost as you would a prospective major donor. First, think about what you are looking for from this person or firm? What personal characteristics or profile are you seeking? Have you researched your prospective consultant well enough to know whether he or she can deliver what it is you need? And what must you do to fulfill your end of the partnership?*

First, Understand Your Need

Why do you need to hire a consultant, anyway?

Perhaps your organization could use the extra help and hiring a consultant is cheaper than hiring a full-time employee. Or perhaps it needs expertise in a specific area, such as revamping its board or organizing a major gifts campaign.

Or maybe what it needs most is a fresh, new, creative perspective and approach that only an experienced outsider can bring.

Consultants also can bring a certain weight to sensitive internal issues and can facilitate change. That is to say, sometimes it's easier for an outsider to say things to board members, an executive director, development professionals or other staff than it would be for an insider. This is especially true if major differences of opinion exist among key players in your organization or if people need to be educated about development work.

More often than not, the expertise you are seeking in a consultant will be needed for a limited time only and must be delivered within a given budget.

The point is, knowing what tasks you want the consultant to perform, what specific outcomes you are seeking to achieve, the time frame for which you require the consultant's services, and how much these services will cost will help to get your client/consultant partnership off to a good start.

> TIP: *Consultants should be viewed as problem-solvers and sources of good advice within reason. No consultant should be deemed all-powerful and all-knowing. At the same time, a consultant should not be used as a "fall guy" to take the blame for program or personnel issues that he or she has merely identified. Nor should you engage a consultant as "hit man" to build a case for what you perceive as poor individual staff performance or to settle some other personal internal strife. In such cases you will be able to identify a good professional consultant by his or her desire and ability to remain neutral.*

What to Look for in a Good Consultant

The stakes may be high. In your search for a good development consultant, you are preparing for a relationship that may be significant both in duration and to the financial soundness of your organization.

In large metropolitan areas it may seem that the world is filled with consultants from whom to choose; in many rural areas the search may be more difficult and entail travel and maintenance expenses.

The fact is, as in all professions, there are good consultants and bad consultants just as there are good clients and bad clients, which we'll get to in a moment. Client/consultant relationships also can mirror some marriages, where you have two good people but a bad fit.

Because you can't really know whether your client/consultant relationship is going to work out until you get into it, you may need to rely on your gut reaction enhanced by certain criteria, namely, the personal characteristics you should be looking for in a good consultant.

When looking for a good consultant, ask yourself the following:

- **Does the prospective consultant have the experience and expertise that match your needs?** This is essential. You need to know how long the person has been in the development arena, if he or she has done work in the specific area you need help in—direct mail, for example—and what his or her track record is for developing successful programs.

- **Does the consultant have the right personality and the patience to work within the culture and framework of your organization?** Every organization has its own way of doing things. Ideally, you want someone you can consider an extension of your staff, someone willing to partner with you and be able to fit into your organization's work style and environment.

- **Is the consultant a self-starter who will be able to maintain momentum, usher you through the process, and keep you on task?** You want someone who is resourceful and independent enough to resolve issues while keeping you apprised of the progress being made on your project.

- **Can this person take ownership of the project?** Good consultants meet deadlines and sometimes push you, the client, to ensure that you're staying on task and meeting your own time lines. After all, this project is probably not the only one you're working on.

- **Does the consultant show leadership and the ability to exercise influence over the decision-makers in your organization?** You know who the key players in your organization will be on this project. Is your consultant someone who can inspire and motivate, someone whom others in your organization will feel confident about, respectful of and take direction from. If your consultant is good in every other area but lacks this characteristic, the result could be something less than a successful development project.

- **Do you want this person to work on-site?** Many consultants prefer to work out of their own offices. This issue should be discussed in your initial contact with any consultant you are considering hiring.

- **Is this someone who will be able to help you articulate and define your task?** You may know where you want to go, but not how to get there. Your consultant not only needs to be a champion for your goals, but someone who brings new insight and sensitive guidance throughout the project.

- **Is this someone you can trust and confide in?** Often you may feel the need to give your consultants sensitive information regarding personalities in your organization or to explain the internal politics that swirl around certain issues. You had better be able to trust them to use this type of information wisely and confidentially or things could become very unpleasant.

- **Will this person be able to evaluate your situation and deliver a product tailored to your needs rather than something he or she "pulls off the shelf"?** Many consultants have boilerplate responses to development issues. You want someone who listens, learns, then proceeds to create a product or program that specifically meets the needs of you and your organization.

- **Last, but certainly not least, is this someone with an interest in the work of your organization, someone who understands your mission and goals and feels comfortable working to help you and your organization achieve them?** If not, then you definitely have the wrong person for the job.

TIP: *A good consultant will give you his or her best professional advice every step of the way, but in the end the product, be it direct-mail copy or a new donor-recognition or planned giving program, is yours. The consultant will go on to other projects with other clients. You, however, will need to live, at least for a while, with what it is that he or she has produced for you. Make sure you get what you want, something you feel comfortable with and proud of, rather than something the consultant would like to deliver.*

Are You A Good Client?

Many clients draw a blank on this one. Because they control the purse strings, clients can easily overlook the fact that true partnerships are two-way affairs. Successful partnerships, like successful marriages, are the product of two partners who meet each other's needs on many different levels. So while you're looking for a good consultant, a good consultant is always looking for a good client.

What does it mean to be a good client? A good client:

- **Has a stake in the project.** A good consultant wants to know that the project for which he is being hired is a priority for the development department or the organization as a whole, something that the board, executive director, or development staff truly wants to see accomplished. In fact, he or she will more than likely end up doing a better job knowing that others in the organization are willing and eager to devote their own time, interest, and energy to the endeavor.

- **Has a budget for the project.** You'd be surprised, especially on smaller assignments, how many times a development director has not secured a budget for a project before hiring a consultant. Budgets often define project scope, and a consultant needs to know how much time and effort you want him or her to devote.

- **Makes the consultant feel welcome.** Keep in mind that consultants are strangers to your organization. Make them feel welcome by introducing them to staff and others and by giving them a tour of your facilities.

- **Provides the consultant with ample resources, such as background material.** A consultant cannot do his or her job properly without having the proper resources. But there's a delicate balance to consider here. Too many unnecessary background documents and tangential information can overwhelm a consultant, making his or her task that much more difficult and time consuming. Cull through background material to give the consultant only what he needs.

- **Is responsive.** A good client returns a consultant's phone calls in a timely manner or assigns a responsible staff person to ensure whatever questions or concerns the consultant may have are responded to quickly. More often than not, it's the client's inability to respond quickly to a consultant's requests that can delay a project.

- **Is communicative.** Being responsive also applies to the consultant's work. A consultant can't always know if he's delivering what the client wants unless the client is communicative at every step of the project. Therefore, be sure to set up an approval process whereby you provide feedback to the consultant at various stages of the project.

- **Pays on time**. Because many consultants are their own administrators and bookkeepers, to track down an unpaid invoice takes time for which the consultant does not directly bill the client. This can cause hard feelings. Thirty days from the time an invoice is received is standard, unless other payment arrangements, such as payment upon product delivery, have been made. At the same time, you should never agree to pay the consultant's fee before the work is done.

> TIP: *A consultant's reputation travels faster and farther then he does, especially in a small market. Every good consultant is aware of this fact and will want to do the best job that he can for you. It's your job to help him achieve that end.*

Where to Find a Consultant

Where should you look to find the best match for your needs?

Most major metropolitan areas are awash in consultants. If your organization is located in a small town or rural area, locating a good development consultant may be more difficult. Once you've found a consultant you'd like to work with, however, distances become almost irrelevant. Telecommunication technologies, including e-mail, fax, phone, and teleconferencing are now the tools of the trade and are helping to keep meeting, travel, and work costs to a minimum.

One place to begin your search for a consultant is in the classified pages of magazines that target the nonprofit management community, such as "Fund Raising Management," "Chronicle of Philanthropy," "The Non-Profit Sector," and others. But only in a pinch. Classifieds won't provide you with what you are truly looking for, namely word-of-mouth recommendations and personal insights as to the quality and character of the consultant.

Better places to begin your search are as follows:

• National Society for Fund Raising Executives
1101 King Street
Suite 700
Alexandria, VA 22314-2967
(800) 666-FUND
Web site: http://www.nsfre.org

• National Center for Nonprofit Boards
1828 L Street, NW
Suite 900
Washington, D.C. 20036-5104
(800) 883-6262
Fax: (202) 452-6299
Web site: http://www.ncnb.org

• Your local United Way agency or organizations similar to your own for referrals to consultants with whom they've worked successfully. Check your local telephone directory.

Regardless of how you go about locating a consultant, it's imperative that you schedule a meeting with anyone you may be interested in hiring. Not only will this give you the opportunity to get a feel for him or her personally and to explain your development needs and the specific steps you envision for your project, but it also gives the prospective consultant an opportunity to meet your staff, see your organization and its work environment, and get a feel for its culture and mission.

If you are considering several consultants located outside your immediate area, an inexpensive way to make initial contact is through video conferencing. This will save on travel and maintenance reimbursements. It is still recommended, however, that you interview finalists face-to-face.

TIP: *It's important for you to call references and ask pointed questions related to whether the prospective consultant's experience and expertise match your needs, and how easy or difficult it may be to get along with him or her.*

Requests for Proposal (RFPs)

If your project is significant in size and scope, it may be best to develop a request for proposal, or RFP, and send it to prospective consultants. An RFP is a detailed description of the goals and objectives of your project and the expertise you require to get you there.

Creating an RFP offers several key advantages:

- It forces you to focus on your needs and objectives, to conduct necessary research, and to gather background information that later can be passed on to the consultant.

- It provides a framework and outline from which the consultant can take direction and begin work.

- Consultants who respond to an RFP will share their initial ideas, expertise and knowledge. As a result, you may discover more about what you need done to achieve your project goals.

The downside of writing an RFP is that it can take up valuable staff time and energy. Therefore, reserve writing RFPs for large, multiphased projects only.

When you write an RFP, make sure it is accompanied by a cover letter (see sample on page 90). The cover letter should be relatively brief and include the following:

- The kind of development expertise you are seeking, for example, board development, major gift giving, donor recognition or direct mail.

- The expected start date for your project, if you have one.

- How long you expect the project to last.

- The scope of services you require.

- A request for credentials and qualifications. These may include a letter from the prospective consultant or brochures and other printed materials.

- How you would like the consultant to respond to your RFP, for example, a phone call, a written response or at a scheduled meeting.

  TIP: *It's important that your RFP and its cover letter demonstrate clarity of vision on your part. What's the bottom line? What are you seeking as an end product? And what are you requesting and expecting from the consultant?*

Selecting a Consultant

Your final selection of a consultant is a winnowing process. If you've done your homework, that is, you know your needs and what it is you're looking for, your selection process should be a structured review of what you already know. Hence, when selecting a consultant:

- Review each prospective consultant's resume or RFP.
  - Do applicants have the experience you're looking for?
  - Are they familiar with your organization, or do they have experience working with similar nonprofit organizations?
  - What's their track record for success?

- Call references.
  - Ask pointed questions about the prospective consultant's quality of work and personal characteristics.

- Meet face-to-face with those you may be interested in hiring.
  - Get a feel for them personally.
  - Explain in detail your development needs.
  - Give them the opportunity to meet your staff and board and to see your organization to get a sense of its culture, setting, and mission.

> **TIP**: *Generally, consultants will meet with you once or twice at no charge and submit a proposal (if they haven't already responded to an RFP) based on these meetings. Also, by this time in your selection process, you should have narrowed your choices to between three and five consultants; otherwise the process will become too burdensome.*

- Ask each remaining prospect to submit a written proposal (if he or she hasn't already submitted a response to your RFP).

- Review each proposal.
  - Does the prospect have a good understanding of your organization and its development needs?
  - Has he or she developed a good plan of action, one with appropriate goals, activities, schedules, and budget?

- Determine what the consultant will expect from you.
  - Background information needed to begin and complete the task.
  - Method for approval at various stages of the process.
  - Access needed to board, executive director, development staff and others.

- If you are considering hiring a large consulting firm, make sure the firm clearly identifies the people with whom you will be working.
  - Request resumes of key personnel who will be assigned to your project.
  - If more than one person will be providing you with services, how will individual roles be defined?
  - If you work with vulnerable populations, ask how confidentiality will be maintained.

In the end, it all comes down to selecting the person or firm with whom you feel most comfortable working with, someone who has the experience and skills to help you achieve your development goals. You also want someone who can relate well to you, your staff, your board, and, not least of all, the mission of your organization.

TIP: *If your project is of significant importance to your organization, select a few board members to be included in the selection process. This will help ensure board buy-in and support of both your project and choice of consultant. In fact, depending on the project, it may be that once you've narrowed your candidates down to a few finalists, your board will select and hire the consultant.*

Writing a Contract

Everything is negotiable, meaning a contract can be anything you want it to be as long as both parties agree to it. Therefore, a contract can be as simple or as complex as you would like it to be (see samples at the end of this chapter). Some organizations have standard contracts that they adapt for all their vendors.

At the very least your contract should clearly articulate the "scope of services," including:

- Outcomes

- Benchmarks

- Time lines

- Payment procedures

- Copyright ownership of the work product

Your contract also should include a withdrawal clause so that if your partnership turns sour, you can get out of it.

TIP: *After you have exhausted every effort to make a situation work, it's important to terminate the contract if you are not achieving your goal. However, in so doing it's also important that consultant and client are in positions to save face. Both parties should treat the situation professionally, that is, with respect, sensitivity, and dignity.*

Once the Work Begins

Your job's not over yet. Once you've selected and contracted with a consultant and the work begins, you still need to manage the process.

- Are contract deliverables being completed as agreed upon?

- Are any unexpected outside expenses or liabilities being incurred?

- What feedback is the consultant giving to help fine-tune the work process?

- Is the consultant working well and listening to the needs of you and your staff?

- Have you provided the consultant with all that he or she needs in the way of support and materials so that the work can be done effectively and efficiently?

- Is the consultant being given periodic feedback as to the quality and direction of his work?

This is pretty straightforward common-sense, stuff. But many clients feel that once they've hired a consultant, the majority of their work is done, that the ball is now in the consultant's court. Not so!

At the very least, a "point person" should be assigned to work with the consultant. This person is responsible for representing the interests of the organization with the consultant, keeping everyone on task, responding to the needs of the consultant, and ultimately being responsible for the finished product.

Keep in mind that this is a partnership. If things start to go wrong, your first step should be to step back to see whether you've been keeping up with your part of the bargain. If you can honestly say that you have, then you can in good faith confront your consultant and try to remedy matters. If all reasonable efforts to get back on track fail, then divorce proceedings may be in order.

Evaluating the Consultant's Work

Conducting a thorough evaluation of the quality and effectiveness of your consultant's work may be a difficult task, especially for small nonprofits that might not have the necessary time, money or personnel. Regardless of any such concerns, you should always attempt to evaluate the quality of work performed for you by an outside consultant.

If your project has a quantitative component, such as reaching more people through direct-mail marketing, your job of evaluating the work of the consultant may be somewhat easier. Yet, even the quantitative results of adding people to your mailing list will more than likely take longer to realize than the tenure of your consultant's contract. Most often, therefore, you are left with a qualitative, rather than quantitative, evaluation process.

Perhaps the best way to think of evaluating the work of your consultant is to consider it similar to a performance review of one of your employees. The questions may be slightly different, but the goal is the same, to determine how effective this person or firm has been in performing the work set forth.

Hence, your consultant evaluation may consist primarily of seeking answers to questions, such as the following:

- Did the consultant perform the work specified in the contract?

    TIP: *Project goals that are quantifiable and clearly stated are easier to track and evaluate.*

- Did the consultant meet specified interim deadlines?

- Was the project completed on time and on budget?

- Was he or she easy to communicate and work with?

- Was the consultant professional in his or her interactions with you and your staff?

- In addition to specified deliverables, was the consultant able to create new systems and ways of thinking so that you, your staff, and organization could better anticipate and solve similar problems in the future?

If the answers to these questions, which can be obtained by debriefing your staff, executive officer and board members are positive, it may be wise to consider the same consultant for similar future projects. The advantages to doing so are many.

The consultant:

- Knows your organization.

- Has good working relationships with staff and other key players.

- Will require less background information to get started.

Many clients see good consultants as extensions of their staff, people who are knowledgeable about their organization and who can be brought in whenever the occasion warrants. At the same time, such consultants develop a sense of loyalty to the organization. These types of client/consultant partnerships are often the strongest, producing the best results with great efficiency.

Final Words

As client or consultant we all know there are no guarantees for success. The pitfalls are many, but so are the rewards derived from a good client/consultant relationship.

The formula for success is rather simple. It requires two partners, acting in mutual good faith, who possess the same objective, to produce the best development product or program possible. As the client, you need this outcome to carry out or enhance the mission of your organization. A good consultant also desires this outcome to maintain his professional reputation and thereby sustain his livelihood.

SAMPLE COVER LETTER FOR Request For Proposal

Dear [PROSPECTIVE CONSULTANT]:

The [NAME OF YOUR ORGANIZATION] is conducting a search for an experienced fund raising consultant to assist us in [BRIEFLY DESCRIBE YOUR NEED, FOR EXAMPLE, "DESIGNING A BOARD DEVELOPMENT INITIATIVE LEADING TO A SUCCESSFUL MAJOR GIFTS PROGRAM"].

The primary focus of the consulting task will be to [BRIEFLY DESCRIBE SCOPE OF SERVICES YOUR ARE SEEKING, FOR EXAMPLE, "INCLUDE AN ASSESSMENT OF OUR COMMUNITY'S MAJOR GIFTS POTENTIAL; AN ASSESSMENT OF OUR ORGANIZATION'S CAPACITY TO CARRY OUT A SUCCESSFUL PROGRAM; AND A PLAN FOR BOARD DEVELOPMENT, MANAGEMENT AND TRAINING."]

We would like to contract with a consultant no later than [GIVE DATE], with work to begin [GIVE DATE]. Our expectation is that the project will be completed within [GIVE EXPECTED DURATION, E.G. "THREE MONTHS."]

If you are interested in being considered for this project, please respond to this request for proposal (RFP) by mail no later than [GIVE DATE]. Your response should include your background and qualifications, expertise in the area of [I.E. BOARD DEVELOPMENT AND TRAINING], an outline of how you would help us achieve our goals, and a budget for undertaking the process.

If you have any questions regarding the enclosed RFP, please don't hesitate to contact [GIVE NAME] at [GIVE TELEPHONE NUMBER].

We look forward to hearing from you.

Sincerely,

SAMPLE CONTRACT PROVIDED BY CONSULTANT

[DATE]

XXXXXXXXX

XXXXXXXXX

XXXXXXXXX

XXXXXXXXX

Re: Consulting Agreement

Dear _____:

Thank you for giving [NAME OF INDIVIDUAL CONSULTANT OR FIRM] the opportunity to participate in this project. [CONSULTANT] will perform consulting services for [CLIENT'S NAME] upon the terms and conditions that follow:

1. [CONSULTANT] will use its best efforts, skills and knowledge to provide such services as needed to assist [CLIENT] in [PURPOSE OF PROJECT]. For this project, services shall include:

    • [LIST SERVICES TO BE RENDERED]

2. [CONSULTANT] has negotiated a $_____ fee to provide these services in full to [CLIENT]. Such compensation will be paid within thirty (30) days after [CONSULTANT] submits its "phased" invoices to [CLIENT]: Phase I, [DESCRIPTION OF SERVICE(S)] ($_____); Phase II, [DESCRIPTION OF SERVICE(S)] ($_____); Phase III, [DESCRIPTION OF SERVICE(S)] ($_____).

3. [CLIENT] will reimburse [CONSULTANT] for out-of-pocket expenses incurred from long-distance telephone calls and other expenses approved in advance by [CLIENT] representative. These expenses will be reimbursed in a timely fashion (30 days or less) upon receipt by [CLIENT] of all such receipts from [CONSULTANT].

4. [CONSULTANT] shall perform this Agreement solely as an independent contractor, and not as an agent or employee of

[CLIENT]. [CONSULTANT] shall be responsible for the payment of all applicable taxes associated with the compensation paid hereunder.

5.   All works of authorship prepared in whole or in part by [CON-SULTANT] shall be "works made for hire," the entire right, title, and interest of which shall vest and reside in [CLIENT]. To the extent that any work is not so treated, [CONSULT-ANT] hereby makes an irrevocable assignment of all rights, title and interest in and to the work to the client.

6.   [CONSULTANT'S] principal contact for the services to be performed hereunder will be [CONTACT NAME] or his/her designee.

7.   In the event that either party neglects or fails to properly per-form its obligations hereunder or otherwise violates any provi-sions of the Agreement, the other party may terminate this Agreement by written notice, effective upon receipt of such notice. Either party may otherwise terminate this Agreement without cause upon thirty (30) days' written notice.

[CONSULTANT] looks forward to working with the staff of [CLIENT] on this project. If you agree to the terms set forth above, please sign and return one original of the Agreement to me. The second original is for your files.

Sincerely,

[CONSULTANT'S NAME]
[NAME OF CONSULTANT'S FIRM]

Date _____

Accepted and agreed to this

_____ day of _____, 2000

By _____
[CLIENT'S SIGNATURE]
of the [CLIENT ORGANIZATION NAME]

SAMPLE CONSULTANT CONTRACT

AGREEMENT BETWEEN [CLIENT'S NAME] AND [CONSULTANT'S NAME]

This Contract is made this day of [MONTH], 2000, between [CLIENT'S NAME] and [CONSULTANT'S NAME], hereinafter referred to as the Contractor,

WITNESSETH:

WHEREAS, [CLIENT'S NAME] desires to engage and retain the services of the Contractor and the Contractor desires to accept such engagement;

NOW, THEREFORE, in consideration of the foregoing and mutual promises, covenants and agreements herein contained, and for other good and valuable consideration, the receipt and sufficiency of which is hereby acknowledged, the parties hereto agree as follows:

A.   Services to be provided [BE AS SPECIFIC AS POSSIBLE IN DETAILING EXACTLY WHAT YOU WANT YOUR CONSULTANT TO DO. THE TIME SPENT TAILORING AND DEFINING YOUR REQUIREMENTS NOW WILL MEAN FEWER HEADACHES AND PROBLEMS LATER AND ALSO WILL ENSURE A BETTER QUALITY PRODUCT.]

B.   Products: (Deliverables)

[DETAIL ALL DELIVERABLES AND DATES TO BE DELIVERED. AN EXAMPLE FOLLOWS]

(1)   Deliver a final Report (three hardbound copies and one copy of text on an IBM PC- compatible diskette using Microsoft Word 7.0 no later than (date) and in accordance with the requirements of the contract.

(2)   Provide progress briefings at [SPECIFY INTERVALS].

(3)   Provide a final exit briefing covering the essentials of the report, as well as answering all questions pertaining to the findings and recommendations.

All deliverables shall be camera-ready original work suitable for duplication. The [CLIENT'S NAME] shall have the sole and exclusive right to determine the acceptability of the services provided by the Contractor.

C.   Compensation

As compensation in full for all services to be performed by the Contractor pursuant to this Contract, the [CLIENT] shall pay the Contractor in accordance with the following payment schedule.

[PROVIDE TERMS OF PAYMENT SCHEDULE]

D.   Travel and Maintenance expenses shall be preapproved by [CLIENT] and will be reimbursed in accordance with [CLIENT] travel and maintenance policies.

E.   Payment will be made by [CLIENT] within 30 days after receipt of Contractor's itemized invoice, certified to be true and Correct, and provided that all respective requirements of the Contract have been Complied with to the satisfaction of the [CLIENT] Representative. Invoices shall be submitted to the attention of the designated [CLIENT] representative.

F.   Independent Contractor

The Contractor is furnishing its services hereunder as an independent contractor, and nothing herein shall create any association, partnership or joint venture between the parties hereto or any employer-employee relationship. Also [CONSULTANT] shall be responsible for the payment of all applicable taxes associated with the compensation paid hereunder.

G.   Termination for Convenience

The [CLIENT] may terminate this Contract by written notice at any time (or with ___ days notice) prior to completion of the Contract upon determination that such termination is in the best interest of [CLIENT]. In the event of such termination, the Contractor agrees to cease immediately all work and turn over all work product to [CLIENT]. The liability of the [CLIENT] shall be limited to payment of an equitable amount for services rendered prior to the effective date of termination, determined upon the basis of the relationship between such services and total services required to be performed hereunder had the Contract not been terminated.

H. Termination for Default

The [CLIENT] may terminate this Contract by written notice to the Contractor if the Contractor fails to perform or defaults in any manner in the performance of this Contract in strict accordance with its terms or fails to cure any breach after receiving a Show Cause Notice identifying the failure, and providing the Contractor ten days to cure the failure or nonperformance. In the event of such termination, the Contractor agrees to cease immediately all work and to turn over all work product to [CLIENT]. [CLIENT] shall have no liability to the Contractor in the event of termination hereunder except to pay the Contractor for services rendered prior to the effective date of termination for default, such payment to be determined based on the same formula as set forth, above.

I. Indemnify and Hold Harmless

[CLIENT] shall save, indemnify, defend and hold the Contractor harmless of and from all liability, loss, cost or reasonable expense arising from bodily injury, death or property damage incurred as a result of any negligent act or omission of [CLIENT], its agents, or employees arising from or relating to [CLIENT] under this Agreement. However, in no instance will the [CLIENT] be responsible to the Contractor in any way for an act or omission of the Contractor's employees, agents or invitees. The Contractor shall save, indemnify, defend and hold the [CLIENT] harmless of and from any and all liability, loss, cost or reasonable expense arising from bodily injury, death or property damage incurred as a result of any negligent act or omission by the Contractor, his agents, employees or invitees arising from or relating to Contractor's performance under this Agreement. However, in no instance will the Contractor be responsible to the [CLIENT] in any way for an act or omission of [CLIENT] employees or agents.

J.   Insurance

The Contractor shall be responsible for providing his own workman's compensation, product liability, and property damage insurance as required.

K.   Assignment

This contract shall not be assigned or the services shall not be subcontracted by the Contractor without the prior written consent of the [CLIENT], which consent shall not be unreasonably withheld.

L.   Confidentiality

The [CLIENT] and the Contractor acknowledge and agree that if during the term of this contract confidential information is disclosed by one party to the other, each party shall hold all such confidential information in the strictest confidence as a fiduciary and shall not voluntarily sell, transfer, publish, disclose, display or otherwise make available to any third persons such confidential information or any portion thereof without the express written consent of the other party. The [CLIENT] and the Contractor shall each use their best efforts to protect the confidentiality of all such information consistent with the manner in which they protect their most confidential business information.

M.   Title to Deliverables

All intellectual property created, developed, modified, or expanded by the Contractor pursuant to this Agreement shall be the sole property of the [CLIENT]. All rights, whether protected by patent, trademarks, copyright, trade secret, or unprotected shall belong to the [CLIENT]. The Contractor shall assist in obtaining the necessary protection for such rights when so requested.

N.   Sole Agreement

This Contract constitutes the sole agreement between the parties hereto and no amendment, modification or waiver of any of the terms and conditions hereof shall be valid unless in writing. Any prior oral or written agreements shall not be considered a part of this agreement.

O.   Disputes

Disputes arising from this contract shall be settled by an arbitration panel. The panel shall be constructed by each party selecting one arbitrator and those two then jointly selecting a third and final panel member.

P.   Notices

All notices given or required hereunder shall be deemed sufficient if sent by United States mail, postage prepaid, to the addresses of the Contractor and to the [CLIENT] specified in this Agreement, unless either party hereto shall specify to the other party a different address for the giving of such notices.

Q.   Tax Exemption

The [CLIENT] is a non-profit public corporation exempt from the payment of sales and use taxes.

R.   Contracting Officer Representative Appointment

The CLIENT Representative for this contract is [NAME OF REPRESENTATIVE]. The Contractor shall report directly to the designated representative designated by the contracting officer representative and will submit all deliverables to same. The CLIENT REPRESENTATIVE is responsible for working with the Contractor, reviewing, approving and accepting the Contractor's deliverables, reviewing and certifying Contractor invoices for payment, and overall monitoring of this contract.

S.   Governing Law

This Agreement shall be governed by and construed in accordance with the laws of [NAME OF STATE WHERE CONTRACT WILL BE EXECUTED].

IN WITNESS WHEREOF, the parties hereto, acting through their duly authorized officers, have executed this agreement as of the date first above written.

Agreed to by

(Name of consultant)

Address

_____

[Consultant's signature, date]

By:

Agreed to by

(Name of client)

Address

_____

[Client's signature, date

General Counsel Review and Approval Date: _____

Kathleen Rae King and Larry Checco

If we had a different political system and could choose the first lady, Kathleen Rae King would be the obvious choice. This bright, vivacious, energetic professional can entertain, fund raise, negotiate the politics of any management system and still have the energy and time to encourage and listen to her colleagues and direct reports.

Kathleen is the national vice president for development for Volunteers of America. She has raised money for the arts, human services and emergency relief for nationally recognized organizations.

Born, raised and educated in California, Kathleen is a wife and mother and holds a Bachelors of Science from California State University Long Beach and a Master of Arts from the University of Redlands, California.

Larry Checco is the kind of consultant busy executives love to work with because he is steady, dependable and produces fabulous results they can count on. Since 1983, his writing, strategic planning, and project management skills have helped raise the visibility, fund-raising capabilities, membership levels and impact of some of the nation's most prestigious not-for-profit organizations and government agencies.

Larry is currently the lead contractor on a long-term project to raise national awareness of a major DC-based nonprofit that works in the field of affordable housing. He also maintains a number of clients in the health care industry.

Larry holds a B.A. in economics from Syracuse University and an M.A. in journalism and public affairs from American University.

Kathleen Rae King
Volunteers of America
1660 Duke St.
Alexandria, VA 22314
800-899-0089
www.voa.org

Larry Checco
508 Scott Dr.
Silver Spring, MD 20904
301-384-6007
Larry.checco@verizon.net

FUNDRAISING FAVORITES

CHAPTER 5

Special Events:
Gateways to Giving

Mary Ann Blank

A colleague once told me that she was totally averse to conducting special events. She seemed pretty fierce in her objections, so I pressed her to explain why she felt so strongly. She feverishly explained that special events take too much staff time. "After calculating salary, benefits, the cost of volunteer hours, and overhead into event expenses," she said, "special events are just too costly."

When you look at it that way, she may have a point. Salary, benefits, and overhead notwithstanding, special events have the potential to raise major financial support and to bring in new contacts for your organization. That is not to say that event budgets shouldn't be carefully constructed, honestly scrutinized, and faithfully adhered to in order to bring about the desired bottom line. It takes serious self-control on the part of committee members and development staff not to select the lobster entrée when chicken will do for a benefit dinner. Corporate supporters and generous donors tend to remember if a nonprofit event is overly extravagant. Special events place your organization in the publics eye—good, bad, or indifferent.

Not every event is worth doing. The decision to go forward will often depend upon an association's goals and objectives. It may make sense in some instances to take on a fund raiser with little net revenue potential in its first year but major fund-raising possibilities in subsequent years. Each event is different, and each should be analyzed objectively in terms of profit and loss.

But consider, too, the ability of special events to bring people together. Did you ever watch "The Little Rascals?" Spanky would say, "Let's put on a show." And his gang of kids would set up a stage with an old wool moth-eaten blanket hung on a clothesline as a stage curtain. Before you could say "black and white TV," the back yard would fill up with neighborhood kids who paid a nickel to watch Darla's song-and-dance routine. Spanky and his gang made money. They made friends. People came and saw and heard first-hand what the show was all about. They left knowing Spanky, Darla, and Alfalfa. The kids connected with one another.

The National Society of Fund Raising Executives dictionary defines a special event as "a function designed to attract and involve people in an organization or cause." The dictionary makes a distinction between special event and fund raiser which it defines as an event conducted for the purpose of generating funds. For my intentions in this chapter, I am combining the definitions of both.

There are many occasions when a special event may be for the sole purpose of introducing and showcasing an organization. Many nonprofit associations will ask major donors or key volunteers to host an event in their homes, inviting their friends and other prospective donors to hear about the organization. The goal is to interest this select group of individuals in making a significant gift to a special campaign or other fund-raising project. Other events may be vehicles to recruit volunteers or to invite people to serve on a particular committee. There are all types of special events—from the unveiling of a new educational program to a reception honoring major supporters—that do not include an obvious fund-raising component. However, all these events inform people of your work and draw them closer to the organization. In the final analysis, these events contribute to or support fund raising because the people who attend them are all prospective donors, even if they are already active donors.

The Importance of Pyramid Building

Picture a pyramid. The same architectural construct applies to fund raising—a broad base of support that narrows gradually to an apex.

In fund-raising terms, the apex of a pyramid represents a relatively small number of donors making relatively large gifts. The bottom of the pyramid represents large numbers of donors making smaller gifts. The apex is where the cost to raise a dollar is nil compared with the dollars raised. This is the coup de grace of fund raising. And the only way to get there from here is to fill your database with names of prospective donors, people who know of or care about the work of your organization. Then cultivate them. Move them up the pyramid. One of the best ways I know to add solid prospects to that pool of names is to conduct special events and be fastidious about donor cultivation before, during, and after each event.

It used to be that direct mail was the best way to cull prospects into the database. Things have changed. The cost of mailing to thousands, and in some cases millions, of new names is prohibitive, not to mention the quality (or lack thereof) of names acquired in direct-mail trades or leases.

But special events are another story altogether. Why? Because they are active and alive. They are viable, and you are in control. Individuals may decide to attend your special event for any of a hundred reasons. Regardless, you have the opportunity to set the stage for donor cultivation much more so than if you sent a direct-mail appeal. A direct-mail appeal to the right person from the right person at the right time will probably yield a gift. A small gift. On the other hand, personal contact goes a lot further because it gives you the advantage of eye contact, the opportunity to act as host, and the chance to create your own giving environment. It also gives you the opportunity to gauge reaction. In other words, it's not static. Of course, that means it's up to you to create synergy.

A Gift in the Hand

Remembering the donor pyramid, let's agree that it's crucial to build up the base of names—prospective donors—in the database, and that it's important that the names in the database be realistic prospects. What's next?

The goal here is to convert the database into a **donor base**. That requires securing an individual's first gift. Special events support this by giving people a way to become aware of the good work your organization does and by providing a way for them to support your cause.

The Invitation List. Presumably, members of the planning committee have sent in lists of personal and professional friends and acquaintances to be invited to the event. Review the list with the volunteer who submitted it, and identify any people on the list who could or should be approached personally at the event. Who from the organization or the committee should approach them? Why? Are they prospective volunteers? Are they affiliated with a corporation sponsoring the fund raiser? Does that corporation have a foundation? Does this individual have the means to give to your organization if properly motivated? The point here is to make personal contact. Invite people to meet with you after the event or to talk with you during the event. Don't wait for them to approach you first.

Cultivating People

Many years ago while working for an international nonprofit health agency, I met the executive director of the organization's Houston chapter. She had conducted one of the agency's most successful walk-a-thons, raising hundreds of thousands of dollars in corporate and individual support by the event's second year. At one of the agency's training meetings, I approached her to pick her brain. She gave me valuable insight into the core of the event. One of the keys to success, she said, is to make sure that on the day of the event neither she nor any of the planning committee members had responsibility for logistical tasks. Their sole responsibility was to network, to bring people into the fold. Networking and broadening the base of support are the most essential elements of her chapter's fund-raising success, she said. Another tip: Before even the first committee meeting the event chair is asked to select his or her successor. The chair-designate is usually affiliated with a corporation and becomes part of the planning committee, attending committee meetings throughout the year. From the outset, this dramatically increases the number of key people involved in the event because where the corporate CEO goes, so goes the company.

The day after the event, a thank-you letter is mailed to every participant, donor, and corporate sponsor. It tells how much money was raised and what it will fund, and it invites the recipient to join the planning committee for next year's event. This advice sounded easy enough to me, so I tried it. Guess what? It worked. I admit to having been a bit skeptical. The bookcase in my office is filled with fund-raising manuals that make it sound oh-so-simple. The difference here is the focus on cultivation of individuals, as opposed to concentrating too much on logistics.

I conducted a little experiment with a walk-a-thon my organization held. After the walk, I sent an event newsletter to everyone who had walked with us. I included a postage-paid response card on which I asked people to volunteer on the committee for next year's event. A few cards came back, and we were able to recruit several wonderful new volunteers. One of them, a young woman who had come to the event with a friend, was an executive for a major food caterer. Her company had the market on food concessions at the area's major-league sports arenas and at many of the state's universities. Eventually, her company agreed to cater the walk-a-thon at no cost to the agency. The event grew yearly with more walkers and more money raised. In 1998, it attracted more than 2,500 participants and raised $1.5 million for research. Her company supplied water along the route, with lunch, beverages, and dessert at the end. But this nonprofit agency wanted more.

The catering executive, who had proved to be such an exceptional volunteer was approached to become a member of the board of directors and was elected by the membership. In recognition of her work for the organization, her company made a sizable contribution in her name, which she matched. While she epitomizes my point, other development officers have similar stories to illustrate the benefit of recruiting event participants to become committee members, as well as donors.

On the other hand, I once heard a story about a group that was holding a gala to honor a noted philanthropist. This event brought very different results. The gala was planned by a fabulous high society committee whose members ensured all the proper accouterments. For the elegant invitation, a printer donated the design, the paper, the printing, and the cost of shipping them to the committee for addressing and mailing. The invitation was indeed beautiful—perfect, in fact. Of course, perfection takes time, and the invitation did eventually get mailed, but the committee was so caught up in its production that members didn't really have time to review the invitation lists or pursue corporate support. Then the flower arrangements really needed to be in keeping with the gorgeous invitation, so people really didn't have time to think about follow-up calls to sell tables and to make sure the room was filled to capacity. At the event and after, everyone was just so doggoned tired from tending to all that perfection, that there was no follow up with the committee or cultivation of those who attended. This event failed to bring in new people to the organization, nor did it raise more money than it cost to put on. In fact, it may have resulted in the dissatisfaction of committee members who were unhappy with the outcome. They wouldn't be coming back any time soon.

Successful events don't happen by magic. They take planning and thought. Funds raised through special events are not raised in one day, but rather as a result of months of work. Getting overly caught up in the planning and day-of-event logistics can, if we let it, keep us from achieving the immediate and long-term goals of recruiting more and more people to raise more and more funds.

After the Party's Over

With special event fund raising, the party is never really over. Thinking about the event, cultivating supporters, recruiting volunteers, networking, talking it up, and keeping the event prominent and in the news should be a year-round endeavor.

Start with planning. Develop systems for as many procedures as possible, and work from a checklist. As soon as you secure the location, date, and time for the event, publish it. Print it in your newsletter. Send out "Save the Date" cards. Put it on your Internet homepage if you have one. Inform the board of directors.

If your organization has a calendar of events, get your event registered. Also, many major metropolitan areas and cities have listings of upcoming events. Make sure that you've checked these listings to avoid conflicts with other events in your area. Then make sure to add your event to the metro calendar. The last thing you want is for your event to conflict with another major nonprofit fund raiser. It may or may not ruin your event, but it sure can make life difficult along the way.

Get the right event committee, starting with the chair or co-chairs. You need good volunteer leadership at the highest level to have your event succeed. Volunteer leadership *will* open doors for you. It *will* set the pace for committee members and motivate them. It *will* help to fairly appropriate fund-raising responsibility between staff and volunteers. Whether you are a professional fund raiser or a board member charged with leading a special event, you have probably encountered a board or committee that believes that you, and you alone, are responsible for the outcome of your special event fund raising. Not true. The board of directors, event chair, committee members, and you all share in the responsibility. It is incumbent upon you to help the committee establish and later implement the event plan, to secure board approval, to keep plans moving forward, adhere to the budget, and to alert leadership when or if problems arise.

Sometimes it's easier to accomplish this if your event is the premier or inaugural event of its kind for your organization. You avoid having to combat the "we've always done it this way" syndrome or "Joe has always been the chair" phenomenon. The downside is, of course, that you have to start everything from scratch. A word to the wise: Don't undertake any special event without appropriate buy in from your board, your event committee, and your immediate staff supervisor. If a vast majority of your board will not commit to buying or selling a significant block of tickets, think twice about doing the event. And budget wisely.

The <u>Before</u> Budget vs. The <u>After</u> Math

Do yourself a favor. Budget expenses liberally, and budget income conservatively. Invariably, things cost more than anticipated. Likewise, sure-bet sponsors won't come through at the last minute.

You don't want to conduct an event that merely covers costs. If you have committed to pay for catering with expenses that equal $150 a person with a guarantee of 400 people, then, you have to be certain you can do the following: 1) Bring in 400 people. 2) Charge enough not only to cover the cost per person, but also to make a profit. 3) Secure corporate support to help defray costs. Special event fund raisers are not exercises in breaking even. How much revenue do you want or need to reap after expenses? What is it that makes the event worthwhile after the expenditure of salary, benefits, overhead, and the outlay of event expenses? What is your bottom line?

Planning Musts. As you plan, put first things first. You can have the best committee this side of the Atlantic, but if your event needs a permit from the city and you haven't got one, you will not have a successful event because you will not have an event at all. Whatever time you think you will need to secure a permit, double it. Then double it again.

If your event has the most substantial corporate underwriting in the history of special event fund raising, but another nonprofit reserved the only major hotel in town, then you may not have a ballroom for your event. The devil, unfortunately, is in the details. If you are planning an indoor event, you will need to know the number of people expected. Obviously, you don't want a facility that's too big or too small. Like Goldilocks, you want it just right. If you begin your budgeting with a list of prospective corporate sponsors and individual attendees you will be better equipped to seek out an appropriate venue. Budget conservatively. If you are lucky enough to sell out and raise the maximum revenue for your event, then "Congratulations!" Alert the media that you have sold out because it will heighten the excitement around the event and lay groundwork for a larger crowd next year.

When setting the budget, don't forget to factor in the sometimes hidden or unexpected costs of audiovisual equipment, as well as gratuities. With average hotel gratuities of 18 percent, you can well imagine the impact to your budget if this item has been overlooked. When audiovisuals are involved, make sure you are complying with any regulations that apply. I had this recent experience with a local chapter of my organization. An academy award-winning actress was going to appear at a chapter fund raiser, and a professional audiovisual company was hired to tape a 30-minute question-and-answer session between the actress and the audience. But during the session, someone in the audience, someone with an authoritative voice, instructed the videographer to stop taping as the actress spoke because of Screen Actors Guild regulations. Later, the executive director received a copy of the videotape—the vast majority of which was blank.

Assign key volunteers to oversee areas of vital importance to your event. Tasks like on-site registration, media relations, and event administration are sometimes overlooked. People who haven't pre-registered for the event will show up at the door. The media will come when you least expect them—and—when you don't want them. You will need change for $100. Everyone will want a receipt, especially if you forgot to bring the receipt book. Special events are never perfect. That does not mean they are not worth doing.

One final word gleaned from experience. Bring business cards and plenty of pens and paper. If you work the room the way you should, you will come home with a handful of others' cards and a full cash box.

Back to the Future

What if, in spite of careful planning and cultivation of your key prospects before, during, and immediately after your special event, you come up empty handed? What's next?

Look at your upcoming activities. If you are planning a direct-mail appeal, add the names from your invitation list to your prospective donor pool. Consider contacting the people who did not come to your event with a letter that begins, "Dear Friend: We missed seeing you at the third annual gala dinner and dance for XYZ Organization. But don't worry. There's still time to support the organization's vital research program. We still need your help."

If you are conducting a membership drive, you could direct a letter to the entire invitation list at least once, inviting individuals to support the organization with a gift of membership. Don't forget to invite this list of individuals to attend other events in the area. And if you are feeling really ambitious, you can send them copies of your annual report with brief, handwritten notes that say something like this: "We missed you at the walk-a-thon. Thought you might like to know that we raised $100,000. Hope to see you next year."

You may or may not get an immediate reaction to this type of cultivation. You will get noticed.

Another effective post-event tool is the survey. After a special event, most, if not all of us really don't want to talk about it any more, let alone generate more memos, paperwork, lists, or reports. But if you can see your way through it, try to send a concise questionnaire to the people who attended, as well as those who didn't. Ask them why they did or didn't come. You may get some surprising answers especially if your survey returns are anonymous.

Surveys are tricky to write because it is easy to build in your own bias. Consider composing it well in advance of the event so that you don't bring your own ideas or disappointments into the equation. Make sure to include corporate sponsors among those you survey. You will learn what they need and want in terms of recognition. It is vital to secure corporate sponsorship. It is a pity to lose it once you have it.

Be Careful What You Wish For

People who put on special events are creative, achievement-oriented individuals. They attract similar personality types to help them—volunteers and donors who want to make a difference and have the time, talent, and resources to accomplish great things. Too often, the capabilities of these volunteers and donors, are underutilized because day-to-day tasks and operations get in the way. If there is a single message I would like to impart above all, it is this: Special event fund raising can be a magnet, attracting major corporate sponsorships, donors, volunteers, and funds to your organization. The job of a fund-raising professional or board member is to fully harness and mobilize the energy and potential of these dedicated people for both the short term and the long run.

Recently, I was reminiscing about my early fund-raising days. I recalled learning the lesson of delegation. It was born from desperation and from what I call the frailties of my human condition. Nevertheless, it was born. I picked up the phone and recruited total strangers to help me with an ungodly schedule of special events. And somehow, this wonderful core of people came forward with their gifts of support, their ideas, their friends, co-workers, companies, free time, and days off. They helped every time I called. Some went on to become board members. I don't think another type of fund-raising campaign would have brought them as close to the organization as these special events I did. Just like Spanky, Darla, and Alfalfa, we got to know one another and connect, all for the greater good.

Mary Ann Blank

Mary Ann Blank is a juggler. With great panache, she has managed a full time job in development, motherhood, volunteer work, marriage, and one of her greatest, if sometimes hidden passions, writing. She is also a very young, doting grandmother.

Mary Ann was the development director for the National Hemophilia Foundation until December 1999. During her tenure, she did the equivalent of parallel parking the QEII. She was their first full time development director. She whipped the data base into shape, started a planned giving program, initiated special events, launched a first-ever capital campaign, and worked directly with the board of directors, volunteer committees and working groups.

While working full time during the day, she still manages to be an active participant in the Writers' Studio in New York. In 1998, Mary Ann, who is fluent in Spanish, won a place in the prestigious San Miguel de Allende Poetry Week in San Miguel, Mexico.

In recent years, she has concentrated her volunteer activities on the National Voluntary Health Agencies (now the Community Health Charities). She was a board member during their merger with the Combined Health Appeal.

Mary Ann has been married to her adorable and adoring husband Herb for 15 years. They met when Mary Ann was working for the Juvenile Diabetes Foundation in Philadelphia. She was lugging in huge sacks of direct mail returns when Herb spotted her and asked if he could help. She recruited him as a volunteer, he recruited her as his wife. Herb is a financier and is always goading Mary Ann into raising the bar. When Mary Ann thinks of asking for $10,000, Herb is the first to say, "why not $20,000 or $50,000."

Mary Ann is director of development at The Mount Sinai Hospital and Mount Sinai School of Medicine where she continues her life as a juggler.

Mary Ann Blank
Director of Development
The Mount Sinai Hospital
Mount Sinai School of Medicine
One Gustave L. Levy Place, Box 1049
New York, NY 10029-6574
212-373-4943
maryann.blank@msnyuhealth.org

CHAPTER 6

Making the Mail Work (Better) for You

Eleanor T. Cicerchi, CFRE

R eaching into your mailbox, you find four letters. You know they're fund-raising appeals just by spotting the name of a charity on the envelope, a nonprofit stamp, or "teaser copy" (intriguing phrases printed on the front of the envelope, perhaps a picture of a cute baby cheetah and a hint that it's in danger). Send a check in response to just one, and soon a flood of appeals is coming your way—many of which you'll probably toss before they're opened (or perhaps after you have removed your free, personalized address labels).

Ever wonder if there is *real* money to be made for the charities that send these letters? The answer is yes (hundreds of millions of dollars, as a matter of fact, but not for all nonprofits). Direct mail is not scientific. It's expensive, particularly at the beginning. It takes staying power, attention to details, and continual monitoring. Expertise helps (which is why you'll probably want some outside help in designing your program). But all that aside, direct mail works for thousands and thousands of organizations. Americans and Canadians are among the most philanthropic in the world. And they make decisions in minutes, if not seconds, unlike foundations and corporations, which can deliberate for months before making a grant or even announcing a decision.

This chapter is about direct mail: the technique of raising money by mailing large quantities of inexpensively produced, nearly identical solicitation packages to a great number of people—and then waiting for those checks to flow your way. We want to help you decide whether investing in direct mail makes sense and, if so, how to begin. If you are already using direct mail, we'll provide some food for thought about increasing productivity over time (donor value) and how to evaluate your results. Even if your organization is not a big mailer, chances are that you are already soliciting and renewing gifts by mail in one or more segments of your development program. We hope our hints on how to structure letters can improve your results.

Is a high-volume mail program for you?

Not every nonprofit is a good fit for high-volume direct mail—say, 100,000 or more packages a year to nondonor names (names you have rented from other organizations), and renewal mailings to your own donor file four or more times during the year. The checklist below can help you decide how aggressively you want to use direct mail.

- **Does your organization have emotional appeal?** If your organization helps children or animals in need, feeds the hungry, houses the homeless or in some other way touches people or animals directly, chances are that you can be successful in a mail campaign. On the other hand, research organizations, societies dedicated to intangible issues, and associations that are distant from those who ultimately benefit (say, an association of libraries), can certainly raise money, but usually not from high-volume direct mail. I know of a highly regarded population-control research institute that tested a direct-mail program a few years ago. Unable to communicate the direct human impact of its work, it had disappointing results and abandoned the technique. Membership fees, major gifts from people committed to the cause, and grants are far more effective for this nonprofit.

The reasons for the importance of emotional appeal are easy to understand. What makes you read through a direct-mail package you receive? What makes you write out that check or reach for your credit card? Chances are, it's an immediate connection—a response that is primarily emotional. A photo of a cuddly panda cub, a picture of a skeletal child with big, liquid eyes, the story of an abandoned child helped by a social service agency. Your first response is likely to be anger, fear, or guilt.

Sure, at some point, you need to be convinced that this organization is making a difference. But what gets you into the letter is the immediate emotional connection. This fundamental of direct mail not only determines whether your organization wants to undertake a comprehensive direct-mail program, but also determines how you'll write letters and how you put together the package. We'll offer hints later in this chapter on ways to create emotional connections.

- **Does your organization have name recognition or a recognizable symbol?** This is not essential, but it sure helps. Think of some of the biggest and most successful mailers: the March of Dimes, the Red Cross, UNICEF, and the American Cancer Society. These are nonprofits with considerable brand equity: People know the names, they trust the brands, and they give through the mail, year after year.

But you don't have to be the Red Cross to succeed. If your organization has emotional appeal, and if you have a smart, strategic approach, you can overcome being unknown. My organization, which operates a flying eye hospital aboard a specially equipped jet, fared poorly in mail requests when it used the name "ORBIS" with no other identifying features. But when we created a sub-brand, "SightFlight," and a special logo with a plane in it, we began to do exceptionally well—and we still are.

External factors can also play a role in positioning your organization. The sudden popularity of an issue, say child abuse, urban violence, or a natural disaster, can boost giving to related charities. So can media exposure, such as TV coverage or an article in a magazine or major newspaper. Just being creative and opportunistic in positioning your organization can pay off. In fact, it's possible to see success with direct mail after years of disappointments.

- **Are you, your boss, and your board ready to invest in start-up for two to three years?** By "invest," we really mean "lose money"—at least for a while. This is important to recognize from the start. Most new, or newly enlarged, direct-mail programs don't produce net income for two to three years—not until the people who responded to the initial appeal renew their gifts and their cumulative giving compensates for the high cost of getting that first gift. The number of people who respond the first time (the yield); the size, frequency, and number of renewing gifts; and the cost of the package and support services all have an impact on how much needs to be invested and for how long. Here, expert advice from people with experience in direct mail can make a huge difference. There are lots of ways to manage the risk and to monitor the results all along the way. Just remember that high-volume direct-mail fundraising is not for the faint of heart. But if you don't try, you may never know what might be.

A Dual-Track Effort

Successful direct-mail programs have two separate—and, to my mind, equally important—tracks: The *acquisition* track seeks gifts from people who have never before given to your organization, while the *renewal* track seeks repeat and upgraded gifts from donors who have given to your organization at least once previously. Both tracks are essential to achieving net income and a sustained program. While you can bring in lots of new money through acquisition, the costs are high. It's only in your renewal program that income is likely to surpass your expenses.

To illustrate this, let's look at a sample start-up program. Organization A mails 100,000 packages to nondonors. The "yield" is 1.0 percent, which is considered very good in acquisition programs. That means 1,000 new donors. If the average gift is $18, a pretty typical number, the organization makes $18,000. But each package cost 38 cents, including postage. Thus, the cost of the mailing was $38,000, and the organization is actually in the hole $20,000—even before staff or consultant expenses are considered!

It's the renewal program that will save the day. Two months later, Organization A mails a letter and response piece to the 1,000 people who sent in gifts in response to the acquisition package. This time the audience is "warm": the people who receive the package have not only read or skimmed your first one, they have actually written a check. An average response to the second appeal might be 7 percent. That is, 70 people of the 1,000 send repeat gifts. The piece is likely to be a little cheaper, with no premiums such as address labels to encourage a nondonor to open the package and fewer pieces of paper inside the envelope. This time the cost is 22 cents. The cost is $220 for 1,000 of these packages. The 70 gifts average $20 for total income of $1,400. Finally, Organization A is making money. Of course, there is a long way to go to make up the $20,000 "investment" in the acquisition appeal, but the tide has turned!

A year or 14 months later, after five renewal appeals, perhaps 40 percent of those 1,000 new donors have given at least one repeat gift. If those 400 people have made a total of 440 gifts (because some people made gifts more than once), and the gifts are averaging $20, Organization A has spent $1,100 to bring in $8,800 through the renewal program.

If that doesn't sound too impressive, remember that Organization A may have 2,000 other donors that have been giving for as long as 10 years. These people comprise a very loyal donor segment, and they have a 70 to 80 percent renewal rate year after year. To achieve economies of scale, you'll add them to your renewal program. Chances are that with the new graphics, more frequent or more regular mailings, and a few other improvements to your program, their giving will pick up. As the new donors become long-time donors, the economics look even better. At some point you may recruit a portion of them to a monthly donor program, which works through direct debits from bank accounts. (This is a very attractive program, because it costs so much less to keep the donor.)

You may be asking about now, "If acquisition is so expensive, why not limit that portion of the program?" The answer to this is different for every organization. How fast do you want your direct-mail program to grow? How much money, how fast, are you prepared to invest? One thing is clear: Unless your program has failed miserably, you *don't* want to stop acquisition. The phenomenon of attrition—or donor dropout—haunts everybody in direct mail. Some donors find other causes to support. They die, move, have financial reverses, whatever. Some mail-acquired donors move up: into your major gifts program, where they get more personalized appeals from your CEO or a volunteer fund-raising leader and are no longer in your direct-mail program. Over time, unless you continue to replenish your donor file with new donors acquired through the mail, your list will dwindle away.

Some organizations concerned with their fund-raising ratios have minimal acquisition programs for two years, then mail aggressively during the third year. This way they keep replenishing their lists, and their average fund-raising ratio is within acceptable limits. Consultants, colleagues in other organizations, workshops and, yes, books like this can all help you come to the decisions that make the most sense for your organization.

Getting Started

Understanding Who Your Donors Are Now

Your first step in starting or revitalizing your direct-mail program is to determine what earlier direct-mail activities have worked or not worked, and with which groups of people. This is an important process that you can dignify (just in case somebody in your organization thinks you should be spending your time doing other things) with the term "audit."

The reason for the audit is that to be successful in direct mail, you have to be able to discern trends or patterns of response that work. This means mailing in sufficient quantity to discern patterns. (If you have ever taken a statistics course, or studied survey results, you know that patterns can only be discerned by looking at a large enough population. With too small a population, a few out-of-the-ordinary responses skew the results.) Given the high cost of printing and postage, mistakes or bad guesses are expensive—so you want to be armed with as much information about what works for your organization as possible.

Look for clusters of donors or characteristics shared by the people who already support you (age, gender, where they live, whether they or family members have used your services, and what other organizations they support, for example). Also look at the types of direct-mail packages that have done well (for example, those that tell a story of a person helped by your organization or that carry an endorsement, those that feature a particular part of your program, or those with premiums or giveaways). Don't *think* you know. Take a hard look. You may want to go so far as a mailed survey that seeks answers to some of these questions.

Which Consultants to Hire

For a large program, you'll want the services of several types of specialists: a list broker (who will suggest which mailing lists to rent and then arrange for the rentals) and a shop that does the "creative" work, such as the letter writing and analysis of results. You'll also need a printer, maybe a mail house or letter shop (to assemble all those packages and get them into the mail), and, if you don't have database capabilities in-house, an outside database management firm. Some of these tasks can be handled in-house if you have sufficient staff or volunteers. Just remember that it makes no sense to staff up for peak volume if the work will be cyclical: either you'll have people sitting on their hands during nonpeak times, or the few people you do have will be losing their minds (and donors will go unacknowledged) during peak times.

If you can hire only one outside firm, choose the list broker. Sixty percent of your results in acquisition can be attributed to the lists you use. You don't want to skimp here.

How to Select Your Lists

High-volume direct-mail programs involve renting names from lists drawn from other nonprofits, magazines, and membership organizations. There are thousands and thousands of lists on the market that you can to choose to rent. Your list broker will be of invaluable assistance in recommending those that may work for your organization.

Here are some tips for list selection:

1) *Choose lists from organizations with similar missions.* If your organization is a health organization or if it helps children, you'll want to rent names of people who support other health- or child-oriented nonprofits.

2) *Always look for evidence of mail responsiveness __and__ philanthropic behavior.* There are millions of people who have disposable income and who may be interested in your cause, but who do not respond to mail appeals. That is why you want to rent the names of people who are already giving through the mail to like organizations. Beware of lists of "wealthy college graduates" or subscribers to high-end regional magazines (unless your organization is a museum or other organization that appeals to high-net-worth people). They may not be mail-responsive and, though philanthropic, may not respond to direct-mail appeals from organizations new to them.

3) *Always do a merge-purge to remove the names of your current donors.* People who have been donors to your organization for years are likely to be offended if they receive a "Dear friend" letter purporting to introduce your organization.

Developing Your "Control" Package

Another important element of a high-volume program is the control package for your acquisition program. Because the stakes are so high in acquisition, you want to leave as little as possible to chance. That's why, when you mail in large quantities, you want to mail a package that has already been tested and has proved its value. This is your control package.

Here's how the process works. Your consultant comes up with two different packages. One of the two might have a premium, such as address labels or greeting cards. Perhaps one is sent in a large envelope, and the other has "teaser copy," such as one Amnesty International used recently: "In some parts of the world, answering this letter could <u>land you in jail or even get you killed</u> . . ."

Rather than mailing great quantities of one or both, start with a test mailing. Your list broker has recommended ten lists: 10,000 names from each, randomly selected. To determine which package works best, mail package A to half of each list, package B to the other half. Identify which package each person receives by a code on the reply device (the coupon people send back with their checks). That way you know which package your donors have responded to.

To evaluate the responses, look at the "yield" (the percent of donors who responded with a gift) and the average size of the gift, as well as the cost of producing each package. Each variable is important. If Package A yields fewer gifts, but those gifts are larger than those acquired with Package B, you might be better off making Package A your control. If one package is considerably more expensive than the other, that is a factor to consider, too. Alas, you are going to have to choose just one because it is too expensive to do all the setup for two acquisition packages.

Thereafter, you will continue to test variations on your control package, always trying to improve the yield or average gift or lower the cost. Perhaps you'll test another package entirely. Remember to test only one different element at a time (otherwise you won't know which element made a difference). When you find a "winner," you can stay with it for several years. I once heard of an organization that used the same photo of a little boy for so many years that he had grown into an adult. The control package was too successful to be abandoned.

Learning Which Lists Work for You

The other important piece of information you will derive from your test mailing is which lists work best. Here, too, you want to look at yield as well as average gift size. Some lists are likely to be clear winners, others will be duds, and still others "so-so." Your list broker will probably recommend that in the full "rollout"—a large mailing of your control package—you concentrate on the lists that performed best, dropping the poor performers, and perhaps continuing to test the so-so lists to see what potential they may have.

As tedious as this may seem, what you are really doing is minimizing your risk in a high-risk endeavor. Direct mail is counterintuitive. What you think will produce well in the mail may not, and vice versa. The only reliable way to find out is to test and quantify the results.

Writing the Letter: "Open the Heart . . ."

Writing letters and other pieces that go into a direct-mail package is not easy. Even the experts in the field are occasionally stumped. In my experience, there is a lot of latitude in copy development, as long as you use emotion, are truthful and believable, and document the impact of your organization. Yet it helps to have an experienced direct-mail writer, especially for your acquisition program. It also helps to adhere to three basic rules: 1) Evoke an emotional response, 2) Keep your message simple, and 3) Involve your reader.

Rule One: Appeal to the Heart or the Gut

There is no getting around this rule. Emotion, as we said earlier, is the way you make that first connection with the donor. I once heard a British fund-raiser sum up the order of things: "Open the heart, to open the mind, to open the checkbook." First, connect with the reader viscerally. After that, tell your story in a convincing way. Substantiate with tangible examples, testimonials, even a few statistics about the number of people you have served. Repeat the major messages, highlight your most important messages, and, above all, ask for the gift, not once but several times throughout your letter (the tie-down). This is the basic pattern of a successful direct-mail letter. See page 131 for additional tips.

Which emotions? According to Greg Adams, a principal in Adams & Hussey, a direct-mail firm that has many high-profile political and social-change clients, this is the ranking of emotions that work best in direct mail:

- Anger (that others are suffering, that something you care about is threatened)

- Fear (of illness, harm to your children, loss of income or privilege)

- Self-interest (benefits, financial security, good health)

- Exclusivity ("because you are among a select few . . .")

- Curiosity (This gets your reader into your letter. Put a puzzling statement on the envelope, but be careful not to say too much or you'll take away the suspense. Then, in your first paragraph, make the transition to your case.)

- Validation (An appeal that states that choosing to support your organization was a good decision, citing the group's accomplishments or other reasons.)

The power of emotion is why wildlife groups showcase photos of cute baby animals and tell you why they are in danger and why you should help. If you care about animals, it's hard not to think about helping a starving baby panda or a tiger cub whose parents have been killed by poachers. The reader continues to read (or skim), to satisfy himself or herself that the organization is reputable, does good work, and uses its funds effectively. A gift may not always result, but if it does, emotion played a substantial part in the decision.

By the same token, international development agencies have found success in asking for sponsorship for children. The appeal revolves around stories and photos of children with soulful eyes holding empty bowls. You're angry, perhaps even guilty, that in a world of such plenty, such tragedies should occur. This makes the connection. The rest of the letter returns again and again to how the organization helps, and the difference your gift will make.

The omission of pity in the list above is deliberate and may surprise you. That's because pity alone doesn't work in direct mail. It needs to be paired with another emotion (fear or validation, for example), as well as backed up by a discussion of why this approach to the problem works and deserves the reader's support. Sympathy or pity may elicit a single gift (to help a family that has lost its home in a natural disaster or war, for example) but cannot by itself sustain a direct-mail program.

If you think your organization doesn't have emotional appeal, look deep into your organization's mission and programs. Can you pull out something that will appeal to basic human emotions? I once worked for an AIDS research organization whose work, at first blush, is pretty far removed from the people who will ultimately benefit. But we found that a community program that gave people with AIDS access to new treatments had immense personal appeal to certain market segments. So did appeals that targeted parents, mothers in particular, who did not want to contemplate losing a child to AIDS. "A world without AIDS" has powerful appeal.

Perhaps one of the best known direct-mail letters to use fear as a motivator is the Memorial Sloan Kettering appeal that opens: "You may not ever need us . . ."

It helps to think about which appeals have touched you. That's the same kind of reaction you want to generate with your direct-mail packages. Strong, immediate feelings that will translate into a desire for action. Promise that action in your letter, document your organization's impressive achievements already, and you are on your way.

Rule Two: The KISS Principle (Keep it simple, stupid)

It's natural to want to put a lot about your organization's work into your mail appeals. But resist the impulse.

- *Focus on one theme or one message.* Describe one aspect of your program, not all of them in a single letter. You'll have plenty of opportunity to talk to your donors about your other activities in subsequent appeals.

- *Repeat your core message and your appeal for support over and over.* If the reader does not see these key words on page one, he or she may see them on page two, or on the reply device.

- *Don't include a brochure.* This is not a hard and fast rule, but it's a good one to follow most of the time. It's fine to include a reprint, a circular that is skimmable, a map or perhaps a diagram showing your program in action. A "lift note" from someone other than the signer of the letter can help, too. The text of each of these pieces should reinforce the message in your letter, as should any text on the outside, or carrier, envelope or on the reply device.

Rule Three: Involve Your Reader

It's also tempting to talk about all the good work your organization does and to expect your donor to buy in. But this is risky. The best letters use the word "you" more than "we," "our," or "I." Invite the reader into the work of your organization. Two useful phrases are "You can help" and "Your support will . . . "

Many nonprofits go further and include participation devices. Ask the reader to fill out a survey. The AIDS research organization I mentioned above has used a survey appeal to acquire new donors for several years. No other donor acquisition has beaten or even matched it. A survey arouses curiosity and appeals to the donor's desire to be acknowledged. Answering the questions focuses the reader on the need for the organization and produces gifts.

Another successful appeal for the AIDS organization, this one for renewing and upgrading gifts from current and lapsed donors, was a petition. Donors were asked to sign petitions to be forwarded to their legislators by a certain deadline—to voice their support for renewal of Ryan White legislation. It worked wonderfully on all scores. The petitions were delivered on time in huge sacks. And dollars flowed to the research organization. Most important, the legislation was renewed.

Amnesty International in the United Kingdom is an effective innovator in participation devices. One appeal contained a small pencil that could be felt through the envelope. The pencil was to be used to sign a petition to release a political prisoner in the developing world. Still another included a piece of cardboard with slits for inserting two coins, worth one pound each.

These appeals can be expensive and should always be tested in small lots before being rolled out. But inviting the prospective donor to participate actively in the work of the organization can be extremely effective. Get your best marketers thinking about innovative ways to do this. The results may surprise you.

How Are You Doing?

As satisfying as it may be to see those dollars accumulating, there are a few more calculations you need to make to assess how your program is doing.

- Retention (or the flip side of the same coin, attrition). Expect some donors to drop out; that's attrition. The retention rate is the percentage of those who continue to give. It's tempting to keep all those names in your files. But if a donor has not responded in 36 months, you might want to try mailing less frequently. Sometimes you can get a long-lapsed donor back by mailing the acquisition package again. And sometimes you just archive a name. Calculate the retention rate year after year; you'll get a baseline rate that you'll want to try to beat year after year.

- Donor value. This is an important calculation: the cumulative "value" of a donor over time—that is, cumulative gifts minus the total cost of getting that first gift. Do this donor by donor or for segments of your list (say, the donor value for donors acquired by using list A vs. the cumulative value of donors acquired from list B. If list A donors give less frequently than list B donors, but give higher gifts, you may want to rent more names from list A. You might also want to calculate the value of donors acquired with premiums vs. those who responded to a package without premiums).

Because so much depends on discovering patterns of success, these calculations will help you do more of what works as you continue to innovate, test, and analyze results. Remember, even the giant mailers once started small.

The Basic Structure of Good Fund-Raising Letters

1. The Hook (Grab the reader's attention.)

2. The Ask (Make your request for a donation early in the letter.)

3. Restate the Problem, Opportunity, or Challenges. (Offer facts and vignettes to convince the reader he/she should be concerned about the problem.)

4. Introduce the Solution or Remedy.

5. Juxtapose the Problem and Solution with Your Organization. (Define your niche.)

6. Have Tie-Down Requests Throughout. Repeat the Ask 5 to 7 times.

7. Stress the Urgency for Action.

8. Spell out the Consequences for Inaction (near the close of the letter).

9. Repeat your Financial Need (at end).

10. Always add a P.S. (Give an additional reason for giving NOW.)

Developed by Malchow, Adams & Hussey, Washington, D.C.

Sample of Acquisition Package

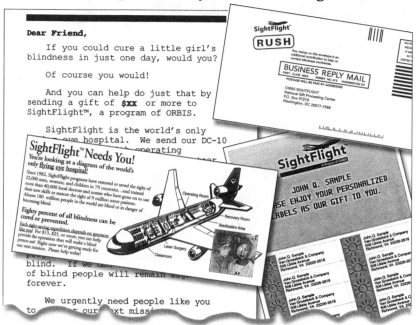

Sample of Renewal Letter

Eleanor T. Cicerchi, CFRE

Eleanor is the queen of direct mail. She really knows her stuff. Eleanor has 25 years of management experience in fund raising and public relations, primarily in health and higher education. She is currently the vice president for development and external affairs/Americas for ORBIS International, Inc., where she spearheaded ORBIS's move into direct mail in the United States and Canada in 1997. The program has been exceptionally successful and has been featured in several national fund-raising publications.

Prior to joining ORBIS, she served as the chief development officer for the American Foundation for AIDS Research (AmFAR), the vice president for institutional advancement for Marymount College in Tarrytown, New York, and campaign counsel with Brakeley, John Price Jones Inc.

Eleanor is not just another pretty face who can raise a buck. She is a Phi Beta Kappa graduate of Mount Holyoke College and a Woodrow Wilson Fellow. She has a master's in nonprofit management from The New School University, where she is now an adjunct instructor. She is also a faculty member for the Fund Raising School at the Indiana University Center on Philanthropy and taught in the graduate arts management program at New York University for nine years.

Eleanor is also very active in community and professional organizations. She is a long-time board member and former chairman of a chamber orchestra, a board member of the American Anorexia-Bulimia Association, and a fund-raising volunteer for Habitat for Humanity and local history groups.

Eleanor lives in New Jersey with her husband Philip. She has two grown kids.

Eleanor T. Cicerchi, CFRE
ORBIS International, Inc.
330 West 42nd Street, Suite 1900, New York, NY 10036
212-244-2525, ext. 206

CHAPTER 7

So, You're Considering a Planned Giving Program . . .

Mark E. Mersmann, CPA and Arthur M. Seltzer, CPA

Where does our organization go from here?

Your organization has worked long and hard to cultivate a core group of repeat donors who are the foundation of your annual fundraising campaign. Everyone on the Board and the staff feels good about that, but there continues to be a concern each year about the success of the current campaign, and about maintaining the relationship with the donors and the level of giving in future years.

Perhaps your Board should take action to build on the past approach to fundraising to respond to these concerns. The Board has heard the term "planned giving" and knows that other organizations have planned giving programs as part of their fundraising.

However, at this point your Board members and staff have many questions:

- Does the charter and/or bylaws permit such a program?

- Are there any other legal restrictions?

- Is planned giving right for your organization?

- Is now the time to start a program?

- Will it ever be the right time?

- Will we need more staff?

- Will it hurt our annual campaign?

- What will it cost to get a program started?

- What will it cost each year to maintain the program?

- Should we target a different type of potential donor?

- How complicated will it be?

- How do we start the process?

All of these are very good questions that need to be answered for your organization. The process of inquiry, study and discussion are very important for the future success of a planned giving program. A less than thorough process will make success less likely.

What is planned giving?

The actual giving is the most important element, but planning is also an integral factor. Planning refers to the donor's process of deciding how to provide financial support to an organization while achieving estate planning, income tax planning and financial planning objectives of the donor. The gifts may be outright donations, testamentary bequests or deferred gifts, where the charity does not assume possession of the transferred property until after the occurrence of specific events (such as death of the donor) or the passage of time.

Where do we start?

Start by consulting with your organization's legal advisors, to determine whether there are any legal restrictions that must be overcome to put a planned giving program into operation. Then, provide general information about planned giving to all Board members and all staff involved in fundraising. Consider inviting a guest speaker who has knowledge and experience about starting and maintaining a planned giving program. Not everyone on the Board will get deeply involved, but everyone needs to have a general understanding of the concepts to develop a meaningful consensus of support for exploring such a program for your organization.

The Board likes the idea; now what?

After obtaining Board approval to proceed with a detailed study, form a task force charged to do the necessary research, and to develop a strategy, a time line and an action plan for Board approval. The task force should be made up of individuals who are enthusiastic about fundraising: analytical thinkers, self-starters who have a track record of following through on assignments. Consideration should be given to including key volunteers and current donors on the task force. Their perspective should be helpful, and their participation can be the first step in marketing the planned giving program. The task force should also include at least one Board member and one or more senior staff members.

Choose a champion to lead.

Soon after the task force is formed, it is essential to identify a key person to be the "champion" of the program. This person should be personally committed to the success of the program and must have the respect of the task force members and, ultimately, of the Board. The champion should have sufficient authority and influence to get the planning implementation moving and to keep a meaningful priority on program tasks and projects.

Prepare a Statement of Philosophy.

A statement of philosophy for the planned giving program should be developed by the task force, through discussion and reflection, to provide a conceptual basis for the program and for use in testing the validity of policies and procedures as they are formulated.

Set targets for progress.

It is important to prepare a time line, to establish a planned sequence of the various tasks and to set target dates for completion of each task. The time line should include regular meetings to discuss progress and resolve interim issues. Meetings will facilitate good communication among the task force members, but the meetings should not be so frequent that they consume the time and energy that should be focused on accomplishing the mission of the task force.

Define your program.

As the task force's vision of planned giving for your organization comes into focus, draft a detailed definition. This will be helpful in clarifying the proposed program for your Board and, later, in developing the explanatory material for prospective donors.

Identify target donors and types of donors.

The task force should develop descriptions of types of individuals and groups of individuals that are appropriate targets for solicitation (e.g., members of certain professions, individuals with personal interest in your organization's mission, known philanthropists, etc.). Based on these conclusions, the task force can formulate marketing strategies and identify needed promotional materials.

Select a trustee.

In many planned gifts, the donor expects the charity to select a trustee to administer the trust and invest the assets. The trustee has a fiduciary responsibility to the donor as well as to the organization. Therefore, the planned giving program must use due diligence is selecting and monitoring trustees. Does the trustee have experience with charitable organizations? What is the trustee's approach to serving donors and beneficiaries? How will trust accounting be handled? What are the trustee's investment policies? How are fees determined?

Should we accept anything and everything?

A wide variety of estate and gift planning vehicles exist for donors. The task force must decide which of these are appropriate and acceptable to your organization. Gifts of real estate may require the organization to deal with various complications, including even environmental problems. Gifts of interests in operating businesses may require active involvement in management until the business is sold. This process requires significant research and deliberation, including consultation with legal and tax advisors.

Prepare draft documents for donor use.

As decisions are made about gift arrangements that will be accepted by the planned giving program, specimen documents should be drafted by the legal advisors to the task force. These will make it easier to demonstrate to the prospective donors and their professional advisors an appropriate approach to structuring gifts. The use of specimen documents will also contribute toward standardization. This is advantageous to the planned giving program. The task force's consultation with existing planned giving programs of other organizations may result in obtaining specimen documents that have been "field tested" and refined.

What is this going to cost?

With tentative decisions made about the types of gifts that will be accepted, types of prospective donors, etc., a cost budget for the first three to five years should be prepared. It should include staff salaries, training costs, costs of developing and printing promotional materials, advertising costs, cost of legal and fundraising consultants, etc.

How will we judge success?

Even as the task force is planning and formulating the planned giving program, it should also define clear objectives and benchmarks for the first three to five years of the program. These should be measurable and realistic to provide a basis for evaluating the success of the program. Ongoing evaluation will increase the probability of continuing success.

Will we continue to need legal advice after the program is in place?

In addition to the consultation and guidance received from legal advisors during the formulation of the planned giving program, it is essential that the task force arrange for the availability of continuing legal expertise in two aspects of the program.

First, the program will require the services of knowledgeable attorneys who will represent the interests of your organization when legal questions arise between prospective donors and the staff of the planned giving program. Attorneys representing the donors may advise their clients to utilize techniques and forms designed specifically for the donor, rather than those used by the organization.

Second, the organization should assemble a list of knowledgeable attorneys, accountants and financial advisors who can be referred to prospective donors who do not presently have advisors with estate and gift planning expertise. These referrals can be very helpful in facilitating the completion of a planned gift. It is possible for an attorney to function in both capacities at different times with different prospective donors, but the donor and the planned giving program should have separate attorneys, to avoid a conflict of interest.

What kinds of marketing material will we need?

Promotional and explanatory materials are very important to attract attention, and to create a positive first impression on prospective donors. Materials from other successful planned giving programs can be a great starting point, but they should be modified to fit the unique personality of your organization and your planned giving program. Explanations about types of gift arrangements must be accurate, but not overly technical. It is advisable to consult with marketing professionals, as well as your legal advisor, as the materials are prepared.

Train your team.

Task force members and staff members who will be actively involved in planned giving solicitation should participate in in-depth training to develop sufficient knowledge and a sufficient comfort level with the program and the material. This will be essential to the ability to interest, inform and persuade prospective donors.

The training should include the general concepts of planned giving, how to market the program in general, how to identify individual prospective donors, how to initiate contact, how to maintain contact and how to finalize the gift.

Market the program.

The initial impact of the program and continuing success will depend on effective marketing techniques. As with development of the marketing materials, seek professional advice on the overall marketing plan. The Board members and staff of the organization can be used as test markets or focus groups to evaluate and suggest refinements to your approach. Mailings and seminars should emphasize the goals and programs of the organization and why the organization is worthy of significant support. The financial and psychic benefits to donors should also be stressed. The marketing program should include extensive and intensive personal follow-up to provide answers and explanations to potential donors and to finalize gifts. Consider naming a prominent, popular member of the community as the honorary chairperson of the planned giving program. This will attract media attention and the attention of potential donors.

Develop target lists of potential donors.

Enlist the help of your Board in developing a list of their contacts. Have them indicate the amount of gift that they think each contact is capable of making to the program. Encourage the Board members to personally initiate the dialogue about planned giving. The dialogue should include a request for a donation of a specific dollar value. Set the sights high; the prospective donor may say "yes."

Manage your solicitation campaign.

As the Board and staff work the lists of potential donors, it will be essential to have a comprehensive contact management system to track all contacts by all team members with each potential donor to document the progress towards securing a gift.

Establish a recognition program for donors.

The recognition program should provide for various levels of recognition from simple but tasteful items of appreciation for small gifts to memorial designations for major gifts. In addition to direct communication to the donor, press releases, press conferences, appreciation banquets, etc. will increase the psychic rewards to the donor and increase the public awareness of your organization and its planned giving program. Procedures also must be in place to honor donors' requests for anonymity.

Monitor and maintain gifts that have not yet matured.

By definition, a planned giving program is an ongoing, long-term process. Securing a planned gift may require months or even years. After the gift is finalized, it may be several years before your organization is able to have initial access to the resources, after which management of the resources and the revenue flow can be expected to continue indefinitely. Accordingly, it is essential that procedures be established to track and monitor all gifts in all stages of evolution and to strengthen relationships with donors. Neglected donors can and do change their minds and their wills!

Tax Advantages Of Planned Giving

The process of soliciting donations involves not only enlisting the prospective donor's support for the objectives of the organization, but also accommodating the donor's needs and objectives. One facet of this effort, which can be facilitated by proper structuring of the gift, involves securing recognition of the donor's support within the community. The other involves utilizing tax incentives to reduce the economic cost of the gift to the donor.

The tax law contains a number of incentives designed to encourage charitable giving, as well as restrictions to curtail abuses. Also, the tax impact of a gift may vary significantly because of nuances in the donor's tax situation, or changes in the tax law.

General rules

The amount contributed to a qualifying charity is allowed as a deduction under the Internal Revenue Code, and under the tax laws of most states. However, the amount of the deduction is limited to a percentage of gross income, and is subject to a variety of other restrictions. Allowable contributions in excess of the limits can be carried forward and used in future years.

Gifts of stock, securities, real estate, and other property that would have generated long-term capital gain if it had been sold instead of contributed, are generally deductible at market value. This favorable treatment does not apply to assets which have been held for less than one year at the time of the gift. The advantage of giving appreciated property instead of cash is that the full market value is deductible, even though the donor has not paid capital gain tax on the appreciation.

There is a special rule concerning gifts of tangible personal property to charity. The deduction is limited to the donor's cost basis, unless the donated property is used by the charity directly to accomplish its exempt purpose; for example, donation of food to an organization that feeds the hungry, or works of art to a museum. The requirement is not satisfied if the charity sells or auctions off the property and uses the money.

In response to a history of valuation abuses, Congress has enacted a number of record-keeping requirements. A cash gift in excess of $250 must be substantiated by a written receipt from the charity, as well as a canceled check. Noncash gifts in excess of $250 must be reported to the IRS on a special tax form. A noncash gift in excess of $5,000 must be supported by a timely "qualified appraisal." There is an exception for publicly traded stock and securities; for securities not traded on an established market, the dollar limit is $10,000 instead of $5,000. If proper substantiation is not maintained, the IRS has the authority to disallow the deduction completely even though the fact and value of the contribution can be established.

Therefore, it is important that the acknowledgment provided by the charity be sufficient to satisfy the charity's obligation to its contributors:

- It must be timely;

- It must indicate the amount of cash contributed;

- It must describe, but need not value, any noncash items contributed;

- It must note whether or not the donor received any goods (other than items of minimal value) or services (*quid pro quo*) in exchange for the contribution;

- If the donor receives a *quid pro quo* worth more than $75, the acknowledgment should specifically indicate that the portion of the contribution represented by the value of the *quid pro quo* is nondeductible, and should provide the donor with a good-faith estimate of its value. "Intangible religious benefits" and objects of minimal value distributed in a fund-raising campaign are not considered *quid pro quo* items for this purpose. Although the charity should estimate the value of the *quid pro quo*, the ultimate responsibility of determining its value is imposed upon the taxpayer.

Where a donor makes a number of contributions within one year, the charity has the choice of providing either a separate statement for each contribution, or a periodic summary.

Corporate Taxpayers

The income, losses and other tax attributes of an "S corporation" are not subject to tax at the corporate level. The various tax items, including contributions, are passed through to the shareholders and are reported on their respective returns, subject to the restrictions and limitations discussed below.

Charitable contributions of "C corporations," which are taxable entities, are subject to a limitation measured by 10% of taxable income, as ultimately determined. Any amount in excess of the limit may be carried forward and deducted to the extent allowable in the five succeeding taxable years.

A gift of inventory results in a deduction of the donor's cost when the transferred items are removed from inventory. Generally, no additional deduction is allowed, because sale of the items would have resulted in ordinary income instead of capital gain. However, where the donated items are used directly by the charity to carry out its exempt function, an additional deduction measured by half of the difference between cost and market value may be allowed.

C corporations which show losses for tax purposes do not derive current tax benefits from their contributions, and may lose them altogether if the carryovers are not used within the five-year period. Therefore, these entities should arrange to have contributions made by officers and key employees who can benefit from the tax deductions. The same rationale applies to "personal service corporations," which normally attempt to zero out their income each year in order to minimize or avoid income tax at the corporate level.

Individual taxpayers

A variety of limitations applies to contributions of individuals.

At the present time, only individuals who have enough deductions to itemize can derive tax savings from charitable contributions.

Deductions for gifts of cash, and property that is not appreciated, are limited to 50% of Adjusted Gross Income (AGI). Deductions for gifts of appreciated capital gain property are limited to 30% of AGI. Any amount in excess of these limits may be carried forward and deducted to the extent allowable in the five succeeding taxable years. Special rules are provided for gifts to private foundations.

The income tax and estate planning needs of wealthy individuals have given impetus to the creation and implementation of a number of tax-saving strategies:

- Contributions authorized in a decedent's will or trust generate estate tax deductions, and can result in savings measured by effective tax rates of up to 50%;

- Contributions during the donor's lifetime not only result in current income tax deductions, at combined Federal and State effective tax rates which can approach 50%, but also result in the exclusion of the donated assets from the donor's taxable estate;

- A "bargain sale" is a transaction in which the donor sells an asset to the charity for less than market value. The difference between the market value and the purchase price is considered a deductible contribution;

- Gifts of retirement plan and IRA benefits, tax-deferred U.S. government bonds and other items of "income in respect of a decedent" (IRD) can be cost-effective ways of making charitable gifts, because they eliminate income taxes which otherwise would be imposed on the donor or the donor's heirs. The combination of estate taxes and income taxes on the IRD items of a high-bracket taxpayer can reduce the portion of the value recognized by the heirs after taxes by 70% or more;

- The "charitable remainder trust" (CRT), discussed more fully below, is another effective technique for disposition of substantially appreciated property;

- CRTs and private foundations can be used by wealthy individuals to provide vehicles for their families to leave continuing, highly visible legacies to their communities extending well beyond their lifetimes;

- The Charitable Lead Trust (CLT) is the converse of the CRT. It can be used by wealthy individuals, where the heirs do not have an immediate need for access to the inherited property. The CLT interposes a charity's interest in the income of the property for a limited term. By judicious selection of the trust's term and the annuity payout, the value of the remainder interest, which is subject to estate tax, can be minimized;

- Other techniques, such as pooled income funds and charitable gift annuities, are available to provide more limited tax-saving opportunities to donors of modest means or limited charitable objectives. A pooled income fund permits gifts of separate donors to be commingled for investment purposes; each beneficiary receives a proportionate share of the fund's income. A charitable gift annuity involves a contractual payout based on the annuitant's life expectancy; the donor gets a deduction for the value of the charitable element, and the annuity payout is partially tax-free.

Charitable Remainder Trusts

The CRT is a useful vehicle, which has justifiably received a great deal of attention in recent years. The essence of a CRT is that in exchange for current tax deductions and avoidance of capital gain tax, the donor ultimately leaves the gifted property to charity instead of to heirs.

The charitable trust receives property which is about to be sold at a substantial profit. Because the CRT is a charitable vehicle, the gain from the sale is not taxed. The trust then invests the property for the term of the trust, making required periodic payments to the donor and/or beneficiaries. Eventually the trust terminates, and the charity becomes the owner of the trust property.

The donor sets the term of the trust. Often the term is measured by the remaining life of the donor and/or the donor's spouse. The payout may be either a fixed dollar amount (annuity) or a fixed percentage of the value of the trust assets (unitrust amount); it is also set by the donor when the trust is established.

The donor derives a number of advantages from this arrangement:

- The recognition of taxable gain, which otherwise would result from sale of the property, is avoided, so the resources available for investment during the trust term are enhanced;

- The trust can be used as a vehicle to convert non-income-producing property into investments that enhance the donor's income. This is a strategy which can be particularly attractive after the donor retires, may have need for additional income and may be in a lower tax bracket;

- The donor's income tax deduction, which is measured by the actuarial value of the charity's remainder interest discounted to present value using the prevailing interest rate, yields an immediate cash benefit to the donor;

- The transferred asset is eliminated from the donor's taxable estate, except to the extent that income interests are held by non-charitable beneficiaries other than the donor's spouse.

A disadvantage, from the donor's perspective, is that the property transferred to the trust is no longer available to bequeath to family members. Where the property transferred has substantial value, creation of a CRT often is accompanied by creation of an irrevocable life insurance trust (ILIT). If properly structured, an ILIT will not only replace the wealth transferred to the CRT, but also will keep the insurance proceeds out of the donor's taxable estate and provide substantial benefits to the family.

The primary advantage, from the charity's perspective, is the opportunity to build an endowment by attracting gifts which otherwise might not be made.

Some donors might not want to transfer the entire value of the trust to a single charity, and the family might wish to maintain the visibility which accompanies continued involvement in a variety of charitable activities. Your charity can increase its opportunity to attract its share of these bequests by providing technical and administrative support to donors, in exchange for defined portions of the charitable remainders.

Attributes of an effective planned giving program

A charity that wishes to establish a planned giving program should have in its armory the weaponry needed to satisfy the tax needs of potential contributors. The attributes of an effective contemporary structure include:

- Staffing the planned giving department with individuals familiar with these tax strategies, and able to assist prospective donors in developing gift programs targeted to their specific needs;

- Developing relationships with attorneys, accountants and financial advisors, who can assist donors in tailoring the transactions and documentation needed to implement their plans;

- Developing relationships with investment advisors, who will manage the charity's endowment and the various investment vehicles required by the donors' gift programs;

- Preparing publications designed to explain the available gifting techniques to prospective donors, and forms to be used in their implementation.

The nuances of the techniques we have discussed are constantly evolving, in response to evolution of the tax law, interest rates, economic conditions and other factors. They will continue to evolve, particularly if proposals for major reform of the tax system are enacted into law.

The major uncertainty affecting charitable gift planning as this is written is the prospective "sunset" of the Federal estate tax which is contained in the landmark 2001 tax legislation ("EGTRRA"). Unless reversed by a future Congress, the Federal estate tax would disappear as of December 31, 2009, but would reappear one year later. As this is written, the House of Representatives is promoting legislation to make the "sunset" permanent and eliminate the existing uncertainty. However, the view of most commentators is that, since the existing Senate leadership is opposed and the country's economic situation has deteriorated since EGTRRA was enacted, this will not happen unless there is significant change in the composition of Congress.

How would charitable giving be affected by the prospective changes in the tax law? The negative implication for charitable giving is offered by some as an argument against a flat tax or consumption tax. The proposed repeal of the estate tax would also impact planned giving by changing the economic consequences of lifetime gifts and testamentary bequests.

The immediate impact of EGTTRA is just to reduce income tax and estate tax rates. This modestly reduces the tax savings generated by charitable transfers. However, if the estate tax is ultimately repealed, much of the financial incentive for testamentary charitable bequests will disappear; the incentives for lifetime planning techniques such as charitable leads and trusts and charitable remainder trusts will be reduced.

Therefore, your planned giving personnel will need to continue to monitor developments on the national political scene, in order to be able to work effectively with your professional advisors and those of your prospective donors. They will need to maintain their skills in this area in order to continue to satisfy the needs of your organization and its contributors.

Conclusion

Planning, initiating, operating and perpetuating a planned giving program for your organization is a significant challenge, but the long-term benefits can make it worth all the effort.

Bibliography:

- Ashton, D. 1996). *The Complete Guide to Planned Giving.* Quincy, Massachusetts: Debra Ashton, ISBN. not registered: Phone. 617-472-9316

- Barrett, R. D. In M. E. Ware (1997). *Planned Giving Essentials.* Gaithersburg, Maryland: Aspen Publishers, pp. 175 pages., ISBN.0-8342-0900-4: Phone. 800-638-8437

- Barron, T. 1997). *Practical Guide to Planned Giving 1997.* Detroit: The Taft Group, pp. 950 pages., ISBN.0-930807-47-2: Phone. 800-877-8238

- Clough, L. G. 1993). *The ABCs of Planned Giving.* Kensington, Connecticut: Planned Giving Specialists, Inc., Phone. 203-224-0289

- Crosson, R. 1994). *A Life Well Spent.* Nashville: Thomas Nelson, Inc., pp. 246., ISBN. 0-7852-8015-4

- Fry, R. P. J. 1998). *Nonprofit Investment Policies.* Somerset: John Wiley & Sons Inc., pp.298., ISBN. 0-471-17887-x: Phone. 800-225-5945

- Greenfield, J. M. 1997). *The Nonprofit Handbook.* New York: John Wiley & Sons Inc., pp750., ISBN.1-15658-2: Phone.800-879-4539

- Schoenhals, G. R. 1997). *19 Other Articles You Can Use to Acquire Planned Gifts-Book 3.* Seattle: G. Roger Schoenhals, pp. 60., ISBN.0-9645517-3-x: Phone. 206-546-8505

- Schoenhals, G. R. 1997). *Doing Planned Giving Better.* Seattle: G. Roger Schoenhals, pp. 60., ISBN.0-9645517-5-6: Phone. 206-546-8505

- Schoenhals, G. R. 1997).*Gaining More Planned Gifts.* Seattle: G. Roger Schoenhals, pp. 60., ISBN.0-9645517-6-4: Phone. 206-546-8505

- White, D. E. 1995).*The Art of Planned Giving.* Somerset: John Wiley & Sons Inc., ISBN.0-471-08149-3: Phone. 800-225-5945

Mark E. Mersmann, CPA and Arthur M. Seltzer, CPA

Once you've met these two, your can see their names in lights: the Mark Mersmann story with the late Jimmy Stewart in "Mr. Smith Does an Audit." and Art Seltzer played by Rick Moranis in "Honey, I Shrunk Your Tax Bill."

Mark and Art are real opposites. You notice it when you enter their offices. Mark's office is extremely orderly with his prized porcelain horse collection. In Art's office, there is a recruiting poster from the IRS that says "Only an accountant could catch Al Capone." His housekeeping style is far more casual than Mark's.

Mark is a fatherly Midwestern family man. He is the youngest child of 8. His Father was a sharecropper and neither parent finished grade school. He is the father of 5 grown children and a proud grandpa. He is active in his church and for many years was involved in marriage enrichment. He has been married for 38 years. He is the kind of person who could do a very difficult audit, deliver bad news and not make you cry. His nonprofit clients are an eclectic group ranging from labor unions to electrical cooperatives to a national association.

Art started as a chemistry major in college and in his junior year fell in love...with bridge. He took a year off to play bridge, discovered accounting in the process, and eventually went back to school. He took a job with a CPA firm the day after he graduated. He fell in love again, this time with his wife. He doesn't play bridge much any more, but is still an avid reader. He is fascinated by politics and current events, enjoys science fiction, and is a devotee of classical music. He loves to solve problems. His idea of a good time is trying to figure out what the folks in Washington are going to do to our tax law, and helping his clients leave as much money to family and charities as is possible.

Art has been married for 28 years. He loves to speak and write, usually in plain English, about tax subjects.

Both have spent decades in accounting. Despite very different personalities, it's clear that they have one thing in common, they are both consummate pros at what they do.

Mark E. Mersmann, CPA
Kiefer Bonfanti & Co.,LLP
701 Emerson Road, Suite 201
St. Louis, MO 63132
(314) 432-6704 ext. 1305

Arthur M. Seltzer, CPA
Brown,Smith Wallace,LLC
1050 N. Lindbergh Blvd.
St. Louis, MO 63141-6741
(314) 432-6001

CHAPTER 8

Let's Get a Grant to Do That!

Jeane Vogel

S top me if you've heard this one: You're in a board meeting. It's time to review the financial statements. Oops. Too many expenses. Not enough income. "I think we need a big grant to get us through the rest of the year," someone says. Great idea!

Or how about this one: Same board meeting. You've been planning for months to expand your services. The director wants to hire staff and get the project rolling. The cupboard's a little bare. "Hey," you say, "we can get a grant to do that!"

Grants. The all-purpose answer to funding problems. Right? I truly wish they were.

But before I discourage you too much, let me reassure you that grant-seeking can and should be a vital part of your overall fund raising program. To be effective, grant proposals must be well crafted, properly targeted and given enough time to allow a strong relationship to develop between your agency and the funder. And your agency must be *ready* to accept grants—meaning that you have your finances in order, your board is active, your staff is credentialed and competent, and your program meets a need.

In other words, can you meet the grant-makers' Triple E Test: Are you Efficient, Effective and Essential?

The next few pages will give you a down-and-dirty crash course in preparing for and writing grants for your agency. Whether you have to write the grant proposal yourself or you have a staff of ten to do the job for you, you and your board members you have a tremendous role to play in the success of your grant proposals.

First, The Basics

It might seem a little obvious, but sometimes just the definition of a grant is a little fuzzy. For most nonprofit organizations, a grant is a sum of money given in support of a specific project from a private foundation, a corporation or corporate giving program, or a government agency. Individuals sometimes give grants, but they often have a private foundation that they draw from.

The process of acquiring a grant is simple enough. An agency fills out a form or submits a proposal detailing exactly why a contribution is sought and what the money will be used for. The proposal can ask for operating funds, which are considered "unrestricted" funds, or money to support a specific program. Funding for specific projects is considered "restricted" because the funds are only to be spent on the project outlined in the proposal. "Unrestricted," or operating funds, can cover any legitimate agency expense.

TIP: Because "restricted" funding proposals give the funder more information about how the money will be used, they are generally easier to fund. Instead of writing a proposal for general operating funds, consider writing only project-specific proposals, and incorporate bona fide overhead expenses into your project budget. That way, you will cover administrative expenses and be able to produce a proposal that is more appealing to potential funders.

Getting Ready to Ask for a Lot of Money

At least once a week I get a telephone call from a bright, well-intentioned person with a great idea for a project or a new organization. To get started, he or she decided that the group will need a grant. Can I write it for them?

The conversation goes something like this:

Me: Well, let's talk about your organization first. Do you have a board of directors?

Caller: Oh, sure. My wife, my brother-in-law Larry, my neighbor's friend and my stepdaughter are listed on the incorporation papers.

Me: I see. Have you thought about diversifying your board, getting more people from different professions? People who might have new perspectives?

Caller: Oh, we're fine the way we are. We don't want to spend a lot of time in meetings.

Me: (Already I know I can't help him, but maybe I can steer him in the right direction.) OK. Well, can you tell me how much of your budget is contributed by the board members?

Caller: They give a lot of their time. But we don't really have a budget yet. Is that important?

Me: Kinda. If the board members aren't making gifts to the group, how are you funded?

Caller: That's why I'm calling you! Can't you find us some money?

You think I'm kidding. I'm not!

There's a common naiveté among board members that good ideas get funded on their merit alone. Not true. Good ideas are funded when an agency has done its homework, has a variety of funding sources, is financially and programmatically competent, has shown a demonstrated need, and presents its case to the *right* funder at the *right* time in the *right* way.

I know that sounds like a lot, but we can take it step by step.

Before the first word is written for a proposal, the agency director and board members must have a firm grip on the organization's mission, programming, finances and long-term goals. If you are a board member, your responsibility is awesome. You, not the director or the staff, but you and your colleagues on the board set the direction for the agency. When you are ready to be serious about seeking grant money in your community, ask yourself these questions:

1. **Do we have a clear mission? Is it consistent with what we actually do?**

If you've answered "no" to either of these, it's time to revisit your mission. Assign a board committee the task of clarifying the mission. Bring their recommendations to your full board at a meeting dedicated to this issue. Give yourself time. Try not to include every single suggestion, but reach a consensus. A mission statement should be short, 25 words or less, and state your purpose *clearly*. Don't include goals, vision statements or wishful thinking.

> **TIP:** *If you can, and it might be a good idea to figure out a way to do so, hire an outsider experienced in facilitating board discussions. A consultant can give you a fresh perspective and expose that smelly elephant in the room that nobody wants to talk about. Rely on your outsider to help you sort out your mission, goals and long-range plans. Local United Way agencies and Junior Leagues often have volunteer facilitators to help you.*

2. **Does the board buy into the mission? Do the staff members? Does the community?**

If your board members have strong disagreements about your mission, it's time to rethink it. If your staff and board have different opinions about the mission, you have three options: fire the staff, fire the board, or talk to each other and find out where the differences lie. Often staff members, who are the frontline people, will have a drastically different view of your organization. Listen to them and take their opinions into account, but set the mission yourselves. The board is accountable to the community and responsible for the health of the organization. The mission statement is yours.

You might have a public relations problem on your hands if your board and your community do not have similar ideas about your mission or how you are accomplishing it. Don't let a PR problem fester. Address it immediately. Recruit a PR professional for your board or hire a consultant to help you for a few months. (It's always a good idea to have professionals on your board, but be warned: Lawyers, PR and marketing pros, accountants and fund-raisers are in demand and know why you want them on the board. Consider hiring a professional to help. Sometimes you *do* get what you pay for.)

3. Do our programs contribute to meeting our mission?

There are lots of good ideas out there. And there are plenty of people in need. If you offer a program that doesn't fit into the mission, you might be wasting time, resources and energy. Take a hard look at your programs and keep the ones that directly address your mission. Funders pay attention to little details, like mission. It will be hard to fund a program that is inconsistent or far afield from your organization's stated purpose.

4. Do we know what our competition is? Do we know who our clients/customers are?

I know these seem pretty basic, but ask them anyway. You might be surprised at the different responses you get from board members and staff. Use their answers to position yourself in the community and to show how unique and valuable you are.

5. Are our budgets in order? Does every program have a clearly defined and consistent budget? Are our finances in order?

Funders will spend more time poring over your financial statements than in reading your eloquent prose. Make sure that every program has its own budget that shows expenses and revenue. And don't forget to put overhead and supervision costs in your project budgets. It's easier to fund a project than to fund your rent. And because you have to have a building to provide your service, a proportional share of the rent and other administrative costs is a fair addition to a project budget.

Board members have fiduciary responsibility for their agency. Board members should set an annual budget, review financial statements monthly, and set spending policies for the agency. This is the hardest work you will do, but it is the most important.

6. Do we tell the community how we spend our money?

Publish an annual report. It doesn't have to be fancy. Even if you don't get a dime of outside money, you are getting a form of public support if your agency doesn't have to pay taxes on its income. So let the public know what you are doing and how you are doing it.

When you get a sizable amount of money from a corporation, foundation or individual, let them know how you spent it. Send them a one- or two-page report on the project, how the money was spent, what impact the project had and what your plans are for the future. A progress or year-end report will further your relationship with that funder, add to your credibility and give you an opportunity to ask for that next gift.

7. Can we demonstrate how effective our programs are?

Grant-makers are a funny lot. They're always asking if their money made a difference. Did the grant meet the stated need? Did the project have the intended outcome?

What they're really asking, of course, is this: "Did I throw my money down a hole, or did it do some good?"

The only way to answer that question is by evaluating the programs. Board members should be prepared to ask the agency director what evaluation tools are used to assess the effectiveness of Program X. How do you know you met the need? If there's a problem in the project, how will the director know about it? How can you use evaluations to improve your product or service?

8. Do we have a diversified funding base? Do the board members make financial contributions to the program?

From your vantage point, yours is a terrific program. Anyone would want to fund it. But you and the grant-maker have different purposes and different perspectives. The grant maker does not want to be the sole funder of a project. What will happen when the grant is gone? Will the project collapse?

Position yourself well with funders by having a diversified fundraising plan. Some of your money should come from special events, such as golf tournaments or dinners. Some of your budget should be unrestricted annual gifts, such as $50 contributions from the general public in response to a direct-mail solicitation. (The "unrestricted" part means that you can use the money for any legitimate agency purpose, not just one project. Grant money is generally "restricted" for a specific purpose.)

Finally, most foundations want to know whether the board members contribute money to the cause. They know they give time, but are they willing to make a financial investment in the organization? Will the board members put their money where their mouths are? Most board members are willing to make some charitable donations, but often balk when asked to give to their own groups. A board member's gift is seen by foundations as a sign that the board members believe in the cause and consider it a good investment of their time *and* money.

If hesitating to make a gift to an agency, board members should remember one of the first rules of fund-raising: You can't ask for a gift until you have made one yourself. The rule applies to grant-makers also. If you are soliciting the community for financial help, make sure you believe in the cause enough to write the first check.

The Board as the Grant Proposal Cheerleader

Most board members want to see the results of the grant proposal, not dirty their hands with the proposal itself. That makes sense. Grant writing is generally not a good use of a board member's time. Besides, board members have much more important things to do in securing grant money.

Here is where another primary rule in fund-raising comes into play. You've heard it a thousand times before but it bears repeating: People give money to people.

While you're in the midst of a fund-raising campaign, counting every dollar, this simple axiom might be forgotten. People, not foundations or corporations or committees, give money to other people, not agencies or programs or good ideas. Sure, a foundation might send a check to a worthy cause without any people actually meeting, but *people* are still making the decisions to support the work of other *people* or to help other *people*. It's so elementary, it is easy to forget.

As a board member, you bring to the grant table two very powerful tools: Yourself and your address book.

Foundations and corporations that make grants want to give to people they know and trust. They want to hear from volunteers who feel passionately about the program and can bring a personal touch to the proposal.

Before a grant proposal goes out, the board should review the list of trustees who will make the decision. Do you know any of them? Do you know anyone who knows them? Are you willing to pick up the phone and call one of the trustees and introduce yourself and your program?

I can't tell you how many times I've told an agency that Funder Y would not consider a grant because the agency doesn't meet the guidelines. But a board member knows someone there, and poof! Two weeks later we have a check in hand. I might look a little foolish but as a professional, I must abide by the foundation's rules. The board members don't, and they can get results.

> **TIP**: *Include cover notes from board members with your proposals. Even if you don't know a foundation officer or trustee, your sincerity and enthusiasm will help your proposal get noticed and will demonstrate that your board is active and in charge. Also, ask your staff to make current grant requests a part of your meeting packet. Look over the list every month and tell staff when you or other board members have a relationship with any of your prospective funders.*

Board Member as Grant Writer

As mentioned earlier, grant proposal writing is seldom a good use of board members' time. And staff members might find it difficult to give constructive criticism to a board member. Despite the warnings, in some smaller or young agencies there might be no one else to do the work, so jump in.

A grant writer needs three vital skills: the ability to follow directions *exactly*, the ability to write well and convincingly, and a thorough understanding of the agency's mission, programs and funding needs.

Whether the board or staff members write the grant proposal, here are a few tips to make it easier and more effective:

- Choose one person to write—no writing by committee is allowed. One person should craft the proposal, with perhaps one other person to review it. Ideally the reviewer will be the executive director.

- Do your research. Does the foundation or corporation make grants? What are their requirements? Do they have a deadline? What kind of information do they want? What format should the proposal be in? Do they want a letter first, or a full proposal?

- Know what you want to ask for before you start. Do you need money for a specific program, operating costs, program expansion or capital expenses? Be very clear about your needs, then you can start to research the grants available to help you.

- Get to know the research or reference librarian at your local library. The reference librarian knows which books, newspapers and internet web sites will help you in your search for funding.

- Talk to prospective funders—often. Call them before you submit a proposal. Confirm all the details of submission: to whom the proposal should be addressed, the types of information requested, how many copies to submit, deadlines? Talk about the type of project you will be proposing. Would that be of interest?

- Ask their advice, then follow it. Submit what they want, when they want it. This isn't a college term paper (though it might seem like it while you're writing it). You cannot appeal for a time extension or special favors. Fifty agencies got their proposals in on time and in the proper format. Guess who gets considered and who ends up in the trash?

- Ask the grants officers at the foundations or corporations for examples of projects they have funded in the past. They might be willing to share an example of a proposal they funded.

- If you get criticism about the proposal or the organization, *listen up*. It might be hard to hear that the funder thinks the finances are shaky, or that your board members seem uninvolved and misinformed, but this is valuable information. Feedback from a grant-maker is your reality check. It lets you know if you are presenting yourself the way you want to or if you are actually doing the work in the community that you think you are. *Don't let your ego get in the way of improving your organization or your proposal-writing skills.*

- Thank everyone for their gifts. This is the point where lots of groups fail. Remember, even if a check came from a large, impersonal corporation, there was still a person who made the decision to send it. Thank them—often. But don't neglect your smaller donors, either. Every dollar counts and spends the same way.

- Follow up successful grants with progress reports on the program. Let the funder know how you spent their money. How has the grant made a difference in the level or quality of service? How many people benefited? How were their lives changed?

- Invite funders to your special events *as your guests*. Show off your programs.

Getting Your Proposal Noticed

Yours might be one of 300 proposals considered by the grants committee this cycle. What will get yours noticed? There's no magic formula, but these ideas will help:

- Give the funder the proposal they asked for. If the guidelines say fill out a form, fill it out. If the guidelines restrict you to five pages, don't write seven. If they ask for a specific format, follow it. If they say they don't fund religious institutions, don't ask for funding for the Summer Bible School.

- Neatness counts. Misspellings, sloppiness, contradictions in the text, and unclear writing will count against you. Have several people proofread the proposal before it goes out.

- Address it to the right person. You were supposed to call the foundation to confirm details, right? Don't trust foundation directories to give you accurate information. It's not humanly possible to keep up-to-date information in print.

- Write clearly and succinctly. Grant officers might be reading hundreds of proposals. If yours gets to the point quickly and is easy to read, it might be passed onto the next review level. Hard to read or lengthy proposals are often tossed before anyone realizes that a great project has been passed over.

- Print in color and include some photos. Funders and clients alike tell me that the proposals I produce that contain photographs of the program in action are more informative and easier to understand. Don't rush out and buy a new printer, but the next time you need one, buy one with color capacities. A picture really is worth a thousand words, but don't overdo it. I put photos right in with the text, not on appendix pages where they might be counted as extraneous additions to the proposal. Also, keep all the text in black and save the color for the graphics.

- Use graphics sparingly. Don't use clip art in your proposal. *Ever.*

- Scan in your logo and use it on your cover sheet. Personalize your proposal as much as possible. Many board members are computer-savvy and can help with this step.

- Use a typeface that is easy to read in a size no smaller than 12 point. Don't mix typefaces or you'll have a proposal that looks is if it was submitted by the Mad Bomber, not your respectable agency. Whether you chose to double space every line or only between paragraphs, chose a format that *you* can read.

Working with Staff and Consultants

There is no other professional relationship more fraught with the potential for misunderstanding and ill will than that of board members and professional fund-raisers, be they staff or consultants. Why? Because their expectations of each other's responsibilities can be so different.

But, when everyone understands his or her role and follows through, the results can be fantastic for the agency and the people involved.

The problems begin if board members believe that the grant writer is solely responsible for the failure or success of the fundraising plan. Sometimes boards even consider the grant writer to be the agency's sole breadwinner. On the other side of the board table, grant writers often find board members unwilling to participate in the process that so desperately needs their attention, and are afraid that board members will hold them accountable for circumstances well beyond their control.

Already you can see that this is a recipe for trouble.

People who write grants are first and foremost program developers. The grant writer is the person who actually takes an idea and gives it shape. The grant writer is often the person who realizes that there's not enough money in the budget to fulfill all the tasks of the project. The grant writer helps mold the goals and objectives into a project description that the lay person can understand and feel a part of.

The grant writer *does not* bring the money in. That's where lots of problems begin.

The first time I meet with a board, often I'll hear how tired they are of raising money. They're so glad they hired me so that they can rest.

Sorry. It doesn't work that way. Grant writers and board members are *partners* in fund-raising. The successful grant proposal has the mutual cooperation of board and grant writer, *and* these elements:

- An agency with a good track record, responsible money management, and the proven ability to do the job.

- A program that meets a need that isn't duplicated elsewhere in the community.

- A diversified board of directors that sets agency policy and provides management oversight.

- A clear, well-written proposal that meets the funder's submission requirements.

- Human contact between the agency and the funder, preferably from board members.

A brilliantly written proposal will not be funded if the board has been unable to control expenditures and the agency has been in the red for three years in a row. Conversely, a poorly conceived proposal might be funded if the board president and the foundation trustee were college roommates. There are so many variables at play in successful grant-making. Be sure you manage the ones you can.

If you are thinking about hiring a consultant to help you with fund raising, there are a few additional things you might want to think about.

- Remember that consultants are not staff. They cost more per hour than staff because you are paying for experience and expertise that you don't have on staff. And consultants are paying for everything themselves: taxes, benefits, rent, equipment, supplies, postage, telephone. *Everything.*

- Consultants are paid to give you the bad news. They're also paid to show you how to turn a dire forecast into funded programs. It's a good idea to listen, but *you* still make the final decision.

- Consultants are specialists. Staff members often have to be generalists. The fund-raising professional on staff might be running a special event one minute, writing a grant the next, and producing a newsletter in her spare time. If your staff is overwhelmed or you want to add some expertise, hire a consultant to help out. Involve the staff in the decision to prevent staff members from feeling intimidated, inadequate or threatened.

- Don't expect a guaranteed result from a consultant. If someone promises to get a certain percentage of your proposals funded, or a guaranteed amount of money raised, be very suspicious. There are no guarantees in fund-raising. It might be tempting to ask for guarantees, but there are too many variables in the funding process to guarantee anything. Instead, demand excellence and expect that the work will be done professionally and with the expertise you are paying for. Proceed with caution.

TIP: *Check references. Some consultants are good salespeople who know how to present themselves well but can't follow through with good work. Ask around and get recommendations from people you trust. Ask the consultant for names of funders he or she has worked with. The grant officer will give you a valuable perspective of the consultant—very different, perhaps, than you would get from an agency director.*

Funding Pitfalls

There are two mistakes that organizations commonly make in the grant-seeking process: They chase grant money and they rely on grants too much.

First, the money chase. **Don't let a foundation drive your program.** For example, you want money to expand your women's shelter to accept families with children. You find a foundation that likes to fund shelters for men. You're tempted to change your program to include men if it means getting that foundation's attention.

Don't be lured by the promise of money and change your mission and program needs. A funder might present you with a good idea, but it's not what you need to do right now. Find the right match for your program and pass on the grant money if it doesn't suit your purpose. The board, not grant money, should be in charge of program development.

Once you've gotten over the temptation to apply for every dollar out there, remember to diversify your funding base. Grants are not always a reliable source of funding. Foundations like to spread their money around, and today's sexy charity is next year's budget hole.

Try to limit the amount of revenue from grants to about one-third of your total budget. Less is better. It's a desperate agency that relies on grant money and suddenly is getting rejection notices instead of checks. Don't risk your programming on grants alone.

If it's appropriate, consider charging a fee for your service. Even a small fee can bring in substantial revenue, and it might make your clients feel better about themselves. Schedule special events that raise friends and funds. Conduct an annual fund drive that seeks contributions from individuals. If you get 500 gifts of $50 in one year, you've raised $25,000! And you've made valuable connections with people who believe in you. Maybe one of them has a foundation . . . .

Basic Components of a Grant Proposal

OK, you've planned, you've assessed, you've researched and you've made contact. Now, what should go into that proposal?

Again, follow the guidelines published by the foundation or government agency. If no guidelines are published, you can use this basic formula for a standard proposal:

- A one-page executive summary with your agency name, executive director's name, address and telephone number, mission, project summary, purpose of the request, amount of the request, agency budget amount, project budget amount.

- A formal proposal that includes:

  - Mission statement

  - Agency history

  - Statement of need

  - Detailed description of the project and expected results

  - Method of evaluating the project

  - The role played by volunteers in the project, if any

  - Collaborative arrangements or relationships with other agencies, formal or informal

  - Detailed project budget with narrative description

  - Explanation of how you expect the project to be funded in the future.

- Think of your proposal as your agency's resume. Keep it simple, short and easy to read.

- Focus on the program and the need you will fill. Give statistics, realistic goals and measurable results.

- Ask for funding to perform the service, not to hire staff. Funders hate to pay salaries, but they will fund the personnel necessary to operate the program and meet the goals. Yes, it's the same thing, but presentation is everything.

- Demonstrate your ability to meet the goals. What have you done in the past? Why is your agency the best one to perform this service?

- Show how others might be able to duplicate what you have done. If you can provide a needed service *and* teach other groups how to do the same thing, you will get more notice and favorable treatment.

- Be judicious with your attachments: Always include a copy of your 501(c)3 tax determination letter from the IRS, recent financial statements or an audit, your annual budget, your board roster, preferably with the business affiliation and board expertise (such as law, accounting, PR), and an annual report or newsletter, if you publish them.

- Consider including a narrative description of your project budget. A short explanation of each line item will help the funder understand the project.

- Letters of support from sister agencies, local officials or religious groups sometimes can be helpful. Ask the funder if letters of support are desired.

- Always document agreements with other agencies if the project is dependent on the collaboration.

Now, do you have everything you need to know about writing a winning proposal? Maybe not, but it's a start. As you start your grant-seeking, keep in mind that not every proposal gets funded. Even the best are rejected. Don't take it personally. Be tenacious. If a funder turns you down, ask why. Can they point out where the proposal was weak? Or strong? Ask if you can apply again next time. Start a relationship.

Once you've got your house in order, you're clear about your organization's mission and vision, program and budget needs, it's time to make grants a part of your fund-raising plan. Now you're ready to spring into action the next time you're in a board meeting and someone says, "Let's get a grant to do that!"

Jeane Vogel

Jeane Vogel started her fund raising career in 1965 organizing backyard children's carnivals to benefit the Leukemia Society. Her first effort raised almost $20. She was nine years old.

Not realizing that her destiny lay in the nonprofit world, Jeane went to work as a newspaper reporter after college. Two of the three publications she worked for went out of business within a year of her hire. No connection has even been proven. She ended her newspaper career as editor of the daily newspaper in a Missouri resort town, where she wrote liberal-minded editorials for a conservative readership.

After a stint working for a US Senate candidate, Jeane settled into the quiet nonprofit world, taking a job as the Public Affairs Director of Planned Parenthood of the St. Louis Region. She left Planned Parenthood just two years later to launch the second half of her fund raising career with a women's counseling group (and because she was marrying the only man who worked at Planned Parenthood, who happened to be the Public Relations Director).

Jeane founded Fund Raising Innovations for Non-Profits, a fund raising consulting firm in St. Louis, in 1994. Fund Raising Innovations specializes in grant proposal writing, annual fund development and strategic planning for nonprofit boards. Clients include groups in the fields of health care, education, environmental protection, shelter and counseling for battered women and children, legal aid, housing, seniors and the arts. Before starting Fund Raising Innovations in 1992, Jeane was the Vice-President for Development at Paraquad, a nationally-recognized advocacy and education group for people with disabilities.

Jeane is a volunteer moderator for seven Internet discussion forums on philanthropy and fund raising for the Charity Channel, (www.CharityChannel.com), reaching more than 10,000 corporate, foundation and nonprofit professionals daily.

She and her husband, Steve Sorkin, have two children, Aaron and Hannah. When not raising money or trying to be a decent parent, Jeane spends her time learning to convert her film photography skills to digital, throwing pots (on a pottery wheel), and chasing fat rabbits from her vegetable garden.

Jeane Vogel
Fund Raising Innovations
36 Queensbrook Place, St. Louis, MO 63132
314.991.0143
jeanevogel@earthlink.net
www.nonprofit-innovations.com

CHAPTER 9

Soliciting (Major) Gifts That Make an Impact

Mike Schroeder

H ey, we've already got a problem here. Just what is a major gift? Is it a gift of cash or sixty cases of soda and sport replenishment drink for the upcoming 10K run? If it's cash, how much are we talking about, and is it given now or sometime in the future? If it's not cash, and it's not given now, then isn't the gift called a planned gift?

I'd like to offer a different term to consider. Let's talk about gifts that make a significant *impact* on your organization, and let's not, for now, limit ourselves to the type of gift or the mechanics of making the gift. After all, gifts that impact your organization come in many shapes and sizes and are made by a variety of individuals at any number of times. Each organization will be different in how it defines impact. A gift of impact may help you achieve your annual campaign goal, it may push you over the top of your capital campaign or it may help guarantee the success of your special event. Yes, the concepts I'll introduce in this chapter are applicable for soliciting corporations, too. When all is said and done, people give to people.

Impact gifts occur when individuals make a gift which goes beyond the scope they originally thought they could accomplish. Doing so allows them to significantly *impact* the current and future efforts of the organization. An impact gift focuses on expanding the *donor's* vision in terms of giving. This process often includes more than annual support, and, conversely, it may include gifts in addition to deferred gifts. By making an impact gift to your organization, the donor will develop a greater stake in your organization. Your job, as a paid or volunteer steward, is to help the donor find ways to make an *impact*.

Getting Our Fair Share of the "Discretionary Dollar"

Marketing executives in the for-profit world, at least those involved with the fast-food industry, talk about "share of stomach." In any one person's stomach, there is only so much room, and each of us has our own capacity for how much food will fit on any given day and at any given time. Many of my roommates in college seemed to have an exceptionally great capacity for McDonald's products. The Friday night consumption choices of my friends would have made the company happy. Each time they selected a Big Mac they were not selecting Burger King's Whopper—neither were they going home for one of Mom's home-cooked meals.

McDonald's and Burger King go head-to-head every day with each other. They also fight for share of stomach with a variety of other food-product makers, including Mom. That's why those marketing executives are **not** most concerned with the activities of their fast-food brethren. They **are** most concerned with eating habits. If fast-food consumption takes a downturn—and Mom feeds my friends—they're all in a sinking boat. It's important for them to create loyalty to their brand, but it's absolutely essential that the industry—and our culture—create consumers who are adopting fast-food consumption as a part of their lifestyle.

Similarly, it's essential to the continuing health and growth of the non-profit sector to make philanthropy an accepted part of the culture. The more the concept of philanthropy is stressed the greater the likelihood we will continue to generate the dollars necessary to carry out our missions.

Like the myriad companies involved in the fast-food industry, hundreds of thousands of non-profit organizations are in competition for the discretionary income of individuals. If an affluent individual is defined as someone with, say, $3,000 per year in discretionary income, rest assured there are a bevy of organizations, probably all quite worthy, positioning themselves for a share of that discretionary windfall. Those that are most successful are the ones that focus on the donor as a partner and investor in the mission of the organization. Just as a consumer shows favoritism each time she selects a Big Mac, a donor makes a purchase each time she makes a donation. She invests in an organization, makes an impact and expresses her philanthropic intent, presumably receiving something in return. At least the donor *should* be receiving something in return. What is that something? Nothing less than an opportunity to change the world, or at least a small part of it. The paradigm of the future for non-profits is that sacrificial gifts will no longer be made. Our job is to provide our donors with solutions for their needs, nourishment for what we hope are their philanthropic cravings.

Understanding The Art of Giving

- People give to extend their own values.

- People want to have a positive effect on other lives.

- Giving is a highly personal decision.

- Individuals don't give unless they're asked.

- Donors don't make large donations unless they're asked to consider large donations.

- People give to opportunities.

- The old axiom is true that people to people.

Understanding The Art of Asking

- Offer hopes and vision.

- The actual decision to make a gift is rarely made on a first ask.

- Wise fund raisers gratefully nurture a small gift into a later large one.

- Make tax considerations secondary. They are well down the list of factors in most cases, but they **are** a factor in **every** gift of impact.

- Recruiting donor prospects as volunteers and board members for your organization is critical to securing future impact gifts, because volunteers are 75% more likely to give than someone who has not volunteered.

- Introduce the concept of gift planning earlier in a donor's relationship with an organization.

- Involve wife **and** husband, as well as adult children when appropriate, in the cultivation and solicitation process.

- The best person to ask for the gift is the one known to be the most respected by the donor. This is peer to peer cultivation.

- The most important factor in asking is the enthusiasm and passion the solicitor brings to the activity. This person must believe in the cause and be able to articulate the vision.

Our Primary Job is
Building Relationships

This concept of viewing the donor as a partner, an investor, in your organization is critical to creating an atmosphere attractive to those who want to make impact gifts. Essential to this method of soliciting gifts are highly personalized relationships with donors. This process begins with identifying individuals with philanthropic intent and then helping them fulfill their individual stewardship desires. I like to think of a classroom when I think about identifying giving prospects. In any classroom of 25 people, perhaps five have had some sort of contact with my organization. Each of the five might have volunteered at an event, three of them might have made a contribution via our annual campaign and two of them might be consumers of our service or are related to someone who is. These five are raising their hands, asking for more attention.

While most people may not get up in the morning feeling charitable, most people **do** feel the need to be connected with the world around them, to somehow make a difference and have an impact. That fact is especially true for those who already have some relationship with a non-profit organization. Through their actions, they've satisfied one of the important elements on their hierarchy of needs. I once read a study that said more than a fourth of Americans would make charity their first priority if given an unlimited supply of money, choosing making a financial impact over taking a vacation, paying bills or buying a house. Our job as non-profit stewards is to give people the means to satisfy their need to positively impact the world.

There are a variety of tools available to us in our effort to nurture and deepen relationships. Let's go back to our classroom. All five of the event volunteers are candidates for other volunteer work. Such work might include committee, task force or board involvement. The greater the maturity of the relationship with an individual the greater the likelihood he or she will take a leadership role, and a leadership role usually includes being involved with planning and strategic visioning. There is no stronger incentive for expanded involvement than to be presented with the opportunity to do work important to the organization, work that really matters. Conversely, doing work the donor/volunteer perceives as unimportant is the most effective way to end someone's relationship with your organization.

At this point, the donor/volunteer from our classroom—perhaps now a board member with a significant stake in the organization—is invested in helping to create the vision for the organization. It's probably time to turn this person loose on the 20 people in that classroom who have not been touched by your mission. Besides having a terrific prospect for an impact gift, you now have an active disciple for your organization.

Your Organization's Readiness for an Impact Gift Solicitation

People often ask if there is a simple formula for soliciting gifts, and the answer to that question is, no, there is no easy answer that fits all situations, since each gift solicitation presents its own unique challenges and opportunities. But there are several basic guidelines that might be helpful to keep in mind.

I have talked about positioning your organization to have success and developing a donor cultivation paradigm that focuses on the interests and values of the donor rather than the needs and, perhaps, distress of the organization. Accomplishing that point of view is the first step in your organization's readiness to solicit impact gifts. There are several other pragmatic steps in the impact gift solicitation process, including the preparation, the solicitation itself and the follow-up after the solicitation visit (or, much more likely, visits). Like an iceberg with 90% of its mass hidden under water, the process of impact gift fund raising is concentrated on what goes on behind the scenes and prior to the actual solicitation. The steps of prospect identification, research and cultivation are much more effective predictors of success than how the ask is made or even who makes it.

First and foremost, it is essential to do your homework. Define your prospects, working from the inside out. Focus on those individuals whom you know best, or who know your organization. This group most obviously includes board and committee members, staff members, consistent corporate supporters, consumers and those related to consumers. It might also include single-day event

Prospect Cultivation

"Friend-raising" activities might include any or all of the following. Use your imagination (and listening skills) to come up with ideas to engage your impact gift prospects. Keep these activities personal, meaningful and don't ask for money.

- Send clips from the newspaper or local business journal regarding an item of interest to the prospect accompanied by a handwritten note.

- Send a book your donor prospect has mentioned, or send one you think might be interesting based on your knowledge of the prospect's interests.

- Facilitate interaction between prospects and current donors and/or Board members.

- Mail highly personalized letters that do not request funds, but rather tell of some important activity at the agency.

- Consider individualized strategies such as invitations to speak or present at organizational gatherings, or one-on-one sessions seeking advice.

- Invite participation as a member of a special task force or focus group.

- Make invitations to small luncheons or breakfasts with the Executive Director, Board chairperson or other Board members.

- Send an invitation to the annual meeting or to tour the agency and its facilities, or events that it conducts as part of its mission.

- Process prompt (and handwritten) acknowledgment of any contribution (time, cash, advice, etc.).

- Be sure that every prime prospect has been the recipient of at least one non-fund raising cultivation method every six months.

- Maintain continuity in this program by keeping an accurate data base, including information like birthdays and anniversaries. Development staff may change, but you can minimize the effect change has on your donor/prospects by keeping accurate records of their relationship with your organization.

- Be willing to allow another person to get involved in the cultivation process if you are getting nowhere with a prospect.

volunteers and individuals who have made gifts to your organization on a consistent basis. In the latter case, a regular pattern of giving is as important an indicator of a prospect's impact capability as size of the gift.

Review the prospect's file to become familiar with the prospect's situation. How long has the individual been associated with your organization? What is the person's special interest in your organization and which programs and projects have special appeal? Is there a giving history to your organization, or a record of involvement with other non-profits? Is the prospect married, divorced or single? Does the prospect have children and grandchildren? There are many sources of information about individuals within any community. Pay attention to the newspaper's business section and specialized business journals, as well as corporate annual reports and donor listings for other non-profit organizations. Be an avid collector of programs from events conducted by other organizations, especially those with clearly defined giving levels. Note who is serving on what boards. Remember, you're looking for evidence of community connections, so don't forget niche newspapers and magazines that often cover charity events extensively or very specific neighborhoods within a large city. There may also be on-line resources that can be helpful in a search for local information.

Ultimately, you're looking for some indication of the values that are important to the prospect. Defining values often means gathering evidence of the individual's interests and giving habits. You may not be able to get all the answers to all of your questions, but the more information you can gather about the prospect, the more comfortable you—or a member of your organization—will feel when you go to talk about an impact gift.

Finally, educate yourself to know and understand your organization's case, and be ready to answer your prospect's questions. Solid preparation can make all the difference in your ability to effectively communicate later, during the actual solicitation meeting.

The next step in the process is to decide who should make the solicitation. Is there a peer of the prospect who could "open the door?" Should the call be made by a volunteer or staff member? If

---

Questions to Consider so You Know
What You Need to Know

- What is the prospect's financial status and relationship to your organization? You absolutely need to know these two things.

- Name of board member, other volunteer or staff who is personally acquainted with the prospect and/or spouse. Another must-know item.

- Are family members financially independent?

- Are there currently, or may there be soon, dependant family members?

- Does the prospect have a stock portfolio?

- Does the prospect own his or her business, or work for a corporation?

- How about hobbies and outside interests?

- Any indication of assets that might be given?

- Political and religious affiliations?

- Is there a planned gift already in place?

- Who are the person's advisors?

---

you don't know the prospect well, talk with someone who does and determine the best solicitation strategy. Then tailor your approach to the individual situation.

It is imperative that the people soliciting impact gifts believe thoroughly in the mission of the organization. Many people have

What to Look for When Prospecting

- **Evidence that the prospect is acquainted with someone in your organization.** Someone in your organization has to know the prospect or know someone who knows the prospect. The person who finally asks the prospect for the gift does not have to know the person at all, as long as they know someone in common.

- **Evidence that the prospect is committed to your cause, even in a broad sense.** Be broad minded when considering this factor. Discover whether the prospect has made gifts to similar organizations or participates in a meaningful way with another group. Listen during your interaction with the prospect and uncover connections within your community, however community may be defined.

- **Evidence that the person has the ability to make a gift of substance.** Don't just look for the most obvious signs of wealth, like the size of a house or make of automobile. Look for signs of disposable income spent spontaneously. Would this person spend $200 on a single item of clothing? Do they eat out often in nice places? Are they season ticket holders to the symphony, professional athletic team or theater?

discovered that doing face-to-face fund raising reminds them of their commitment. They remember why they became involved in the first place and why they think the work is important. It is an optimum situation if they have also demonstrated their belief in the organization by making their own contribution. The size of that contribution is not important, but it must be a contribution significant for that individual.

It is often helpful to send a letter to the prospect, introducing yourself if need be, describing the project or objective and stating that you will call to set up a meeting. Describe some of your recent achievements and share the vision of your future plans. Invite the prospect to be a part of a group important to your organization. Share the joy of your accomplishments and dreams. While you're composing your letter remember that the prospect wants to make a difference, and you're offering an opportunity to do so. Tell the prospect how important the project is to your organization and the community at large.

Soon after the letter is sent, call to set up an appointment. This step can seem formidable at first. You can ease yourself into the discussion by talking about your shared interest in the organization, explaining your role as a solicitor and sharing your enthusiasm about the project.

Then, ask the prospect when you can meet to discuss the project further. When asking for a meeting, be sure to suggest alternative dates to give several options. Finally, agree on a specific time and place for your meeting and after you're off the telephone be sure to send a short note of confirmation.

Before the meeting, review the prospect's file again and think about how you will approach the subject of the gift (role-play with a colleague). If you are going to make the solicitation call with another person, develop a plan and rehearse it. Be ready to suggest several gift possibilities. Direct gifts are a possibility at every call, but will not necessarily come up with all donors. All fund development staff and other key personnel should be in tune with all types of giving, but keep in mind that the technical will always give way to the practical. The vision you share with the prospect will drive the gift. Tax benefits are well down the list of motivations for a majority of impact donors, although planned giving prospects in particular should be approached with their financial circumstances in mind. In general, focus your skills, and the skills of your organization, on defining your vision, building relationships and painting a picture the donor can help paint.

Solicitation Strategy: The Steps to Success

- Identify qualified prospect(s) and match with qualified solicitor(s).

- Meet with the qualified solicitor(s) to review the action plan.

- Seek a first appointment of the solicitor team with the prospect.

- Conduct the first meeting with the prospect and plan a follow-up.

- Arrange a second meeting, perhaps a site visit, and ask to make a formal presentation.

- Prepare a full presentation and brief the team, preparing them to ask for the gift if the situation is right to do so.

- Make the full presentation and include the solicitation if prudent to do so.

- Receive a gift decision and get closure.

- Send a thank you and begin the donor recognition program.

- Begin preparing for the individual's next gift.

The Solicitation Visit

Remember asking your parents for something special as a kid or teenager? The car for the night, permission to stay over at a friend's house, an hour extension on your curfew. You probably laid some groundwork first. Asking for big stuff was a process. If you wanted the best chance for success, you did some research. You listened at the dinner table when they talked about their friends and the access they allowed their kids to the family car. You made a mental note when they talked about curfew times for the kids down the block. You also probably strategized about how the ask should be made, and where. You wanted to avoid situations of high stress, where your important question might be lost in a sea of other priorities. You might also have worked in the days, weeks and perhaps months in advance of your request to prove yourself worthy of such a gift from your parents. You may have dropped little hints during this time. Your goal was to get what you wanted, and you kept your eye on the prize throughout what was most likely an extended period of paving the way for your actual solicitation.

Similarly, a vast majority of impact gift solicitations will be extended processes and involve more than one visit with the prospect. These visits are part of the process of cultivation and should be viewed as an investment in your organization's future. It may take a year, or more, to facilitate an impact gift. Several visits may be required to inform your prospect and involve him or her in your cause. Keep your eye on the prize.

The solicitation visit need not be as intimidating as it may seem. First of all, the prospect knows from your letter and phone call that you will be talking about making a contribution. Since he or she has agreed to see you, the answer to your request is not an outright "no." The prospect is considering saying "yes." Your job is to move the person from "I'm considering giving" to "I'd be delighted to give."

For the purpose of this section of the chapter, I will condense the process into one visit. In analyzing the solicitation visit, you should consider the four basic phases of an impact gift solicitation: The Opening, The Involvement, The Case Presentation and The Closing. Keep in mind that the actual solicitation visit should occur in a setting most comfortable for the prospect, and a place where you can conduct business. Provide a concise letter/proposal to leave as written backup for your oral ask.

The Opening

The first five minutes of the meeting are critical to obtaining and retaining the prospect's trust. Be relaxed, smile, look the prospect in the eye. Open the meeting with pleasantries. Break the ice by discussing an interesting object in the house or office, mutual friends or something else of shared interest. Get the prospect to talk about his or her involvement with your organization and its programs. Establish a warm, friendly atmosphere and rapport.

The Involvement

Listen carefully for cues and clues about special interests, family situation, health and financial concerns. Try to focus the conversation on four Fs: the prospect's family, friends, finances and fervent interests. Be an interested, active listener and summarize your experiences with the prospect. Begin to explore the prospect's opinion about your organization.

The Case Presentation

Describe the project and talk about what it means to the future of your organization. Make it come to life. If it's appropriate, talk about your own gift and why you are involved in this important project. Stress the importance of the prospect's support, and what the gift will accomplish. Describe the gift levels and recognition opportunities. This may help to raise his or her sights and lead to a larger gift.

Be positive. Don't get defensive and by all means don't get into an argument. You must appear poised, enthusiastic and confident. If you are well prepared for the interview, this will not be hard. It's OK to bring along someone who has been with the organization a long time to assist in answering difficult questions. It's also fine to answer a question by admitting that you don't have the answer. Volunteer to find the answer and get back to the prospect (then make sure and do it). Throughout the conversation, continue to show your interest in the prospect and in his or her concerns, needs and interests.

The Closing

If you've done your homework and completed your cultivation process, then the purpose of the ultimate solicitation meeting—which will probably not be the first face-to-face meeting you have with a prospect—is to get a commitment to give. Everything else revolves around that purpose. It's fine for the conversation to drift off on a tangent, but you must keep bringing it back to the opportunities provided by your organization for the prospect's involvement—and investment. Help the prospect to see that giving to your organization is a logical and natural extension of his or her values. Ask questions with the intent of engaging the prospect.

Ask for a specific amount. I read a newspaper account recently of a study of New York City panhandlers. The panhandlers who asked for a specific amount, or for a specific purpose ("So that I can get on the subway") were more likely to get something than those who asked for the vague "spare change." The same is true for impact gifts. Simply saying "We would like your help," or "We need some money for our important work, and we would like you to help," is too vague. The prospect doesn't know how much money is needed, or what an appropriate gift would be. Is $100 too cheap? Is $1,000 ostentatious? Walk the prospect through your gift levels. Keep in mind that it's probably better to overshoot the target in terms of your ask amount than it is to ask for too little. What's the appropriate target amount? I've heard various answers to that question, including 5% of a person's adjusted net worth for a stretch gift (with 1% being an acceptable target), 10 times the person's largest previous gift or 5 times the individual's aggregate giving total. This formula will be different for each organization and each project.

After introducing the amount, listen. Wait for the prospect to respond. Do not start talking again until the prospect has made some response. You have asked for a significant gift—which may be the most meaningful charitable gift of the donor's life. People don't make such decisions easily or quickly. Give the prospect time and space to think about it. Once the individual responds, focus on that response, which could be one of several.

What to do if you hear, "Yes"

If the prospect says "yes," you have accomplished your objective and achieved resolution. Thank the prospect and be ready to follow up with appropriate materials, meetings, discussions with advisors and so forth—until the gift is closed. Resolution and closure are the two distinct parts of this end-game process. Resolution is coming to agreement, and closure considers what could go wrong and involves "dotting the I's and crossing the T's." A gift isn't complete until closure is achieved, so continue to cultivate and involve the prospect in your cause even after you've heard "yes."

If you hear, "Maybe"

If the prospect doesn't seem particularly interested in the project or seems reluctant to make a gift, ask questions to determine the reasons why. Any complaint about the organization should be taken seriously, and you should provide as much information as possible to clear up any misunderstandings. Listen with empathy. Clarify and reflect what you're hearing from the prospect. Focus on the feeling words the prospect is sharing with you. Combine prior points of agreement to advance to a new point. Express understanding of the prospect's points without conceding agreement. Try to elicit as much information as possible about the prospect's feelings and reactions so you can go back to the office, discuss and evaluate the situation and strategize the next steps. A response that shows you understand the prospect's concerns can go a long way to alleviating them.

If you hear, "No"

If the prospect says "no," don't take the rejection personally. The "no" may really mean "not now" or "not under my present circumstances." People make impact gifts on their own time schedules, when the time is right for them.

As you bring the meeting to a close, thank the prospect for meeting with you, no matter the response. If appropriate, set up a specific time and place for the next meeting or contact. Don't leave a pledge card with the prospect. If he or she has not made a commitment, further personal cultivation will be necessary.

> ## Elements Influencing a Donor's Decision to Make an Impact Gift
>
> - A worthy project
> - Complete information
> - Competence and readiness of the organization
> - Confidence in the leadership
> - Public benefit value of the organization
> - Donors' being part of a larger story
> - Visible association with a success
> - Donors' being well asked, for the right amount
> - Appropriate recognition

Doing More Homework

As soon as you leave the prospect's home or office, make a written record of your conversation and the issues discussed. Do this as soon as possible, while the meeting is still fresh in your mind. Evaluate the prospect's response.

Follow up with a note of thanks for the meeting. Include any information you promised to send, and provide answers to any questions the prospect may have raised. Follow up by telephone to make sure he or she has received the materials and to answer any additional questions. Keep the door open and the dialogue going.

Get together with colleagues to discuss strategies for continuing the cultivation and securing the gift. Keep your eye on the prize. Identify possible gift opportunities based upon the prospect's expressed interests. Continue cultivating and involving the prospect in your organization.

If further visits are necessary, the four phases of solicitation will be repeated over again until the prospect decides to make a gift or definitely—and finally—decides against it.

Although it can be anxiety-producing to ask for an impact gift the first few times you do it, it is thrilling to get a commitment from an impact donor. It's also a good feeling to know that you were able to set aside whatever discomfort you may have had about asking for the greater purpose of meeting the needs of your organization. Knowing that you can talk comfortably about the financial goals of your organization is also empowering. Boards are often immeasurably strengthened when each member feels able to ask for a significant gift.

You can get what you want and need, but you need to ask for it. There's a world of folks out there ready to help you achieve your organization's dreams.

General Impact Gift Solicitation Pointers

- An impact gift is best asked for in person, face-to-face.
- Do your homework, know your organization and share your passion.
- Make your own impact gift before asking others to do so.
- Recognize that individuals give to satisfy their needs.
- Practice active listening skills.
- Lead the prospect to a commitment by removing objections.
- Don't give up too soon.
- Prepare for a continuing cultivation effort.
- Find creative ways to keep the prospect engaged with your organization.
- Don't leave the responsibility for follow-up to the donor's advisors.
- Find creative ways to say thank you.
- Use common sense and practice your skills of basic human interaction and relationships.

Recognition

The most effective recognition for any impact gift is to continue to engage the donor in the organization after the gift is made. Keep in mind that the chances of another gift coming from someone who has already made a gift are quite good. For example, more than 60% of the planned gift donors to Harvard give again during their lifetime. Keep in mind that an investor/donor in your annual campaign is a prime candidate for a planned gift and vice versa.

Any basic recognition plan should include an honors and recognition policy, an analysis of the cost-effectiveness of the elements of the plan and an outline for maintaining donor relations. Each organization will have to answer some basic questions. Is recognition based on cumulative giving or one-time gifts? Are planned gifts recognized separately? What opportunities exist for naming (an area, program or event)? Is there a plaques program or donor wall? In general, start with a basic plan that fits the project or opportunity, then consider enhancements and finally how you will recognize gifts in perpetuity (planned gifts).

In any gift scenario, follow-up and ongoing communication is essential to effective individualized donor relations. The prospect, now donor, wants to know that his or her gift made a difference, as you said it would during the cultivation process. It's your job to keep the lines of communication open with each impact donor and to be accountable for the actions—and in some cases, providing the services—identified as important to that donor. You've asked people to invest in your organization and thus help you change the world. Recognize your partner investors as such.

Changing the World

Our world desperately needs those of means to be involved and engaged in their communities and to philanthropically invest their resources in ways that make a difference. The greatest gift you can provide them is an opportunity to be involved with your organization, to join you in affecting one small part of the world you both care about deeply. You succeed if you put yourself in a position to present your mission, and you fail only if you don't share the opportunity. Invite individuals to make an investment in the values and vision of your organization, and don't forget to have fun and share your own passion.

You've Successfully Prepared for the Solicitation if . . .

- You have the right prospect
- You know the prospect's interests
- You have cultivated your prospect
- You get an appointment
- You know your gift strategy, including target gift amount

* * * * *

When You Make a Solicitation Visit, be Aware of . . .

- The fact that the purpose of the visit is to ask for a gift
- Talking about opportunities and not charity distress
- Your listening and observation skills
- Being quiet after you've asked for the gift

* * * * *

Conduct Your Solicitation Visit With These Steps in Mind . . .

- Open with pleasantries
- Get to the subject
- Get to the asking and ask for a specific amount
- Be ready for any number of responses
- Leave on a positive note
- Follow up

Mike Schroeder

If Steven Spielberg ever decides to do "The Mike Schroeder Story," his first call will be to Tim Robbins to play the lead. They share the same tall, athletic build and ready smile. Mike smiles a lot these days as the Executive Director for ALS Hope and founder of Blue Sky Coaching. Blue Sky Coaching provides personal and business coaching services to working professionals.

Mike previously served as the Planned Giving Officer for Special Olympics, Inc. where he oversaw the launch of the Special Olympics Planned Giving Initiative, an effort to coordinate planned giving activities in each Special Olympics chapter in the United States. Before that, he worked for almost five years as Vice President of Development and St. Louis Metro Director for Special Olympics Missouri.

Throughout his career, Mike has managed to combine his three loves—athletics, nonprofit management and writing. His days as an athlete have been compromised by back problems secondary to the onset of middle age, but he still enjoys writing both fiction and nonfiction.

After beginning his career as a journalist and college public relations practitioner in his native Minnesota, Mike moved in 1984 to Colorado Springs, CO, where he worked for USA Hockey, first serving as its Public Relations Director before being promoted to the new position of Director of Fund Raising. In that role, he coordinated marketing, licensing, fund raising and public relations for one of the U.S. Olympic movement's most successful national governing bodies.

In 1993, Mike moved to St. Louis, where he started the St. Louis Vipers, a professional in-line hockey team. It was a for-profit venture that ended with very little profit, but he had great seats to the games.

Mike Schroeder
6175 Kingsbury, St. Louis, MO 63112
Phone: 314-721-6064 • Fax: 314-721-3669

CHAPTER 10

Claiming Your Organization's Piece of the Corporate Pie!

David M. LaGreca

Introduction

I n 1996, corporate[1] contributions to our nation's nonprofit organizations totaled $8.5 billion. This growing philanthropic investment in the nonprofit sector equals almost three-quarters of the $11.8B contributed by private foundations. For those nonprofits able to position themselves clearly and strongly, this pool of money represents an opportunity that many organizations do not pursue. Happily, with a little knowledge, experience and determination, corporate funding can be open to your organization. It may take some energy to implement your corporate fundraising strategy—but for many organizations it can be a recipe for getting a piece of a growing pie!

Baking Hint #1

Don't assume your organization is too small. While you may not qualify for corporate sponsorship, your programs may meet a company's need.

---

[1] The word "corporate" is used here to refer to a wide range of businesses including traditional corporations, financial service corporations, professional firms (such as accounting and consulting), and all commercial enterprises in between.

1. Why Do Corporations Contribute to Nonprofits?

Before developing a corporate fundraising strategy for your organization, you need to understand the motivations that Corporate America brings to the distribution of its philanthropy. Here are some of the most commonly expressed reasons for corporate philanthropy are:

- **Marketing the corporate name.** This is often seen in event sponsorship and cause-related marketing. In the past decade, a major trend in corporate philanthropy has been a shift from direct grant of money to sponsorships. While not new by any means (Mobil Oil's sponsorship of PBS programming goes back decades), corporate sponsorship is proliferating both in terms of numbers of events and dollars contributed[2]. Here are a few examples:

  - 5K, 10K and marathon races: From local backing of a community race to Chase Manhattan Bank's support of the New York City Marathon, we have become used to seeing corporate names on the backs (and anywhere else they can fit their logo) of runners and walkers.

  - Cultural events: A glance at the program you receive at almost any national, regional or community theater or dance company's performance will show a growing group of corporate sponsorship either for the organization or a program that the organization runs.

  - Local events for social service organizations: In a New York City suburb, local offices of professional and accounting firms compete for sponsorship of an annual golf outing benefiting a major child care agency.

  - Cause-related marketing: McDonald Corporation's support for Ronald McDonald Houses across the country is a prime example. (See Chapter 11.)

---

[2] This is not limited to nonprofits as a visit to any number of sports stadiums across the country will reveal. Major league sports teams now play in stadiums with names that include 3Com, Busch and Continental Airlines. In an interesting mix of corporate sponsorship and higher education, college football bowl games now carry corporate names, such as FedEx, Nokia, and Tostitos, in front of their traditional names.

- **Positioning the corporation as a good citizen.** Banks and financial services firms have taken the lead in this area with the encouragement of the federally required Community Reinvestment Act (CRA) which assesses their impact on the communities that they serve.

- **Ensuring that their employees have good communities to live in.** This is seen particularly where corporations have clustered their headquarters. In those areas, corporate philanthropies often collaborate on funding for community services, such as schools, YMCA's, and Boys & Girls Clubs.

In addition to "investing" in the communities where their employees reside, a recent trend is fueled by today's tight labor market:

- **Positioning the company as responsible and responsive to the community in recruiting and retaining employees.** As competition for qualified employees intensifies, many corporations point to their community activities as a way to "humanize" the workplace. For example, one major office of an international accounting firm highlights to all prospective employees the office's commitment to a workplace-mentoring program for high school students.

2. Where Are the Decisions Made About Who Gets What?

From the perspective of your community-based organization, corporate philanthropy can appear to be monolithic and centralized. However, this is not often the case. **Within a corporation, funding decisions can be made in a number of places. And to make things more interesting, funding can come from multiple sources in one corporation** (smorgasbord style!). With decisions about grants and in-kind support being made in multiple places, nonprofits have **more work** to do in approaching corporations. But, the nature of how business funds the nonprofit community creates **more opportunities** as well!

Nonprofits that are successful in the corporate fundraising arena need to be familiar with all the places where philanthropic decisions are made.

- **Centralized corporate foundations**: Many well-known major corporations have centralized corporate foundations. Among these are American Express, AT&T, Citigroup, General Motors, General Electric, Lucent Technology, and Mircrosoft. Centralized foundations also exist in most professional firms such as : Arthur Andersen, Ernst & Young LLP, and McKinsey & Company. These pools of corporate philanthropy are guided by "headquarters" and usually have clearly defined giving objectives. Fortunately, this information often can be accessed through corporate web sites.

- **Local branches/manufacturing centers/ service centers**: These offices often have access to philanthropic funds to further their standing as "good neighbors" in their particular communities.

- **Public and community relations departments**: Many corporations and smaller businesses have departments called either public or community affairs where contributions can be sought.

- **Marketing and special projects budgets**: The largest corporations and firms have marketing and special projects budgets with money to "sponsor" events and activities in an effort to raise their visibility in particular communities.

With decisions on funding being made in any or all of the places described above, nonprofits need to be clear about both:

- Which corporations to ask.

- Which part of the targeted organization to ask.

Baking Hint #2

If you choose to approach different parts of the same company—for example, the centralized foundation and the marketing department—make sure that the right hand knows what the left hand is doing! You can really burn the crust if you don't!

3. A Word About Mutual Self Interest

A more subtle fact of corporate philanthropy can be seen in the movement toward defining the mutual self-interest that exists between the corporation and the nonprofit organization. For example:

- With environmental issues a major concern of battery manufacturers, several such corporations provide funding for nonprofit recycling efforts, as well as educational programs aimed at encouraging the next generation of scientists.

- Many industries (for example, banking, hospitality and retail) support job-training programs run by nonprofit organizations to ensure a steady supply of qualified entry-level employees.

- Pharmaceutical companies often support disease-related organizations. This gives them a pipeline to efficiently and effectively market their products directly to consumers.

Situations like these allow the corporations to do well for themselves, while doing good for the community. Because of this, **organizations approaching the business community for support need to articulate the value that support for your organization can bring to the company.**

Baking Hint #3

If you have a publication that is shared with a select audience, corporations may be interested in advertising in it. For example, companies manufacturing drugs for AIDS will often advertise their prescription drugs in periodicals targeted at those who are HIV+ or at risk.

How Do You Begin?

You are a $700,000 organization with a tradition of governmental support and a small amount of private foundation funding.

Over the past ten years, you have never raised more than $25,000 from local corporations. How do you begin to claim a piece of the corporate pie for your organization's mission?

Before you commit the first word to paper in applying for funds, there are two simple—but often exhausting—steps you must take:

- Research YOUR business community

- Strategically assess your organization

1. Research YOUR Business Community

No matter how small or large your organization is—or for that matter the size of your community—the business sector that surrounds you is complex. The easiest way to begin this research is to gather a few people together to brainstorm. The goal here is to list:

- All the **employers** in your community (from the largest to the smallest).

- All **companies who do business in your community** even if they are not in your community.

- **Business associations** in your community, such as Chambers of Commerce and county organizations.

- Who **employs the members of your organization's extended family?**

Baking Hint #4

Make sure you know where each volunteer (and the significant other of each volunteer) works. In addition, know where the significant others of all staff members work. You may find fundraising opportunities in their companies.

Generating a list

An ideal group of brainstormers for this exercise would include[3]

- A bank branch manager—preferably where your organization— or a board member has an account!

- A board member

- A corporate funder (one who knows your organization)

- Executive & development directors

- Individual contributors

- A local small business owner

- A volunteer

Now ask the group to generate a list of businesses to research.[4] Be creative! Don't overlook any business. Ask yourselves these questions:

- If you live in a rural community with no major retail stores, which catalogue do most people order from?

- If you live in a farming community, which agribusiness company sells the most seed and fertilizer in your area?

- Which contractors are building the most new homes or stores in your area?

- If your local economy depends on tourism—which hotel or motel chains are in your area? Credit card companies? Note: Whether your organization is a rural development corporation developing eco-tourism in the north of Poland or in a summer community in northern Michigan, companies that derive income from these activities may be interested in supporting you!

- If there is a financial services company in your community that deals with trusts—track it down. Their trust officers often know about trusts seeking to fund specific types of programs. They can be a great help!

---

[3] Don't worry if you don't have everyone on this list—just get started.

[4] After almost a decade of interviewing business executives, this one is crystal clear—business people enjoy having their brains picked! Everyone loves being asked his or her opinion!

Researching the list

Now that you have a list, you need more specific information about these businesses. For large corporations (such as American Express and ADM) or a local branches (for example, your bank) **you can find information about their corporate giving on the Internet.**

For local businesses and branches, phone calls will be necessary. Your public library or The Foundation Center (www.fdncenter.org) can be helpful as well.

Baking Hint #5

We know there are not enough hours in the day. So ask a volunteer, a student intern, or a retired individual to lead this research for your organization!

You are looking for **information about each company's:**

- Funding guidelines: Do they fund programs just for children and education? Are they interested in science? Because of a baby boomer employee pool, have they recently become concerned with services for the elderly?

- Plant locations: Where do their employees actually work and live?

- Matching gift programs: companies will often have matching gift programs, matching employee donations to nonprofits sometimes one-to-one (or sometimes more!)

- Grantees: What organizations have these companies supported in the past? Is your organization like these beneficiaries!

Baking Hint #6

By way of policy, make sure you know where each of your individual donors works. Many employers sponsor programs in which they match employees personal charitable donations.

2. Strategically Assess Your Organization

While research on your business community goes on, take a cold hard business look at your organization. Define the work that you do by program and the value you create for your consumers. For example, **a well-run, community-based day-care program for active elders has great value to:**

- The **participants**—by providing activities, companionship, and volunteer activities.

- The **family's** peace of mind.

- The **employer** of the elderly person's children—who are less likely to take days out of work.

- **Small businesses** that provide services for the elderly, for examples pharmacies, would benefit from having multiple customers in one place.

Develop a similar "value equation" for each part of your program. Then compare it to each corporation's funding guidelines.

If your program doesn't match their guidelines for giving, do not give up. You may be able to provide a direct service to their employees or employee families that even they have not thought up. Be creative!

Program Assessment

For each program your organization has (or wants to develop), ask yourself which companies

1. Care about your organization's activities?

2. Have an interest in the populations you serve?

3. Would purchase your services for their employees or employee families?

4. Have funded other organizations like yours?

5. Would benefit from allying themselves with your organization?

6. Articulate giving priorities that include your program area?

7. Have in-kind donations (furniture, printing, office equipment, marketing or advertising expertise, for example) that you need?

Deciding Whom To Ask

As Chase Manhattan Bank's motto proclaims, *The right relationship is everything!* This is particularly true with fundraising, and so the first rule of corporate funding is "**ask people that you know.**" The second rule of corporate fundraising is "**Get to know those people you need to know!**"

Baking Hint #7

Make up any excuse to collect business cards from anyone concerned about your organization. Collect business cards at productions, fundraisers, meetings and other events—even if you have to raffle off a prize by using business cards as the raffle tickets. You never know who employs the folks who attend your programs— and you need to find out!

Remember: Asking those you know is easier than getting to know those you need to know—but the latter is not impossible.

How should you begin? Here are some tried—and true—strategies for getting to know someone—even if you are not sure who it is!

Good corporate lead but no name: You know a company that supports programs like yours, but you do not know anyone at the company. First, review all the business cards that you have been collecting. If no one works at that company, try people you know in the same business (for example, Community Reinvestment Act officers at one bank often know their counterparts at another). Your board can also help a great deal.

Baking Hint #8

Ask your funders if they have contacts with other corporations and foundations that might support your program. The great thing is that your funders have already invested in you and most are happy to help you find other sources of funds.

As a last resort, write a brief letter of introduction to a targeted foundation, asking whether you could brief them on your organization's programs. Make sure you make it clear (in one paragraph) why you think they would be interested in your program.

Good corporate lead and you have a name! Follow the same process as above—but also check to see whether the individual serves on any boards in your community. Also find out what he or she did before going to work for a corporate foundation. Many of these individuals worked in program areas they now fund, and you may be able to develop a connection in this way.

In both these scenarios, the goal is to write to them—at the suggestion of someone they already know if possible—and to ask whether you can bring them up-to-date on your program.

Two other facts are critical to remember:

- You may work a great deal at getting a small grant from a corporation. But—as with major donor cultivation, you are beginning a relationship that will develop farther. Today's $500 could be next year's $5,000.

- When you are turned down, bear in mind how children view being told no by adults. "No" could certainly be "yes"—only later. Fundraisers, like kids, must learn to ask again. Or if a sports analogy helps, baseball players who do not hit the ball 7 times out of each 10 times at bats, are all-stars (and paid accordingly). If you get three yeses for each ten times you ask, you're an all-star, too!

Role Of The Board In Corporate Marketing

Board members are critical to an organization's corporate fundraising strategy. In fact, without business expertise and experience on your board of directors, there is little chance of success. Board members can help in a number of ways:

- Board members' companies should be the first corporations approached in initiating a corporate fundraising strategy. Many corporations (no matter where the funding decision is made) look more favorably on an organization when one of their "own" sit on the board of directors. When a fundraising proposal arrives on the desk of a corporate funder with a personal note from an executive at that company, attention will be paid.[5]

- Board members function as ambassadors for their organizations. Beyond their own companies, they can be valuable in

---

[5] The next time you are looking for a board member with a particular set of skills and expertise, you might want to look among the corporations in your community you have targeted for contributions. Corporate funders often receive requests from executives looking to get involved with the community. Adding them to your board could be the beginning of a long-term relationship!

approaching other corporations for funding on a business-to-business level. For example, if your organization is approaching a large accounting firm's foundation for a grant, a note signed by the accountant on your board communicates volumes—peer to peer.

- Board members with business expertise also are critical in shaping presentations to corporate funders. Government contract applications require a certain bureaucratic language, as do private foundation ones. Approaches for corporate funding should be clear, concise and to the point. The financial fundamentals should be reviewed by a board member with financial experience. Remember: You are speaking to business people—have someone who speaks their language guide the development of your approach!

- Finally, no corporate fundraising contact should be initiated without asking the executives on your board whether they have any contacts at the targeted company. One truism of networking: *We often don't know we know whom we know*! Got it? For example, asking board members for their corporate contacts usually produces little results and often a yawn. But, asking board members whether they know someone at a specific corporation usually jogs their memory and can result in some great contacts.

Baking Hint #9

Many board members worry that if you take corporate money, your organization will be owned by that corporation. Corporations have better things to do than own you! Don't hesitate to give them an opportunity to help the community by helping your organization!

Board members' assistance may range from attending a meeting with their own corporate foundation personnel, to joining the executive director in meeting with another corporate foundation, to writing a note to a friend who works at another corporation, asking for assistance in contacting that foundation. Because your board's personal network is critical to successful fundraising, pay particular attention to the individuals your board members bring to events or add to mailing lists. Always ask for their business affiliations.

Setting up your organization's corporate fundraising infrastructure

It's about information, information and more information! Organizations that succeed at corporate fundraising manage information about their business contacts well. There is no one way to do this, but here are some suggestions that might be helpful:

- Find a board member who will be the point person on all the other board members' business contacts. With e-mail you may be able to do this painlessly with a monthly reminder. This information should be fed to the staff member responsible for corporate fundraising. Some larger organizations may have someone dedicated to this, but in most organizations the executive or development director is in charge. Having a board member volunteer to collect and collate this information can be a great gift!

- Read the business section of your local paper daily. While this may seem far removed from the critical mission issues of your organization, knowing your own business community is crucial.

- Find out whether your local chamber of commerce has regular meetings. Many organizations overlook the small businesses in their communities and small does not mean poor!

- Share your corporate funding calendar with your board members at each meeting. A simple spreadsheet—with which companies are being pursued for which programs and when—goes a long way toward strengthening board members' participation and accessing their networks.

- Regularly review your program and articulate the value it may bring to the members of the business community.

Finally, enjoy yourself. Fundraising in the business community brings you in contact with some great people who are committed to both their corporations and the communities around them. Enjoy meeting them—even when they say no. Eventually "no" may turn into "yes"!

Positioning, Positioning, Positioning

Finding a piece of the corporate pie to nourish your program ultimately comes down to *positioning your organization as having value in the eyes of the business community*. If you believe in your organization's mission, you should be unafraid of adopting the language of marketing to present your case to corporate funders.

You may run the best early childhood education program for low-income families in the world. And you may believe you deserve funding because that is so. But if you can't make the case that your program has an impact on the work force of tomorrow, why should a business fund you as opposed to the three-hundred other organizations requesting their assistance?

Corporate funders must be engaged in ways that address their corporate needs. Perseverance is necessary, and the "pie" may take a very long time to come out of the oven. But winning the corporate funding "bake-off" is an important way to ensure that your organization will accomplish its mission.

David M. LaGreca

David LaGreca is still a man with a past—one that now includes his contribution to the "SECRETS OF SUCCESSFUL BOARDS: The Best from the Non-Profit Pros." In 1999, David established his own consulting practice—The LaGreca Company—working with nonprofit organizations and corporate community relations and human resources programs.

Prior to 1999, David LaGreca spent eight years as a consultant at the Volunteer Consulting Group (VCG). His responsibilities included nonprofit board recruitment and consulting, meeting facilitation, the corporate placement program (American Express, PSE&G, Ernst & Young LLP), VCG's national initiatives and overall management of VCG's information systems.

Before joining VCG in 1991, Mr. LaGreca was the Administrator for the Department of Surgery, Memorial Sloan Kettering Cancer Center. He also taught at Boston College, wrote a weekly newspaper column in Rhode Island and has spent the last twenty years working with community-based health care organizations caring for terminal patients.

A graduate of the Katholieke Universiteit te Leuven, Belgium, Mr. LaGreca received his MBA from the Columbia University School of Business. As a former diocesan and Jesuit priest, he has worked with a wide variety of nonprofits addressing issues covering education, health care, homelessness, and human rights.

A native of Rhode Island, Mr. LaGreca has lived, worked and studied in Belgium, England, Germany, Italy, Jamaica, Massachusetts and Tanzania.

Mr. LaGreca served on the Boards of Hospice Care of Rhode Island and McAuley House (Providence, RI). He served as Chair of the Board of Body Positive of New York—a position he held for five years. He currently sits on the Board of Directors of the Vocational Foundation, Inc. and on the Advisory Board of the MBA-Nonprofit Connection.

David M. LaGreca
The LaGreca Company
4 West 104th Street, #LB, New York, NY 10025-4318
(212)-222-3892
dmlnyc@aol.com

THE CUTTING
EDGE

CHAPTER 11

Is Your Name for Sale?
Cause-Related Marketing

Jill F. Osur

Any successful fundraising campaign should be sure to tap into one of today's hottest streams of revenue: cause-related marketing. In cause-related marketing, a company creates a fundraising promotion that integrates its sales efforts with a nonprofit organization. IEG Inc., the world's leading provider of independent research and analysis on sponsorship, projects that corporate investment in cause programs will reach $630 million this year. In addition, IEG reports that monies raised through cause programs jumped 335%, from $125 million in 1990 to $544 million in 1998.

Cause-related marketing has evolved into a huge piece of the sponsorship pie because companies have realized that instead of just writing a check to support a charity, they can tie their corporate and philanthropic priorities together by creating a promotion that will increase sales, improve community goodwill, increase employee pride and morale, and differentiate themselves from their competitors.

Cause marketing campaigns can be extremely creative. Many of the most successful campaigns structure their promotions in one of the following ways:

- Percentage of sales goes to the charity

- Specific donation to the charity entitles the consumer to promotional offer

- Fixed amount goes to the charity with every rebate mailed in

- Fixed amount goes to the charity for each product sold.

The outcome of such campaigns can create a win-win-win partnership. The companies win because they move product, differentiate themselves from their competitors, and create goodwill. The consumers win because they feel they have made a contribution with every purchase. And the charities benefit because they receive a tremendous amount of exposure and a nice big check. Successful campaigns reach revenue that is not accessible to traditional fundraising vehicles.

Consumers have become accustomed to seeing products in the store tied to a cause and have come to expect this business practice from blue-chip companies. The 1999 Cone/Roper Cause Related Trends Report states that two-thirds of Americans say they would be likely to switch brands or retailers to one associated with a good cause, when price and quality are equal.

The study goes on to say that two-thirds of Americans agree that cause marketing should be a standard practice, and that eight in ten Americans report having a more positive image of companies who support a cause they care about. Consumer enthusiasm for such campaigns has spurred the huge increase in cause marketing campaigns and the outcomes indicate that this trend will only continue to grow.

How to choose a partner

Before you embark on an ambitious cause marketing campaign, your decision of whom to partner with can make or break your campaign. Just because a corporation would like to conduct a cause marketing program with you does not mean that you should jump in with no questions asked. It is critical that the nonprofit and the corporation are a "good fit."

For example, if the tobacco industry wanted to donate a dollar to local schools from every pack of cigarettes sold, you would have a recipe for disaster. The campaign would create a tremendous amount of exposure, but all of the wrong nature. The media would jump all over the tobacco industry for trying to promote cigarettes to youngsters, and would reprimand the school for encouraging such a promotion.

As a staff or board member involved in fundraising, your first responsibility is to research the company and find out whether any potential negative issues might arise during a campaign. Look at the history of the company to see whether it has received any bad press related to its product or personnel. Finding negative information does not necessarily mean that a partnership won't work, but it will help you put all of the issues on the table for discussion. In addition, you may be able to help your corporate partner improve its image.

Remember that your cause and its mission are of the utmost importance. It is your job to maintain the integrity of your organization and to never commit to a campaign that could potentially damage its reputation.

It's amazing how often partnerships arise from a board member having a casual conversation with a personal or professional acquaintance. Whether your organization has a professional development staff or not, never underestimate the power of your board. Many boards state in their criteria for board membership that an individual must be willing to help raise funds and open doors. Board members are ideal for this because they are passionate about the cause.

At the next board meeting, don't miss the opportunity to have an open discussion about potential prospects. You will be quite surprised at what happens when a group of executives sitting around a room begin to share ideas. Egos take over and the contacts start flowing. Create a list that the board can utilize or the development staff can work on with the board. Begin a process in which board members proactively help generate leads. A board member can be having lunch with a client or vendor and have a conversation about his board involvement in the nonprofit. During the discussion he can ask the simple question, "Have you ever considered conducting a cause-related marketing campaign with a nonprofit?" That one sentence is the hardest part of the whole process. But once the question has been asked, the door has been opened. If the prospect is receptive, it's time to set up a formal meeting to discuss the opportunity.

Conducting an interview with a potential partner is extremely important. Some novice fundraisers and board members may feel intimidated by this process, believing that they should be grateful that someone else wants to raise money for them. Always remember, however, that you are entering into a partnership, and that you would not be acting in a professional manner if you did not do your homework and ask the appropriate questions. Corporations will appreciate your level of expertise and feel more confident about the partnership knowing that you are committed to making the campaign as successful as it can be.

Knowledge of every detail of a cause marketing campaign is critical. Whether a board member or staff generated the lead, you will have to go back to your board of directors and go over every detail of the campaign for their sign-off. You will ultimately be responsible for the outcome of the campaign, so the more informed you are, the better you will be able to respond and react to any situation.

Always ask for all of the specifics of the relationship in writing. Getting the specifics on official company stationery will make selling the promotion to your entire board much easier. A written contract that details the campaign allows both partners to be clear on expectations.

The following are recommended questions to ask a potential sponsor:

- What are the details of the promotion?

- What is the exact time frame?

- Why do you feel our cause is a good fit for you?

- How will you incorporate our cause into the campaign?

- What kind of advertising will you put into place to promote the campaign, and what is your budget?

- Will your company be doing an employee kickoff prior to the campaign?

- If so, can we educate your employees on our cause and help them understand how their success can directly affect our mission?

- If not, can we provide you information on our cause to distribute to your management to help educate your employees on our cause and to help them understand how their success can directly affect our mission?

- Will we have the opportunity to approve all collateral material with our mark and logo on it, including press releases?

- What are your expectations of our organization's participation?

- Will there be a minimum cash guarantee to the cause for the promotion?

- Can you provide us with a list of staff members who will be working on the campaign along with a list of their job responsibilities?

- Can you provide us with a fact sheet and a promotional kit with all collateral material so that we can educate our staff and board?

- Are you willing to create a contract outlining the promotion and expectations?

If the promotion calls for consumers to make a donation directly to the charity in order to receive product, make sure to ask the following:

- What forms of payment will be accepted?

- Are the checks or credit card payments made out directly to our organization?

- How is the money collected and sent to our organization?

- How often will we receive money?

- Will the consumer get some kind of receipt thanking them for their donation and stating what amount, if any, they can use as a tax write-off?

- Who thanks the donor?

- What kind of accounting structure will you use?

- Can you provide us with a detailed campaign activity report monthly and at the end of the campaign?

If the campaign involves a check coming from the corporate partner, make sure to ask the following:

- What kind of accounting structure will you use?

- How often will checks be disbursed to our charity?

- Can you provide us with a detailed campaign activity report monthly and at the end of the campaign?

- Can we capture names?

- Who thanks the donor?

You may feel that the list of questions is long, but asking them will not only instill confidence in your partner, but also help with the management of the campaign. Most campaigns fail when there is a lack of communication or miscommunication on expectations. If you can create a working document with all pertinent information included in it, you will be able to manage the campaign and most likely have a successful outcome.

Staff from your organization will probably have a few questions themselves. Remember that if you conduct a campaign that covers a significant geographical area, the campaign will impact everyone in the organization. Whenever you conduct a cause marketing campaign, spend a lot of time educating your own staff. The last thing you want to have happen is for a newspaper to call one of your local offices to ask where the money raised from this campaign will be used, and for the person taking the call to have no knowledge that the campaign even exists. Focus a lot of time and energy getting all staff behind the campaign and knowledgeable about the campaign details.

What Is Your Name Worth?

Far too often, organizations lend a corporation their mark and logo, invest significant staff time and resources, and make little or nothing for their efforts. Of all the information in this chapter, the most important is that you must know the market and what your name is worth. You want to make sure that the potential partner is willing to make your cause an integral part of the promotion and to prominently display your mark and logo in all collateral materials and advertising.

Never participate in a cause-related marketing campaign without a rights fee or a minimum guarantee. Whether or not the campaign makes a dime, you should be paid for the right to use the name of your organization and its logo. The credibility and reputation of your organization will play a significant role in the success of the campaign, and you should be compensated for that.

If your organization has never charged fees like this before and you have no idea what your name is worth, I suggest that you begin by looking at your current sponsorship levels. If you have done a cause marketing campaign in the past, look at how much these campaigns have typically produced.

If there has been no consistency in pricing or if you feel that you are underselling your organization, a great resource for placing a value on your sponsorship packages and creating a price for rights fees and minimum guarantees is IEG Consulting's weekly Sponsor Report (www.sponsorship.com). The report is an inexpensive way to keep on top of the sponsorship market; finding out what corporations are paying for sponsorship and cause- related marketing programs; and what nonprofits are charging. IEG Sponsorship Report, along with IEG's consulting expertise, can be a tremendous help in getting any nonprofit up and running and in laying a solid foundation for successful campaigns.

Knowing as much as possible about cause-related marketing is extremely valuable when placing a price on a promotion. The other "must have" industry information is the Cone/Roper Trends Report. This study covers American consumers' feelings about cause-related marketing. Cone (www.coneinc.com) is also considered one of the nation's foremost consultancies in the field of strategic cause-related marketing, and has been at the forefront of creating and implementing innovative programs for national companies for more than 17 years.

If you don't have the budget to consult with these industry experts, you may also find the Internet extremely useful. Log on to any major nonprofit's web site and you usually can find the details of their cause-related marketing campaigns. You can also find some very useful information by searching the web for articles on cause-related marketing.

How To Open The Door And Sell Your Organization

You may have the most creative, lucrative campaign ever developed but no one to sell it to. Getting in the door and seeing the right person is half the battle. As mentioned above, research is critical. Based on your research, create a list of companies that you would like to align your cause with. Create two columns, one with a list of eight to ten "A" companies representing your top choices and the other with a list of eight to ten "B" companies. Focus all of your energy on column A first, and move to column B only when you have exhausted column A. This type of cultivation is no different from the strategy used to go after a corporate gift or sponsorship.

Use your network of contacts, including board members and other friends at nonprofits to try to get a warm lead. Send the list to the whole Board. If someone knows a key executive at one of these companies, ask him or her to help set up an appointment for you to meet with the head of marketing, or the key person in the marketing department who works on acquisition marketing or promotions. Through your research, you should have obtained their name and title.

If you have a fundraising board, more than likely someone on the board will know someone at one of the companies on your list, or would be glad to make a call to a senior level executive in that company.

Sometimes the most successful cause-related marketing campaigns are not generated with new partners, but rather develop out of relationships with existing partners. Look over your current list of partners and sit down with those that might be most appropriate to conduct such a campaign.

If all else fails, cold calling is an option. If you are calling the right person with a good opportunity, persistence may pay off.

Once you have secured a meeting, it is imperative that you go into it prepared. Your job is to impress the person you are meeting with and to make him or her want to do business with you. It is not your job to say what is best for them. You can, however, talk about your impressive track record, tout the reputation of your organization and discuss a campaign that would be a win-win-win.

Your knowledge of the industry and of the power of cause-related marketing can spur a very creative meeting that may lead to the beginning of a successful partnership. Prior to the meeting ask for an annual report and review it carefully. On the day of your meeting, look up the day's stock price and read the business section of the newspaper for any pertinent industry news. Asking questions about the company's priorities and objectives can give you enough information during this first meeting to begin creating some scenarios for a campaign. Make sure that the corporation is willing to be a partner in this process. If the company expects you to do all of the creative work, that is an indication that it will not be an active player in the campaign. Your primary objective in the meeting is to sell yourself and to get the person you are meeting with excited about the prospect of conducting a great campaign.

What Do You Get For What You Give Up!

If you have done your homework, chosen the right partner, secured a rights fee or minimum guarantee, and agreed on a written contract, you should not have to give up anything for what you get. Part of the process of placing a value on your mark and logo is knowing how much your time is worth. For example, if you end up spending 30 hours a week for four weeks and the promotion generates

$5,000, you are probably going to feel as if you gave up quite a bit. On the other hand, if you know the campaign is going to give you a tremendous amount of exposure and generate significant money, then the time commitment will be worth it. Make sure that you calculate every aspect of the campaign before signing any contract. You need to know your net bottom line when it comes to revenue versus expenses and staff time before you can agree to any proposal.

The word partnership has been used throughout this chapter because in any business venture, both parties should bring an equal amount to the table, and at the end of the day you should have a win-win situation for both organizations. If you can be a partner in a great campaign and deliver more than you promised, you have successfully set yourself up for negotiating a long-term partnership. Another key finding in the 1999 Cone/Roper Cause Related Trends Report says that eight in ten Americans would like to see a company choose one cause over a long period of time rather than many causes over a shorter period. Americans feel that a longer investment by the company demonstrates its commitment to the cause. Your success as a good partner will help dictate the longevity and prosperity of your partnership.

Case Studies

If you follow the advice in this chapter, you should be able to create, implement and achieve success. There have been some great cause-related marketing campaigns and some real bombs. Following are some examples:

What Not to Do

Example One: (from Cone Inc.)

The American Medical Association (AMA) negotiated an exclusive five- year sponsorship and endorsement with Sunbeam Corporation. Sunbeam would pay AMA royalties tied to product sales in return for use of the AMA's name in promoting a wide range of Sunbeam products, including such health-related products as blood pressure monitors, heating pads, thermometers, humidifiers and vaporizers. Under the arrangement, the AMA was to be mentioned prominently in Sunbeam's marketing and advertising of the products endorsed or recommended by the AMA. The AMA seal was to appear in advertising and on product packaging. Written healthcare information from the AMA was also to be included inside the packaging of the products.

Almost immediately following the announcement of its deal with Sunbeam, the AMA faced a virtual blizzard of public criticism from a variety of sources, including newspaper editorials, consumer health advocates and from within the AMA's own membership and board of trustees. Criticism centered on the exclusive nature of the endorsement arrangement, the fact that the AMA apparently had not tested or evaluated any of the products involved and the questions that the arrangement raised about the AMA's credibility as an independent organization.

Before the marketing campaign was implemented, the AMA terminated the arrangement. Sunbeam then filed a lawsuit against the AMA, which was settled in July 1998. As part of its defense, the AMA maintained that the agreement was against public policy and would violate state and federal laws prohibiting unfair or deceptive trade practices. In the settlement, Sunbeam agreed not to require the AMA to participate in the marketing campaign, and the AMA paid Sunbeam $9.9 million for damages and expenses.

This mess could have been avoided if the AMA had done adequate research upfront and gone through the proper internal channels of approval. It turned out that the AMA was selling its endorsement of products it had never tested. In addition, the campaign never went through an internal approval process. It was not until after the contract had been signed that the AMA analyzed its mistake and decided to withdraw from the agreement.

It's much better to do your homework and to agree not to do business because you cannot come to terms than to have your botched agreement make the front page of a major newspaper.

<u>Example Two (from the IEG Sponsorship Report):</u>

The Arthritis Foundation found itself in hot water during the creation of a cause marketing campaign with Johnson & Johnson's McNeil Consumer Products Co., the makers of Tylenol. The agreement included a minimum of $1 million a year, establishing the Arthritis Foundation line of pain relievers, named for the cause and bearing its logo. The product would be offered with a free foundation membership offer in every package.

The advertisements for the Arthritis Foundation pain relievers falsely claimed that a portion of each purchase price would go toward finding a cure for arthritis, when in fact McNeil was contractually committed to pay $1 million annually for the use of the foundation's name and logo, regardless of sales.

The assistant attorney general of Minnesota got involved and claimed that the advertising violated state consumer laws by misleading consumers into believing that the products themselves, rather than the brand, were "new" medications, when all four product lines already were available to consumers. David Woodard, assistant attorney general said, "If there are going to be tie-ins between for-profit sponsors and non-profit organizations, and a commercial product is sold as a result, the ads about that product have to apply to legal standards. An ad campaign linking a corporation with a non-profit that is recognized by millions of consumers as unbiased help for people who suffer from arthritis undermines public trust."

Again, unfortunately, the media caught wind of the promotion and smelled a scandal. McNeil Consumer Products Co. has settled its suit with the district attorney and has agreed to pay 19 states a total of $2 million to settle allegations that its sponsorship of the Arthritis Foundation misled consumers.

Doing it Right

There are plenty of examples of great national and local cause-related marketing campaigns.

<u>Example One:</u>

On a local level, Special Olympics Northern California partnered with Pacific Bell Wireless for a four-month period, creating a campaign called "Give a little, Get a lot." For a $20 donation to Special Olympics Northern California, the consumer would receive a free wireless phone, a free pizza, and five free video rentals. The package was valued at more than $250.00. The campaign generated more than 100,000 new customers for Pacific Bell Wireless and raised more than $2.1 million for Special Olympics Northern California.

Pacific Bell Wireless dedicated its entire marketing budget during the four-month period to promoting the campaign through television, print and radio ads. Pacific Bell Wireless and Special Olympics created the campaign to focus on the Special Olympics athletes from Northern California who would be attending the World Games that summer. By placing the focus on the cause, it was possible to put together a media tour featuring the athletes. It also gave Special Olympics an opportunity to ask the public for its help in sending these athletes to the games by participating in the promotion.

Within the first month of the campaign, there was so much public awareness from the promotion that Pacific Bell Wireless pulled back on all television advertising. An entirely new demographic of buyers had come forward to support the campaign. Consumers said, "You mean if I write a check to Special Olympics, I get all this?" Customers felt good about their purchase and consequently felt good about Pacific Bell Wireless.

Special Olympics Northern California had the right to approve all collateral material and press releases; to participate in the planning process; and to have a staff member and athlete speak at the employee kick-off. A written contract outlined the campaign and the minimum guarantee, and an accompanying document outlined roles and responsibilities. In addition, Special Olympics trained its staff and created an internal handbook that included a fact sheet, Q & A sheet, and other pertinent information.

The campaign yielded not only the largest contribution the organization had ever received, but also the creation of a new database and public relations exposure. Special Olympics could never have afforded a public relations campaign of the scope this campaign achieved, and the exposure helped every part of Special Olympics program.

<u>Example Two (from the IEG Sponsorship Report)</u>:

In this example, the organization raised money above the rights fees. The Boys & Girls Club partnered with Coca-Cola Co. and created a campaign that used artwork from Boys & Girls Clubs members on 12-packs of soda. Three cents from every purchase was donated to the Boys & Girls Club. The campaign resulted in $500,000 for the cause on top of the rights fee Coke agreed to pay under its 10-year, $60 million deal.

The promotion provided exposure for the cause on 44 million packages last year. "There's no way we could buy that kind of exposure," said Kurt Aschermann, senior vice president of the Boys & Girls Club.

The promotion was simple but effective. The demographics of members of the Boy & Girls Clubs fit perfectly with those of Coca-Cola. Coca-Cola was able to move more product; the promotion helped to expand the reach of Boys & Girls Clubs to more kids. "The nonprofit now serves three million children, up from 1 million a dozen years ago. The number of clubs has increased to 2,300, up from 1,300 and we've just exploded in size," Aschermann said.

Conclusion

Corporate marketers are always looking for new, innovative ways to differentiate their products and get a leg up on the competition. What better way to assist a company than by helping it create an integrated marketing platform that combines its philanthropic, sales, marketing and human resources objectives into one campaign. Only cause-related marketing can do this. Given this tremendous resource that reaches revenue not accessible through traditional fundraising vehicles, it's strongly recommended that cause-related marketing practices become a standard part of your annual campaign.

As with any business plan, there are the do's and don'ts to keep in mind. To summarize, remember the following:

DO

- Make a list of companies that have similar missions and products that would make for a great cause-related marketing campaign.

- Check with your board of directors, friends and network to help secure a meeting with the appropriate person from the corporation's marketing department.

- Be persistent.

- Research your partner thoroughly.

- Create a list of questions for your partner.

- Be up-front about expectations of time, resources and responsibilities.

- Ask for the value of your mark and logo in a rights fee or as a minimum guarantee.

- Ask for the partnership to be drawn up as a contract.

- Make sure to receive a full accounting of all product activity and funds generated.

- Ask for access to the campaign database.

- Always deliver more than you promised.

- Be clear about staff time involved.

DON'T

- Don't enter into an agreement without an up-front rights fee or minimum guarantee.

- Don't undersell your mark and logo.

- Don't allow your partner to use your mark and logo as an endorsement.

- Don't align your organization with a company that has a bad reputation or is not a good fit.

- Don't agree to any promotion that is not in writing.

- Don't allow any collateral materials or press releases to be created without having the right to approve and make changes.

- Don't allow your partner to use your logo as an after-thought. Make sure your logo is prominent in all collateral and advertising.

- Don't sign any contract without going through the proper individuals in your organization, including a review by legal counsel.

You are now geared up with all the appropriate tools to go out and secure your next partner. Remember that you represent your organization and that it is your responsibility to raise funds while always maintaining the integrity of your mission. If you choose to embark on this wonderful field of marketing, patience and persistence will pay off. There are plenty of companies looking for the right partner. Who knows? Your call may be the one they've been waiting for!

Jill F. Osur

Jill Osur is a woman to watch. She is young, dynamic and will be a force in development and nonprofit management in the years to come. She is a tall, beautiful, athletic California blond with a brain and vision. She is the Sr. Vice-President for Marketing and Development for Special Olympics Northern California. Since the program's inception 6 years ago, Jill has taken this organization from a revenue base of zero to over $10 million dollars. Jill is responsible for the Cingular Wireless national partnership, resulting in $40 million dollars over 4 years for Special Olympics.

Before coming to Special Olympics, Jill served as senior vice president of national marketing and sales of The Registry Companies, a national pre-employment screening and resume verification service in Danville, California.

Jill also has extensive experience in special events and political fund raising. She has worked for clients such as Geraldine Ferraro and was the director of advance to Dianne Feinstein during her 1990 bid for Governor of California.

Jill has had a life long love of athletics. She went to University of California at Berkeley on a NCAA Softball scholarship where she received her B.A. in sociology. She continues to volunteer with various sports and social service groups. She is a member of the board of directors of the Contra Costa Jewish Day School and the Catalog for Giving, Bay Area. She has served on the boards of Bear Backers and the Big C Society, both affiliated with her alma mater. She is an active volunteer for Battered Women's Alternative in Contra Costa County. She has been active in Big Brothers/Big Sisters of Oakland since 1991. The University of California at Berkeley awarded her the Most Valuable Player award for personally raising $163,000 for Women's Softball.

Jill lives with her husband Dean and is the mother of three beautiful, lovely children ages 9, 7 and 5.

Jill F. Osur
Sr. Vice President of Marketing & Development
Special Olympics Northern California
3480 Buskirk Avenue, Suite 340, Pleasant Hill, CA 94523
925-944-0594, ext. 209 • Fax 925-944-8803
www.sonc.org
email: jill@sonc.org

CHAPTER 12

Surviving Fundraising on the Internet

Steve Epner

Anyone who has to communicate with others had better be able to do it online. Many people have already made the Internet and e-mail their preferred method for connecting with the world. For many in the new generation, if you are not on the Internet, you do not exist.

But what does the Internet have to do with fund-raising? AT&T said it best with this comment: "It isn't about technology; it's a new dial tone."

Think about the telephone. You do not need a telephone science degree to use one. No one needed to read manuals written in "geek" or had to spend years learning archaic commands.

Watch an eleven-year-old on the Internet, and you'll see that young people are as comfortable online as their elders are on the telephone. The kids have been raised in an electronic, connected world. This is how they communicate with one another.

Writing a book chapter about the Internet carries a high degree of risk. Technology is changing at such a rapid rate that anything written one day may be out-of-date the next.

The concepts and ideas presented in this article represent the best information available at the time of publication. Use the following guidelines as a starting point. Then, as you develop ideas and strategies, review them with a thirteen-year-old to make sure they are current and valid.

Do not try an idea once and then dismiss it forever. In some cases, an idea that doesn't work has failed only because critical mass has yet to be reached. Keep revisiting ideas. As more people become part of the connected community, early failures may become future successes.

So what are the basics? First, you must have a presence on the Internet. There is a limited pool of money and the goal is to get your share. When another organization finds your traditional donor or attracts their attention online, the dollars that might have gone to you in the past may now go elsewhere. Once gone, a donor will be harder to win back.

Every nonprofit must have a domain on the Internet. Getting a domain is neither difficult nor expensive. Registration can be accomplished online. There is a site, www.internic.net, where anyone can research and select names. Each domain ends with a dot (.) and an extension. The ending "dot O R G" (.org) was to have been reserved for nonprofit organizations, but this limitation has not been enforced.

Still, this extension is preferred for charities. Some nonprofits have reserved their names with the "dot com (.com)" extension—designated for businesses—as well to make sure they do not lose anyone who is trying to locate them by browsing on the Internet.

In July 1999, the cost of registering a domain was $70 for two years and then $35 per year after that. In addition, internic (which was started by the National Science Foundation and AT&T) lost its monopoly for name registration. New extensions are to be released. Current information on these matters will be available from any Internet Service Provider (ISP), a local college or university.

So many domain names have been registered already that few three- and four-letter acronyms are still available. Try for yours, but do not be surprised if it has been taken. Then look for names that the public will associate with your cause, disease or group. If multiple names might apply, register them all. Even a half-dozen names will cost only $420 for the first two years. Why let a potential donor miss you when the cost is so low?

Search engines look for domain names, but so do individuals. Many people looking for information will initially skip the search engine and enter a name followed by dot ORG to see what they find. For example, someone trying to find information on lung cancer might try entering www.lungcancer.org to see what might be available.

Select natural names. If you find that the name you want is taken, enter it into your browser and see what pops up. Many names are unused after registration, some are used by "kids", and others were taken by "squatters," hoping to sell them later for a profit. Get in touch with the people who have your name to see whether they will allow you to gain control of it. As charities, your chances of reclaiming a domain name are much better than for-profit corporations.

Once your identity is established, you are ready to proceed. For this discussion, fund-raising is divided into two distinct areas: proactive and reactive. Proactive is the process of "pushing" information to a target audience. It is not much different from bulk mail or blast fax, just faster, cheaper and with a greater reach.

Reactive fund-raising involves, first, the ability to get someone's attention once he or she accidentally or purposefully finds your site. Then you have to take care of the site visitor's needs and ask for help. It is really no different than a potential client's finding your organization by phone or in person and asking for information. You gladly provide the information and include a request for funding.

On the proactive side, an organization's most important asset is its mailing list. For online fund-raising, the list will contain e-mail addresses instead of street addresses. Software is available to track, sort and manage these lists, also known as databases.

"De-dup" computer programs are used to eliminate duplicate names and addresses, just as with standard mailing systems. The lists must be kept up-to-date to maintain their value.

Anyone who sends e-mail can be accused of "spamming" (the electronic equivalent of junk mail). Be careful. All e-mail solicitations or other documents should carry instructions for having a name taken off the list. Requests for removal from a mailing list should be honored.

Many business people today are inundated by unsolicited e-mail, so much so that they have opened multiple e-mail addresses. One address is allowed to get all of the spam that is sent. It is reviewed infrequently and often just deleted.

The other is used for important or business e-mail. This address is carefully guarded to reduce the number of people who might mail to it. Any unwelcome e-mail may elicit a very negative response. Instead of making a friend, you may find you have an enemy who will not only refuse to donate, but will tell friends to stay away as well.

What should you be sending? The jury is still out. A few suggestions follow. Consider doing small group tests to see how each mass e-mail message might work for you. Periodically review message content with your colleagues to learn what is working and what isn't.

Start all e-mail with a quick grabber (not unlike any fundraising letter). But in this case, limit it to one or two sentences. Most regular users of e-mail like brief messages that they can deal with quickly. Long messages are filed for later reading. The only problem is that later rarely arrives. When the backlog becomes too large, the unread messages are just deleted.

Next, give the reader a link to your site for more information. Most of the people you reach with e-mail also have access to the Internet. Having an embedded link makes it easy for them to check you out for more information.

Each campaign should use a different internal page (thus, a different embedded link) to serve as the introduction to new visitors. Your Webmaster or Internet Service Provider will be able to provide counts of how many responses you have by day to any specific area within your site. This will make it easy to measure the success of each mailing. More sophisticated response-measuring tools will allow you to better understand which audiences react best to which letters.

Some solicitations will use surveys and other methods common to standard mail campaigns. The difference with e-mail and the Internet is that the survey can be completed online and results processed in real time (while you wait—no delay). In some cases, you may want to use the survey results to establish an immediate dialogue with a prospect.

For example, in the case of a disease, a survey question might ask whether any relative has the illness. If the answer is yes, the system can immediately ask whether information is needed about the latest research or treatment news. Making it easy to get personal is what this technology is all about. Instead of creating a larger gulf between people, it may allow you to be more helpful to more people in a shorter time.

Once an online dialogue has been established and assistance has been offered, you have probably found a donor and a friend. Help first and then follow up (by e-mail, of course) to see whether the material you sent was of help. It is then that a subtle request for funds to help continue the activities of the organization may be most effective.

Requests for funding should also be spread throughout the Web site. Make them simple, not obnoxious. Wherever you have a page that offers assistance, it is appropriate to request help to be able to continue to provide these services to those in need without regard to their financial ability to pay.

When people arrive at your site, it must be designed to make it easy for someone to find help or be encouraged to donate.

Designing sites is an inexact science. Some Internet users like great amounts of action, sound and information. Others argue for simple and fast. Whichever way you go, there are some basics to consider.

The first is to be consistent with your mission and message. A poorly designed site can trivialize your message. At its worst, it will anger or even antagonize the very people you want to reach.

Consider that most users do not have high-speed access to the Internet. Therefore, the fancy animated cartoon with stereo music that seems so "cool" when viewed at the developer's site becomes a pain in the neck for site visitors having to wait two or three minutes for downloads before they can see anything. Any download that takes longer than about fifteen seconds can seem like forever on the Internet.

When getting started, look for common denominators. Sure, new machines all support high-density graphics (in other words, very high resolution). Just remember that the most common resolution is one step back from technology's latest. Use the lower resolution, and more people will be able to get full value from your efforts. The same is true of colors. Sure, you can get some neat effects working with 256 million colors, but a fast site using less than 32 will look just as good to most viewers. More importantly, even those using older machines will see it properly.

Many people incorrectly refer to the site as a "home page." The home page refers only to the first information retrieved when a site is visited. It may be one or more screens full of information. Length has nothing to do with it.

A Web site is a collection of pages, each of which can be located for viewing from one home page. The information may be open to the public or restricted to select individuals. Some Web sites require preregistration for access; some even charge for the services they provide.

Having a Web site used to mean that a charity had erected a billboard along the information superhighway. As such, the stakeholders hoped that people passing by would notice it and take some action. The problem is that most sites have been built without a good definition of expectations or goals.

So if a Web site is a good idea, and it is part of your overall plan, what separates a good site from a bad one? Five issues make the difference.

First, the site must be fast. We live in an MTV world. If the first page does not "pop" in ten seconds or less, some of your viewers will be gone. The best sites have a short, uncomplicated home page that is brought up quickly. It has limited graphics and provides an introduction or overview of the charity. Then, there are "buttons" or links to other parts of the site by key words.

Once a person is interested in a site, he or she will wait longer for information to load. The goal is to quickly capture interest and then to provide a map that lets interested parties rapidly find the information they want.

Second on the list is to make the site clean. Remember when desktop publishing first came out? Everyone wanted to play. Newsletters were created with seventeen different fonts using six different sizes of type. Each page (sometimes each article) had a different border. Then there was clip art everywhere, with no space unfilled. The document looked like a mess.

Designing a Web site could end up the same. With the latest tools, anyone can design a very sophisticated site. But before opting for something fancy, ask: "What good will all of this animation, flashing lights, moving signs and so on do toward increasing donations?" Most of the time, the answer is: "I don't know."

Hire a good designer to make sure that the site makes the impression you want, that a consistent message is sent, and that the message fits as part of the complete fund-raising program. Stay on top of the "techies" to make sure they do what you want, not what they want on their resumes. This is not a technical project, but a marketing one.

Third, always print out all of the pages on your site on an inexpensive dot-matrix printer to test for legibility. Current research suggests that some 75 percent of all Internet access is from home, not the office. This means that the majority of your potential donors find your site in the evening. If they see something they like, it will be printed to show around or share.

But that carefully crafted page with interlocking colors that produced a three-dimensional feeling on screen may end up looking like a black blob on a standard black-and-white printer. Then all of the time, effort and money spent setting up the site and attracting a prospect will have been wasted.

Next, the site must be regularly updated. Anyone will visit a site once, maybe even twice. But if nothing has changed, they are unlikely to return for a third visit. The best sites have new information added no less than twice a month. Some sites are updated multiple times a day. People want the latest information. Being current with the latest and greatest is an advantage on the Internet.

A nonprofit with a limited budget may need to find volunteers to help keep a site changing. The home page should highlight new information as a service to return visitors.

Finally, the site must be accurate—informationally and grammatically. Nothing will turn off the public faster than a sloppy site. Maintenance of the informational part of a site is not a technical job. Get an English major or a person with public relations training. This is how the world will see you. Do not leave that important image to someone more familiar with bits and bytes than with P's and Q's.

What should you do on the site to encourage donations? The home page should contain a link to a "Getting Involved" information section. In it, all of the options should be explained. Provide a link to an online page where a pledge can be completed, and make it easy to find.

It is wise to be able to accept credit card and debit card donations. These can be validated while a prospect is online. It is the option of choice for more and more donors.

There are other ways to find small, but continuing donations. Ask your donors to go shopping using your site as a "gateway." One good example is Amazon.com, the online bookstore. If a donor buys a book as a result of a link from your site, you will receive a small commission. It is easy for your organization to sign up online and to establish the link from your site.

The rules and methods of Internet shopping will be in constant flux, so check out all of the sites that may be of interest to your donors, clients and stakeholders to see if it is possible to earn money by having an active link from your domain.

Just as important is the ability to measure the effectiveness of your site. Certain tools can be used to measure the length of time spent in each segment of your Web site. This is important to your being able to fine-tune your site for maximum effectiveness. Once you know which themes tend to grab the visitors, you can expand on them. If readership starts to drop, you know the last change is not working.

Take some time to surf to other charity sites. Keep an eye on what others are doing for hints of what is working. No one knows the answers. All we can tell you is that the future generations will communicate and interact on the World Wide Web (or its successor). If you want to continue to be relevant, you must be there.

The Web provides a new way for you to provide many of your traditional services. Support, education, referrals, and even access to care-givers can all be offered online to anyone, anywhere, anytime.

Finally, we must all consider costs. Many "hosting sites" (where Web pages are stored) will provide free or reduced costs if you agree to publicize their service at the bottom of your site. Any charity can afford a basic Web site.

Design services often are available from colleges and universities with computer science and design classes. Students need to create portfolios to show what they can do. Charges can be minimal and the results amazing.

Better yet, the ongoing cost of fund-raising can be reduced. There is no incremental cost for sending e-mail as there is for fax or hard-copy mail. Processing electronic donations is a breeze, and the back office workload is greatly reduced. Plus, the value of being available twenty-four hours a day, seven days a week is hard to measure, but it could be worth a fortune in new donors and volunteers and in terms of helping more people.

The Internet and its connected society are like a train coming right at you. There are only two choices. You can get on the train or you can ignore it, but you cannot stop it. The choice is yours.

Steve Epner

To know Steve Epner, just take a look at his office. Most offices have "work stations," Steve has "play stations." Among his piles of computer literature and family pictures, are magic tricks and toys of every description and type.

His fascination with all that surrounds him is what makes Steve a sought after consultant, speaker and author. He makes technology simple and the simple magical.

Steve has been directing traffic on the information super highway since 1966. Beginning as an operator in a "tab shop" environment, Steve has progressed through the computer age serving in various roles including operations, programming, system development, project management and general management.

As a consultant, Steve helps bring businesses and technology together. Clients learn to effectively utilize their information resources to help them reach the future. Clients have learned to count on Steve's enviable reputation for working with teams to develop business plans that do not end up collecting dust on a shelf. As president of BSW Consulting, Steve is also known for finding ways to use information as a competitive tool.

Steve understands that technology is valuable only if it solves real business problems. By encouraging active involvement from all levels of management and staff, "project teams" take ownership of decisions, diagnose situations, focus on high priority issues, discover unique solutions and manage for success.

Facilitating strategic and tactical planning meetings for both technical and non-technical groups are among Steve's talents. He is an expert who encourages competing views, while preventing a shouting match. Many sessions include training the client organization to manage future meetings. Steve appears at conferences, shows, and meetings across the country. A highly regarded industry expert, Steve is widely published and has provided comment for national business publications including the Wall Street Journal.

Steve is the founder (1976) and past president of the Independent Computer Consultants Association. Steve continues to be active in leading the consulting industry toward goals of professionalism and responsibility to the client community. Steve is a past president of the St. Louis Gateway Chapter of the National Speakers Association.

Steve Epner, CSP
BSW Consulting, Inc.
1050 N. Lindbergh Blvd., St. Louis, MO 63132
314-983-1214 • Fax: 314-983-1329
E-mail: sepner@bswc.com
www.bswc.com

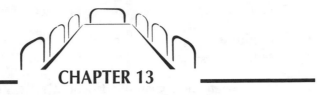

CHAPTER 13

Social Entrepreneurism as a Fundraising Strategy

Peter C. Brinckerhoff

B ecause the subject of this book is fundraising, why a chapter on entrepreneurism? It may surprise you to learn that I think you should regard fund raising, that very interesting and very important board function, as a business, particularly an entrepreneurial one. But, at its core, it is just that. In this chapter, we'll look briefly at what social entrepreneurism is and then apply its tenets to your fundraising efforts. I'll give you some benchmarks of what you should expect as a board member, and some ideas of how to apply the ideas of entrepreneurial fundraising immediately to the benefit of your mission-based organization.

1. What is Social Entrepreneurism?

Social Entrepreneurism. A long, tongue-twister of a term. So, at times throughout this chapter, I'll refer to it by the shorthand SE. But what does it mean? To me the core of social entrepreneurism is good stewardship, and board members like yourself are stewards of your organization. Good stewards don't just rest on their laurels, they try new things, serve people in new ways, are lifelong learners, try to turn their organizations be centers of excellence. Social entrepreneurs have the following characteristics:

- They are constantly looking for new ways to serve their constituencies, and to add value to existing services.

- They are willing to take reasonable risk on behalf of the people that their organization serves.

- They understand the difference between needs and wants.

- They understand that all resource allocations are really stewardship investments.

- They weigh the social and financial return of each of these investments.

- They always keep mission first, but know that without money, there is no mission output.

These are crucial traits for you to mull over as you consider your organizational adaptation to the SE model, at least for fundraising How do you, your staff and fellow board members view risk? As something to avoid, or as something that is part of steady improvement of services to the community? What about services? Are you doing the same old thing you were five years ago, or can you specifically list what the organization did to improve services last week, the week before that, and the week before that? Steady, consistent improvement in services, and the constant adding to the value of those services from the point of view of the people you serve and the people who pay for them is an absolute necessity if you are to become and remain a social entrepreneur.

Budgeting as investment is another concept that entrepreneurs are comfortable with, and another important part of fundraising. When you allocate staff, property, volunteer time, or cash to an issue or a project such as fundraising, it is really an investment in that part of your mission. But is it a good one? Does it give you the best mission return and financial return for the dollar, or are you just doing more of what you have always done? Social entrepreneurs constantly question whether their investment decisions are the best for the community, their constituency and their mission. The question they ask are this: Is this a good investment in both mission and financial outcome? And, even though the answer is yes, they don't stop there. They ask a *second* question: Is there anywhere else we can get a better mission/money return?

This is not to suggest that all your current programs are bad, or not producing the needed return. Undoubtedly you have some excellent, high mission return programs and services But just because you have always done something, does not mean you should continue to do it, particularly if you can no longer do it well in comparison to the rest of the world.

Next, a social entrepreneur knows the difference between needs and wants, and this is a very important realization. For some managers that I have talked to or worked with, it has been a true revelation. Here's the problem: entrepreneurs must be market-sensitive while still being mission-based. To do that, you have to regularly ask your markets (the people you serve, as well as the people who fund you) what they *want*. Now, most of us in the not-for-profit sector are driven by what people *need*, and we are very good at discerning that through observation, interview, testing and the like. We do community *needs* assessments, talk constantly about meeting unmet needs, in short, we're *need* fillers. So, we focus on needs, not wants. The danger is that people seek what they want, not what they need. If we are to add value to our services, we must focus on wants, and never assume we know what they are until we ask. If we give them what we think (or know from our experience) that they need—and force it down their throats, it probably won't be what they want, and then they won't get the needed service.

The most common example of this is a person who needs alcohol or drug rehabilitation. Everyone around this person knows he or she *needs* help, and right now. But they won't seek help until they want it. Put it another way, until the treatment agency can provide services in a way that this person *wants*, their *needs* can't be met. Social entrepreneurs always seek ways to improve services, but by first asking the recipients of those services what they want. This has real impact on fundraising, which we'll cover in a few pages.

Finally, social entrepreneurs always focus on mission outcomes. They remember that the first rule of not-for-profits is *"Mission, Mission, and more Mission!"* But they are more keenly aware than their non-entrepreneurial peers that the second rule is *"No money, no mission!"* and that it is a close second.

2. How Does Social Entrepreneurism Affect Fundraising?

You are probably thinking, "That may be all well and good, but what in the world does all of that have to do with fundraising? Well let's look at each of the characteristics of a social entrepreneur again, but this time through the lens of fundraising.

Social entrepreneurs are willing to take reasonable risk on behalf of the people that their organization serves.

> Let's be frank with each other: fundraising is risky. Why? Because it is so incredibly competitive. As you read the other chapters in this book, you have learned many, many great techniques to improve your organization's fundraising skills. But none of the highly learned and experienced authors of the other chapters in this book gave you the key to unlock the secret of how to make fundraising a sure thing. There is no such key, because there is no such secret. Fundraising is, like any other function of a not-for-profit, a risk. You invest a lot of money, staff time (and thus more money) and volunteer time. The question for you as a board member is this; is this a reasonable risk to take? I believe it is, *if and only if* you develop some core competencies in fundraising, research, write and follow a fundraising plan, and have quantifiable, *realistic* expectations of outcome that turn your fundraising efforts into what the business community would call a *profit center*.

> *Profits* in a not-for-profit?! Does that term make you wince? It shouldn't. Profits are just fine in a 501(c)(3) organization. In fact they are crucial if your organization is to grow, innovate, and find new ways to serve your community. The problem is not that your organization makes money. The problem is how we name our sector: not-for-profit or nonprofit. That labels us with what we are not. I would so much prefer that we called ourselves community service organizations. I digress, but to make a point: while it is essential that your

organization make money most years, I am not contending that every part of what you do, every service, every function, make money. Some parts of what you do will have such high mission value that it is totally appropriate for you to continue doing them, even at a steep financial loss. An example of this would be a soup kitchen, where the service (nutrition) is given away. No income, but high, high mission return.

So some parts of your organization may be what I call *high mission return/low financial return*, while others may be *high mission/high financial return*, and still others *low mission return/high financial return* centers.

And fundraising is one of those. It produces no mission directly, therefore to merit your investment, *it better make money*! That is the only way you can rationalize the commitment of time and money. Only if your fundraising becomes a profit center can it contribute to mission, by donating dollars to the high mission/low or no financial return parts of your organization. The need for the fundraising arm of your organization to make money may seem pitifully obvious to you. I hope so, since I see organizations all the time that invest 500 volunteer hours in planning, advertising and running a chili supper that sells 200 tickets at $5 each, mostly to board, and staff. That's $2 per volunteer hour, and then we have to subtract the costs of the meal, and the staff time involved. And the organization is thrilled, because last year they only sold 175 tickets! Of course, there are events that don't make much money, but are great "networking" or visibility events. But remember not to have just those kind of events—the cost is current, and the payback is way out in the very gray future.

So the social entrepreneurism concept here is to take reasonable risk, but to make money to add to the mission capabilities of the organization.

Social entrepreneurs are constantly looking for new ways to serve their constituencies, and to add value to existing services.

The application of this to fundraising is pretty simple: know who you are trying to appeal to, and find out what they want. All donors give for one or more reasons. Some give for recognition, some to feel good, some because a family member was helped by your agency. Some want publicity, some don't want any.

What are the wants of your donors? And don't tell me you already know what they want. Unless you have just asked them, you don't. So target one part of the fundraising market, become an expert in their wants, and constantly be updating your information on their motivations for giving.

Social entrepreneurs understand that all resource allocations are really stewardship investments.

We are way too focused at board meetings on looking at budgets as a set of just income and expenses. I know, and I acknowledge that, as stewards, you need to maximize your organizational income and control expenses, but we need to go further. As we look at an expense, we need to see not just an outflow of cash, but an investment. Is this the best investment of this money for the organization? Could we get more mission out of another investment? In many cases, we don't have a choice about where to spend certain parts of our money. We get funds from a government, foundation, or United Way, and have to spend it on the services we have contracted to provide. But fundraising is different. Most not-for-profits spend unrestricted funds (these are funds that are not tied to a required service and are often raised through fundraising in previous years) to generate newly donated dollars. Here you can ask the question: is this the best investment for this money? Are we getting the most mission for this investment in the short and long term?

Remember, fundraising is a function that, as a not-for-profit, you *can* do. No one mandates that you *have* to do it. If you really can't do it well, and if it generates a loss of revenue for a number of years, think it through again.

Social entrepreneurs weigh the social and financial return of each of these investments.

I covered this in the first section above, but let me reiterate-you need to get some balance of social and financial returns from your investments. Since fundraising provides no mission return in terms of direct service, it darn well better make some money. While you shouldn't expect to make profits immediately (as in any other new service or new business venture) you should be able to see the light at the end of the tunnel, and the staff should be able to demonstrate through its development business plan, that it is *planning to make money.*

Social entrepreneurs understand the difference between needs and wants.

We all have needs. Food, clothing, shelter, love. We all buy wants. Sometimes we want/buy what we need. Sometimes we want/buy what we don't need. But the fact that wants, not needs rule is a crucial fact of marketing. While for-profits often convince us that we need what we don't want, not-for-profit marketers are tasked with making people want what they do need, so that they can provide services.

In fundraising this equation gets pretty simple: People don't need to give away money. Some want to, but don't want to give it to your organization. So, to be a successful fund raiser, you've got to make enough people want to give your organization enough money to more than cover the costs of asking. What do potential donors want? As I said earlier, you have to ask.

Social entrepreneurs always keep mission first, but know that without money, there is no mission output.

The interesting thing about this factor in the social entrepreneurial applications for fundraising is that so many organizations forget to keep mission first when it comes to fundraising. They will spend any amount of money or time to hold a fundraising event, even if mission suffers in the interim. Try, try, try to avoid that. As you look at your fundraising plans, ask the staff what the impact on service provision will be. Additionally, look at the ways you raise money. Are they mission-sensitive? *Mission first.*

That's the way that social entrepreneurship impacts fundraising. Now let's examine the positive outcomes that the concept has on your organization as a whole.

3. The Benefits to the Organization

We've established that your mission will benefit from adapting to the social entrepreneurism model. How about your organization? Here are some direct benefits to consider.

More Income, and long-term stability.

Applying the SE model results in more income and better long-term stability in *most* not-for-profits. Why? Because it helps the organization develop new methods of service delivery and/or income. It is more likely to result in net income in new programs. And, it helps the organization make better financial and mission choices about expansion efforts. Why doesn't it help *every* not-for-profit make more money? Because, whether you are a for-profit or a not-for-profit, business is risky. As I said earlier, the idea of the business development process is to help *reduce* your risk, not to eliminate it. No plan, no matter how well researched, how brilliantly conceived, guarantees business success. That having been said, your business decisions will be more informed and more likely to succeed using this model, and you will begin to seek income from places you never have previously.

A focus on core competencies and customer satisfaction.

As you begin to apply your business development knowledge to the tasks facing you, you will quickly realize that competence and quality of service are crucial, and that no one cares any more that you are a not-for-profit when they gauge that quality and competence. Hopefully, this enlightenment will spread throughout the organization and help you improve the quality of everything you do. I know from experience that business development training turns people who are ambivalent about investing in quality into true believers in such investments. This focus on quality has a corollary: the realization that the organization must set its sights on constant customer satisfaction, not just customer service. We'll talk about this more at length when we get into marketing issues. But, the key issue here is that organizations that are concerned about satisfaction are concerned about whether that customer got what he or she **wanted** *from the customer's point of view.* Organizations that focus on customer service are focused on what the customer **needs**, *from the service provider's point of view.*

FOR EXAMPLE: You order a pizza delivered to your home from a pizza restaurant who promises delivery in 40 minutes from the time of your call. The pizza comes in 35 minutes. The pizza parlor has just met one of its quality standards which states: "Deliver every pizza in the time promised when the order is placed." But you'll never order from them again. Why? Because the pizza was cold. The delivery person left the insulating bag open while she was driving to your home. She also had her window open to vent her cigarette smoke. Thus, the cold pizza. See the difference. The restaurant measured only what *it* thought was important: speed. *You* were concerned about having edible pizza. Would you have been happy if it had been hot, but not delivered for an hour? Probably not. But a customer satisfaction checklist would include a number of things (on time, hot, polite delivery, etc.) that comes from some research into customer wants.

In businesslike not-for-profit organizations, the idea of customer satisfaction is paramount. It can be for your organization as well.

Better knowledge of who you really work for.

By looking at the organizations and people who interact with your organization, you will discover that you actually work for a bunch more folks that you previously thought. Social entrepreneurism requires that you look at the people you serve, the people who are employed by you, the people who volunteer for you, and the people who pay you all as equal markets, whose wants are to be investigated and met to the utmost degree possible. Put more simply, if you think that your only customer is a person who receives service from you, think again. The knowledge of your entire customer base is often a revelation to the management team and board, and begins the process of understanding why there is so much conflict about resource allocation within an organization that was previously thought to be focused only on its service recipients. And understanding that conflict can help you solve a great deal of it.

4. What Should Our Organization Do Now?

What are the steps that entrepreneurial fund raisers go through? I know that in other chapters of this book, you have had much excellent advice on how to do the various components of fundraising. My take on it is, of course, from the perspective of the social entrepreneur. Here's how I would recommend that your board approach fundraising entrepreneurially. The steps are in the order that they should be taken.

Set your preliminary financial goals for the next three years.

First things first. Since we have already agreed that fundraising does no direct mission in and of itself, you need to start with some desired financial outcomes now. Why? Why don't you just do the business plan and see how much you can reasonably raise? Or hire a consultant to tell you what level the community is willing to give? Because identifying your preliminary goals now helps you attach the money to some mission use. You need to link your fundraising efforts to mission outcomes. It makes it easier to sell the extra work to staff and board, and certainly makes it easier to raise funds. This number will be a start, and will almost certainly be amended after you finish your fundraising business plan, at which point it may go either up or down. I like a three-year horizon as it forces you to think beyond this fiscal and budget year.

Agree on how much are you willing to risk.

Time for an early reality check. Is there a number of dollars, amount of staff or volunteer time, or reduction of mission delivery that your board is not willing to go beyond as an investment in fundraising? There is, I am sure; the question is how to agree on the figure. The earlier you have this discussion the better since, if you go ahead with fundraising, you *will* be investing these things. Make sure that everyone knows that this is a risk, and that everyone is on board for the ride.

Assess and strengthen your core competencies.

What is it you do well in terms of fundraising? Do you have people who are comfortable asking for money? Great! But do they do it *well?* Any experienced fund raiser has legions of stories about enthusiastic volunteer fund raisers who are not inhibited about asking for dollars, but also have a gift for alienating everyone in sight. As Max DePree says in *Leading without Power,* "Don't confuse enthusiasm with competence."

Do you have the capacity to manage large numbers of volunteers on a single event? Or great mailing lists? Or excellent access to local corporations? All these, and many others, are key competencies for certain parts of the fundraising spectrum. Find out which areas you are good at and strengthen them by training your volunteers and staff, and perhaps hiring a full time, professional fund raiser.

And, if you can't identify any competencies, don't start fundraising anyway. Get some training first, and see if you can develop a competence. Imagine how successful someone would be who wanted to start a restaurant, realized that they couldn't cook, but went ahead and opened up the eatery anyway. Why should you be any luckier. Remember, while social entrepreneurs take risks, they know how to take *reasonable* risks. Find your competencies and match them with a particular type of fundraising that most fits.

Identify your target markets.

Once you know what kind of fundraising you can be good at, (direct mail, special events, bequests, charity auctions, etc.) then you can go ahead and figure out who your target markets are. Surprise! The target markets may not all be potential donors! They may well be volunteers who help you put on a large event, or give you access to a corporate or private donor. Identify your markets, and then figure out if you know what they want as donors. Some donors (not many) want a tax break, most want to feel that something useful is being done with their money, and many (but certainly not all) want some sort of recognition. So find out what people want.

Develop a business plan for fundraising.

Now that you know what you're good at, who you are going after, and have some agreement on outcomes and reasonable risk levels, it is time to write a business plan for fundraising. This will be very much like a business plan for any other aspect of your organization; it will include a description of the kind of fundraising you will do, an assessment of your target and secondary markets, a look at your competition, a description of your core competencies, financial projections, and goals and objectives. Make sure your goals and objectives have quantifiable outcomes, and deadlines for completion.

The board should carefully study this plan before going ahead with fundraising, and assure that staff are also on board. Make sure that the mission and the financial outcomes are worth the risk!

5. As a Board Member, What is My Role?

So what should you do personally to help your organization succeed in fundraising? My suggestions are as follows:

Assure that your Fundraising Business Plan is Developed.

> Make sure that your staff and fundraising committee develop a fundraising business plan that looks at fundraising as a business and projects it as a profit center in the next few years. Make sure that the plan focuses the organization on the kinds of fundraising the staff and board can do well. Make sure that it calls for improved fundraising competencies for everyone, board, staff, and other volunteers. And, make sure that the plan is kept up to date, with regular revisions and improvements.

Hold the organization (and yourself) accountable for its implementation.

> You've got the plan, now get it implemented. Your fundraising plan should be discussed at board meetings at least quarterly, with a review of the goals and objectives, how far you are along in each area, where you are ahead of projections, and where you are behind. This report and discussion should not take more than 15-20 minutes at the outside. You have many other things to consider at your board meetings besides just fundraising. But that does not excuse you from a total lack of monitoring the plan. I have found that the more that staff and board review their plan implementation status, the more the plan gets implemented, which should be no surprise to anyone.

> The other part of this task is to hold yourself accountable for your role in fundraising. If you agreed to sell tickets to a fund raiser, do it. If you volunteered to accompany a staff person on a visit to a foundation or corporate donor, make sure the appointment is underlined on your calendar in red-and that you don't try to skip out. A plan is really a contract with the organization. Keep your side of the bargain.

Play a personal role in the organization's fundraising

You were told earlier in this chapter about how competitive fundraising is. There just is no way that your organization is going to compete if your volunteers, particularly your governing volunteers are not involved—personally. This may mean asking for funds directly by phone, letter, email or at some large event. It may mean inviting your 5,000 closest friends to a fundraising dinner or other event. It may mean selling tickets to a chili supper and, possibly, even making the chili! It may mean accompanying staff to crucial meetings with foundations, corporate donors, or individuals who have indicated an interest in leaving a bequest. It certainly means writing the first check yourself. This is really part of your job as a board member. I know that it is one that many, many board members would rather pass on, but it comes with the territory. The more personal involvement you and your fellow board members have, the more successful your fundraising efforts will be.

6. Recap

In this chapter, we've covered the idea that your fundraising efforts should be a profitable business, one that matches your core competencies with the wants of people who donate your money.

We looked at a definition of social entrepreneurism, how it affects your fundraising efforts, a list of what your organization can do now, and some ideas for what you as a board member can do immediately to help.

Raising money is a risk, but one of many that social entrepreneurs are willing to take on behalf of the people that their organization serves. The more you think of fundraising in this light, and the more accountable you hold yourself and your staff to develop good fundraising business plans before you go out and ask for money, the more successful you will be. Good luck!

Peter C. Brinckerhoff

Peter Brinckerhoff is an internationally renowned trainer, author, and consultant to not-for-profit organizations. He brings years of experience in the field to his work, as he is a former board member of local, state, and national not-for-profits and has worked on the staff and as executive director of two regional not-for-profits. Since founding his consulting firm, Corporate Alternatives, in 1982, Mr. Brinckerhoff has helped thousands of organizations become more mission-capable.

Peter has had more than 60 articles published in the not-for-profit press, including *Nonprofit World, Contributions, Strategic Governance, Grantsmanship Center News,* and *Association Management.* He is on the editorial boards of *Strategic Governance* and *Nonprofit Management Review,* and is a regular contributor to the international *Journal of Nonprofit and Voluntary Sector Marketing.*

Peter is the author of four bestselling books on not-for-profit management; *Mission-Based Management* (1994), *Financial Empowerment* (1996), *Mission-Based Marketing* (1997) and *Faith-Based Management (1999)* all published by John Wiley & Sons. Peter's books are used as texts in undergraduate and graduate programs in not-for-profit management at more than 50 colleges and universities. Both *Mission-Based Management* and *Financial Empowerment* won the Terry McAdam Award from the Nonprofit Management Association for "Best New Nonprofit Book of the Year." Peter's next book: *Social Entrepreneurism* is due out in the summer of 2000.

Peter can be contacted at:

Corporate Alternatives, Inc.
2707 West Washington Street, Suite C
Springfield, IL 62702
217-787-6993-voice • 217-787-9316-fax

TOOLS AND TECHNIQUES TO MAKE IT WORK

CHAPTER 14

Create a Fund-Raising Newsletter Program

Elaine Floyd

J ust mail out a newsletter and sit back as the donations pour in. OK, so it's not that easy. Even though it's happened to a few lucky organizations, most effective fund-raising newsletters are part of a total news program. "Oh, that's work," you say. "Yes," I say. But with a model to follow and some time-saving tips to boot, your total news program will bring you closer to the people you serve and closer to the people who provide you the time and monetary resources to serve them.

Effective newsletters are powerful community-building tools. When you share news and stories among a group of people with a common interest or goal, the effect is to "connect" recipients in a way that they feel they are a part of the community. This connection can lead to support and an increase in services.

This chapter will show you how to find and format your best news and stories. To make it easy to refer to (in those moments of newsletter deadlines), much of the information is set up in checklist style. We're going to cover how to find six different types of news and then how to format your news using the NEWS model.

Hang onto your steno pad. Away we go.

Newsletters Invite Action

All newsletters promote specific goals. While customer newsletters strive to boost sales and association newsletters work to increase memberships, most nonprofits use newsletters to increase donations, promote services or solicit volunteer time. In general, effective non-profit newsletters:

- Boost donations.

- Bring in new supporters.

- Attract volunteers and members.

- Bring back lost volunteers and donors.

- Add value to your services.

- Reinforce your specialty.

- Establish expertise and credibility.

- Spur word-of-mouth referrals.

- Inform and educate.

- Win support.

- Publicize your organization to the media.

- Network with industry allies and vendors.

- Unify a "community" of readers.

- Inform the public about new services.

- Acknowledge donors.

But, in order to achieve these goals, newsletters must be read. The newsletters people read contain useful information presented in appropriate and appealing ways. Successful promotional newsletters get people to read not only what interests them, but also what the publisher wants them to read.

> **TIP:** *Show donors that their money is frugally spent. Print your charity newsletter on low-cost paper, send it by fax or broadcast it by e-mail.*

What Makes Good News Content

It's the news element of your newsletter that gets it read. Your newsletter needs a feeling of timeliness—so that your "news" isn't the "olds."

Most effective marketing newsletters include six types of content:

1. **News** — services, causes, events, fund drives, survey results, industry trends, forecasts, news from other publications, and insider tips on what's happening in the organization or community.

2. **People** — profiles of interesting clients, members, donors or employees; success stories; recognition; welcome messages for new volunteers or staff; opinions of what's happening in the industry; predictions of trends; calls for volunteers.

3. **Education** — frequently asked questions and answers, tips, top 10 reasons to support you, book summaries, motivation, editorials, letters, definitions of common terms.

4. **Events** — calendars, reminders, deadlines, RSVPs, reports of successful past events.

5. **Entertainment** — humor, fun, quotes, trivia, cartoons, jokes, amusing anecdotes, unusual news or stories.

6. **Response** — reply cards, action lines at the ends of articles, surveys, RSVP numbers, hours to call.

The following lists of questions, developed for each of the six types of content, may help you develop the news that you have. (Often, you are so close to your organization that you forget what you know that others don't.)

News

Make your organization *the* source of information on the cause you support and the services you provide.

*   What has been the biggest change in the organization's area of interest in the past year? The past decade?

- What changes do you foresee in the next year? In the next decade?

- Do you have any opinions or forecasts from your board that you can publish? What is the "inside" scoop on the hot issues?

- What would go on the organization's "wish list"?

- What are some successes the organization has had recently?

- What needs to be accomplished and how quickly?

- What are legal issues affecting the organization?

- What legal or legislative issues should members write to representatives about?

- What can members do in their daily lives to support the organization or its causes?

- Are you launching a new fund drive? How can readers participate?

- Do you have any research findings or survey results to report? (They can be from other publications as long as you quote the source.)

- How are the issues your organization supports or fights portrayed in popular culture and in the media?

People

People love to read about and see pictures of other people (especially themselves!). People donating their time and money usually do so because they support your cause. But chances are, they support other causes as well. Keep their attention by giving them yours. In this section include profiles, success stories, recognition of volunteers and donors and other messages or letters.

- Who are some people who should be thanked or recognized for contributions, donations, volunteering or work for the organization?

- Tell before-and-after stories of the people you've helped. What service or program were they a part of? What made this a special success story? How can donors support similar programs?

- What are your most immediate needs?

- What are some upcoming volunteer opportunities?

- What are the starting dates and ending dates for volunteer opportunities?

- When is the deadline for responding?

- Do you have an interesting staff member you can profile?

- What are some businesses who support the organization or its causes? Why do they support your organization?

- What keeps members, volunteers and staff motivated?

- List your board members.

- Do you know of any members who've undergone a "conversion"—people who used to be against your cause but changed their minds?

- How can you involve children and teenagers in your organization or its causes?

  TIP: *Be careful not to use pictures of vulnerable populations (for example, hospice patients, abused children or rape victims) without permission.*

Education

Include helpful articles on subjects related to your cause.

- What statistics would be useful for donors and volunteers?

- Print your mission statement in every newsletter.

- What terms, initials or other jargon should readers be familiar with?

- What are the top myths or misconceptions about your organization or area of interest?

- What other publications within your organization or area of interest, such as Web sites, magazines or brochures, should readers know about?

- What products should members support or boycott?

- How are dues and donations spent?

- What are other organizations that members should know about?

Events

List your own events or other upcoming events in your community.

- What events, such as banquets, meetings, demonstrations, protests and press conferences, are coming up?

- What happened at past events such as these?

- What volunteer and funding opportunities are there?

- Where can readers purchase tickets?

Entertainment

People need a break from the day's pressures. Include something fun in every newsletter.

- Tell a tasteful joke or story you've recently heard.

- Include an inspirational quote.

- Include a trivia question.

- Include a cartoon.

Response

Here are some questions that will help you think of how you can build in ways for your readers to respond to your newsletter. (Without them, you'll never be able to answer the question, "Is the newsletter working?")

- Do people need to RSVP for an event you've mentioned in the newsletter?

- If you're asking for a donation, be specific about what you need. Consider putting this in the form of a wish list.

- If asking for monetary donations, provide different levels with incentives for each.

- If asking for volunteers, be specific about the jobs you need done. Make them short-term commitments to entice new volunteers to give you a try.

- Do you have any T-shirts, mugs or caps to give away with donations or volunteer hours? Offer something of value, something that people may want or find interesting.

- Do you have any special reports, white papers, copies of handouts or article reprints that you can offer to readers? Can you offer these by fax on demand?

- Do you have anything left over in your supply closet that you can give to readers as incentives to respond?

- Mention the incentive within the article or action line in the newsletter.

- Repeat the offer in a benefit-oriented, active headline.

- List a deadline for the offer or state "while quantities last."

- Repeat your address, phone and fax (the card will get separated from the rest of the newsletter).

- Provide check boxes to make responding easy.

Once you've collected your top news from the six categories of content, it's time to look at how you're going to put it together in a way that attracts your sponsors, supporters and volunteers. You'll do this by paying careful attention to each step of the N-E-W-S model.

Newsletters Sell With the N-E-W-S Model

Publishing a newsletter taps into your most vital marketing resources—time and money. Before deciding to commit either one, make sure a newsletter will benefit your promotional efforts and generate reader response. One of the factors affecting the benefits gained from newsletter publishing is the degree of "reader interaction" you achieve. If you want your newsletter to arrive safely from the mailbox into your readers' hands, follow this N-E-W-S model.

N is for Name

Your prospects need a basic awareness of your organization before they can support you. Tell them who you are, where to find you, and, in general, what products or services you provide. Keep your name in front of prospects in the hope that they'll remember you.

Most readers enter at the mailing panel—the front door of your newsletter. They glance at the mailing label containing their name, your return address and anything else close by. At this point, your newsletter will unobtrusively remind people of your existence. It can help them recall an upcoming event or a mailing you previously sent. Your name enters your prospects' minds as soon as they glance at the return address.

Every newsletter works as a recognition tool. Although the concept is discouraging to hard-working writers, a large part of your newsletter's promotional value is not the quality of the articles but the cumulative effect of your name in front of your prospects time and again.

Place information that spurs interest in your organization on the mailing panel. Use any of these:

- your organization logo and name

- your phone number

- your Web address

- your e-mail address

- your slogan or mission statement

- a listing of the services you provide

- a highlight of the volunteer of the month

- a message line on the label above the person's name

- a box listing the content of the newsletter

- teasers to encourage recipients to open the newsletter

- the date of your next meeting

- an event calendar or event highlight

- a list of donations needed

- a famous quotation

> TIP: *Avoid printing anything on the outside of the envelope that would violate the privacy of the recipient (for example, Parents of Gays and Lesbians or references to AIDs groups or divorce recovery). Sensitive information is better in an envelope.*

You must convince recipients that the newsletter includes timely information they should read now. Because most people look at the front page, this is a good place for teasers, such as an "Inside this issue" box. Discourage readers from putting the newsletter aside with magazines and other materials they don't have time to read while opening their mail. Place the one thing you want everyone to know here.

> TIP: *The most visible areas of your newsletter are:*
>
> *If the publication is mailed:*
>
> - *the mailing panel*
>
> - *the front page*
>
> - *the back page*
>
> *If the publication is e-mailed:*
>
> - *the subject line*
>
> - *your return address*
>
> - *the area on the screen before scrolling*
>
> *Make sure that you put the messages that you want everyone to see here.*

E is for Enticement

The next thing most readers do is open to the front page and glance at the nameplate area. The nameplate signals the starting place for newsletter content. You must project an image that matches what you're all about. A children's program may look fun; a museum, artsy; a disease recovery or research group, serious. In the initial stages of a decision, your prospects carefully evaluate your organization. Why should they give a donation to you instead of someone else? Prove that you run a credible operation.

Through the nameplate, you can catch readers' interest with:

- a newsletter name explaining the benefits of reading

- a tagline that says your newsletter is written just for them

- a nameplate design telling more about what you do

The name and the tagline come together in the design of the nameplate. The nameplate also sets the tone of your publication— through its typestyle, its size and position, and any other graphic elements, such as logos and company colors.

Example: One charity's newsletter for prospective volunteers and donors is called "Making a Difference." The tagline tells readers the result of their support—"How your time and donations are improving the lives of the homeless."

Once people look at the nameplate, they begin to skim the headlines and illustrations. This gives them a feel for the type of information you're providing. (*Beware*: What they're really doing is looking for an excuse *not* to read the newsletter.)

You have about 15 seconds to grab their attention through:

- intriguing or emotional photographs of people or animals (be careful not to turn readers away with anything too gruesome)

- illustrations or charts that condense your message

- captions under each photo that pull readers into the article or that include your most important message

- cartoons illustrating your promotional message

- concise, easily removed calendars

- headlines telling the benefits of reading an article

- subheads that list your main ideas at a glance

- pull quotes that intrigue readers and highlight important messages

- paper, ink colors, fonts and design that reflect your organization's personality or mission

Because most people glance, then skim, then read, here are a few design tips to draw readers' eyes where you want them to go. Take care not to overuse these tools. Use only one or two per page for maximum effectiveness. When you want an area of your newsletter to be noticed use:

- arrows that point to the type

- graphics in the shape of a circle

- a small amount of reversed (white on black) text

- bold typeface

- unusual photographs

- illustrations that "move" toward articles

When recipients glance through your publication— reading headlines, examining photos and scanning for something eye-catching—they absorb your image. If you've used effective promotional tactics, the reader will learn about the service you offer. If the contents are worthwhile, you have a good chance of getting your reader to read on and maybe even to call you.

> **TIP:** *Through your newsletter name and subtitle, make sure that a reader can tell who you are, whom the newsletter is written for, a benefit to reading it and the subject of the news.*

Creating Great Calendars and Event Announcements

Calendars are the best way to summarize and present information at a glance. The events calendar and announcements are important parts of most newsletters. Here are some things to keep in mind:

- Preview events yet to be scheduled.

- List other events around the community to promote your image as a community-service provider.

- If an event is canceled after the newsletter production is final, cover the announcement with "postponed" instead of "canceled."

- Print the price of the event or note that it's free.

- Mention if reservations are required, and provide the phone number for reservations.

- Place your calendar on a refrigerator-friendly insert or in a visible area, such as the back page near the mailing area.

- Mention your top events in more than one place in the newsletter.

- Give each event a name.

- Highlight the event name rather than the date.

- Incorporate graphics and photos into the calendar design.

- Remind readers to call ahead, as dates and events are subject to change.

W is for the Written Word

Amazing as it may seem, much of your strategic news work is done before readers really *read* your newsletter. Your goal in your articles is to give readers information on why they should support you. Show that you're an expert. Give specific features and reasons why they should choose you over your competitors. Make a marketing presentation.

The graphics and headline techniques described earlier provide readers with "points of entry." Points of entry are places for readers to start gathering more specifics. Provide other options for a reader who may not be interested in the first article. Remember, you have only about 15 seconds to capture a reader.

Most readers are front- and back-page minglers. They scan the pages, searching for a place to stop and "chat." Invite them to join several "conversations" by providing at least three articles on the front page. This is the entry point for 85 percent of readers.

If your newsletter includes longer articles, place these on the inside pages or toward the end (but not on the back page). The back page needs short articles, too. This is the entry point for the other 15 percent of readers.

Use the content of your newsletter to:

- Introduce new capabilities and services.

- Tell your success stories in case histories.

- Recognize top members, donors, or employees.

- Report on trends and statistics.

- Show your involvement through lively editorials.

- Give "how-to" information.

- Provide technical advice in question-and-answer columns.

- Share inside information.

Select and write these articles to reinforce your promotional message to volunteers, supporters and prospects.

TIP: *Let your volunteers and supporters sell for you. Keep a list of comments and ideas you hear as part of the daily operation of your organization. Print the most interesting quotes and comments, as well as letters from clients, supporters or volunteers. Or survey supporters, and ask about their experiences of working with you. Print the results.*

S is for Sell

Once your prospects are ready to act, tell them what to do: "Cast your vote this Tuesday." "Call this toll-free number now." "Return this reply card." "Write your legislator today." "Send $25 to help feed a family of four."

Tell readers what action you want them to take and how to take them. This is done by providing:

- A self-mailing reply card

- A money-saving coupon the respondent clips and returns

- A masthead or announcement telling where to write or call for more information, how to send a letter to the editor or how to submit articles or other content

- Ordering information at the end of an article

- A contest in which readers can send in photographs or suggestions

- A readership survey

- A telephone number to call

- A toll-free number to pledge time or money

- Office hours and directions or a map for people who want to drop by your organization

- Pertinent Web addresses

You'll get several types of responses to your newsletter. Some people just want more information. For those who feel more comfortable writing than calling, provide reply cards and coupons. For those who'd rather call, list your phone number and hours of operation. For those ready to respond now, include a reply form. Encourage people to phone in their reply or send it via fax.

To make your newsletter successful, follow up on all responses. Most of your respondents are going to buy someone's product or support someone's cause soon. Make it yours.

Can you visualize your prospects shouting, "I want to join," "Here's my donation" or "I want more information"?

> **TIP:** *Not every organization has the marketing budget to produce fancy multiple-page newsletters. Even those with larger coffers should test the project on a small scale first before launching the Queen Mary of publications. Publishing on a shoestring is easier than you may think. Try a one- or two-page letter-size or even postcard-size newsletter. This shortened format saves writing and design time and cuts printing costs. Finding sponsors for each newsletter also stretches the budget. Suggest sponsorships in memory of or in honor of a loved one, especially in honor of a birthday or anniversary.*

Repetition, Repetition, Did I Mention Repetition?

To be reasonably sure that people remember your marketing messages, they have to see them seven to ten times within a six-month period. This means that your announcements, appeals and special events must appear in least seven different places. These can be:

- Postcard mailings
- Fax or e-mail reminders
- Signs
- Reminders from staff
- Announcements in the calendar sections of newspapers
- Newsletter previews
- Newsletter calendar items
- News write-ups in newsletters
- Ads placed in your own newsletter
- Reports of past events along with photos
- Repeats of the same news on your Web site
- Reprints of an article placed at your location

TIP: *Send your newsletter to any news editor—for newspapers, radio or TV stations or other newsletters, for example—who may potentially write about your nonprofit.*

TIP: *Use a postcard to ask readers for their e-mail addresses. Explain how e-mail can help you better stay in touch. Tell readers how much money the organization will save by converting from paper to e-mail.*

Finding and Motivating Newsletter Volunteers

Now that you know some of what pulling this newsletter together is going to involve, you may just have one word: volunteers. Finding and keeping good volunteers requires a system for coordinating their efforts. Here's how to make it easy for volunteers to work with you on the newsletter:

- **A View of the Big Picture**. Remember that you're leading your newsletter team. Get everyone excited about the goals of the publication. Show volunteers previous issues and tell them about the positive changes or effects the newsletter has had. Sell volunteers on the success of your newsletter. People like to be involved with successes.

- **Short Commitments**. Many people run from newsletter responsibility because it is a never-ending project. Issue after issue, year after year, this thing is going to be around. That's a huge commitment. Do not ask volunteers to make it.

  Instead, break down jobs you need help with into onetime, easy-in/easy-out agreements. If someone enjoys working with you, he or she will volunteer again or agree to take on a longer-term task.

- **Precise Instructions**. Conscientious writers, reporters and photographers fret over every aspect of their work. Providing them with precise instructions helps avoid rewrites or redos and preserves morale.

  One of the most common problems occurs when contributors submit lengthy articles. The editor either must cut material or run an article that's going to turn away readers. If the editor changes the article, the volunteer may become angry.

Protect volunteer morale by providing length requirements. Provide forms that guide reporters to giving you exactly the information you need. Give written instructions to photographers, artists, printers and desktop publishers. Respect the time of your volunteers.

- **Scheduling**. When you have a schedule, you have a better feel for the amount and kind of help you're going to need, and you can recruit in advance instead of always at the last minute. You'll see the difference in every person involved with the newsletter—from contributors to paid vendors.

  Develop a scheduling form for your newsletter. Give everyone involved a copy. Learn to schedule enough time for each step and stick to the schedule.

- **Training and Assisting**. When you think of the people you respect, they are usually those who have pushed you to new heights—teachers, parents, managers, colleagues, and friends—while also celebrating every success you've made along the way.

  You can offer volunteers the benefit of your expertise—improving their news-writing and publishing skills. Someone may be a wonderful writer but one who writes such long articles that few people are reading them. Such a writer may grumble the first time you insist on a 300-word maximum. But the increase in the number of people who read and comment on the shorter articles will ensure that the writer will thereafter support your policy wholeheartedly.

- **Recognition**. Your recognition of your volunteer's efforts is an important first step. Recognition from readers is probably even more rewarding. When someone submits a reporter form for an article, list a byline "as reported by," as is done in many newspapers and magazines. Motivate and train volunteers to do good work, and people will comment on their efforts.

  Give everyone on your newsletter team extra copies of each newsletter that they can give to their family and friends.

Elaine Floyd

Elaine Floyd is president of EFG, Inc. (formerly Newsletter Resources). Her company provides several useful books for creating newsletters, including:

Quick and Easy Newsletters: a step-by-step system for putting together a newsletter in an afternoon. This newsletter kit includes templates and filler materials for creating newsletters, putting news on postcards, using postcards that link to Web sites, writing e-news that drives Web traffic and composing press releases that attract the news media. It includes organizational forms and worksheets that speed up the implementation of effective news campaigns. The CD can be used along with any Windows publishing program.

Marketing With Newsletters: how to boost sales, add members and raise funds with a printed, faxed, e-mailed or Web site newsletter. See hundreds of strategies and examples for using news as a marketing tool.

The Newsletter Editor's Handbook: a quick-start guide to news writing, interviewing, copyright law, Internet searches and desktop publishing. Jump-start your news-writing skills in an evening.

For more information on these guides, see:
http://www.newsletterinfo.com.

To order, call Paper Direct
(800) 272-7377

or write to:
EFG, Inc.,
2207 South 39th Street
St. Louis, Missouri 63110

CHAPTER 15

Accounting Concepts: Look Ma – No Numbers!

Stanley L. Corfman, CPA

This chapter is about accounting.......

Having stood before a lot of groups, I've found that most people have one of three basic (but not mutually exclusive) reactions to a statement like that: 1) Deep yawns with deliberate glances toward the exit, 2) Deep shudders with furtive glances toward the exit, or 3) Bright-eyed anticipation of the delights to come while searching for a seat up front. I can't hope to turn you into No. 3 if you're not one already (you have to be born that way, I think), but in the limited time we have I hope at least to drag you a little closer.

We'll do this in stages. Let's first talk about how accounting can be helpful—helpful because accounting is a tool, a means to an end. Your certified public accountant (CPA) may try to tell you that it's an end in itself, but she or he is probably a No. 3 and sees everything through her or his green-colored eyeshade. Then I'll describe the tool, the basic concepts and principles that make it work. Then we'll look at how we can use those principles to tell an organization's story. We won't get very complicated, because, believe it or not, the basic principles aren't—complicated, that is.

Why?

This book talks a lot about the fiduciary responsibility of not-for-profit board members. Fiduciary responsibility means that the buck starts and stops with the volunteer board of directors. It is ultimately responsible for making sure that the organization uses its resources to meet its mission, whatever that may be.

Commercial organizations have owners, and owners have a very good, built-in reason to keep a close eye on what their organizations do and how they do it—their pocketbooks. Not-for-profits don't have owners. Their profits (we tend to call them surpluses, when we have them) stay with the organization, so the sharp eye of personal self-interest is missing. Because they are exempt from tax (the not-for-profits, not the directors, doggone it), most state laws make the directors formally responsible for monitoring what their organizations do.

Board members have many tools to accomplish these tasks. The most important are their eyes and ears and their knowledge of the organization. Their decisions need to be passed through the sieve of their own experience and measured against what I like to call the "front page of the Times" (substitute the name of your own hometown paper) test. Anticipating what the court of public opinion might say about your decision is often (but not always) your best barometer. How different things might have been if the directors of United Way of America had wondered in advance how their chief executive's salary, perks, and practices would play out when displayed in the media.

Directors also need to bring to the table a bit of skepticism. A certain amount of tension between a board and its chief executive is healthy and ought to be welcomed by both parties as constructive. If the directors of the Foundation for New Era Philanthropy had remembered "if it looks too good to be true, it probably is," a significant blot on their reputation that made some question all not-for-profits might have been avoided.

But let's get back to accounting. An organization's accounting records can be an invaluable aid in understanding how and where resources are being used, but it's important to remember that "aid" is the right word. As powerful a tool as accounting is, it can only inform decisions. It can provide only one kind of information to be used along with other kinds, especially the ones I've been talking about, to make decisions. It should never be given more weight than it deserves and should always be taken with a large dose of salty common sense. After hearing what "the books" have to say, a director needs to decide whether what she or he is hearing passes the smell test, and if it doesn't, questions must be asked.

Many people—the No. 2s—are needlessly intimidated by accounting. The basic ideas are reasonably simple and don't require math any more complicated than we all learned in sixth or seventh grade. It's really just a matter of mastering some basic definitions and concepts. It's true that like many things, the application of those simple ideas can get a little complicated—that's where your accountants can come in handy. But even those more complicated applications can be understood by applying the same basic ideas. As a director, remember that your accountants (and your chief executive, for that matter) work for you. If you don't understand something, it is your responsibility to ask questions until you do. Part of their job is to help you understand it. Yours is to use that understanding and your judgement to keep your organization doing what it's supposed to. For your part, let's start with:

The Basic Building Blocks

There are five basic building blocks for accounting, and they are divided into two groups: those that measure activity over time (revenue and expense) and those that measure balances at a point in time (assets, liabilities, and net assets). First. I'll describe the blocks, then we'll look at how the blocks work together.

REVENUE

Resources (usually money, but not always) an organization receives. It might be in the form of contributions, ticket sales, fees for services, or any of a huge number of ways not-for-profit organizations fund themselves.

EXPENSE

Resources used by an organization to carry out its mission. Again, usually money, but not always.

ASSETS

Things that can be used in the execution of your operations. The most obvious example is cash, because you can spend it, but there are many others. This list is not exhaustive, but here are some examples to show you how far afield from cash we can get and still meet the essential meaning of an *asset*:

ACCOUNTS OR PLEDGES RECEIVABLE—Money people owe you. Eventually you'll be paid, and you'll receive cash, which can be spent.

PREPAID EXPENSES—Services that you've paid for but haven't used.

INVESTMENTS—Ownership of or loans to other (for-profit) companies or organizations—Treasury bills, commercial paper, stocks, bonds, and the like. A collection of investments by a not-for-profit is usually called an *endowment*.

INVENTORY—Assets held for sale or distribution outside the organization. These don't become expenses until actually distributed. (We'll talk about *matching* and *revenue recognition* a little later.)

FIXED ASSETS/EQUIPMENT—Buildings or equipment that you've built or bought that you'll use for long periods. As these are used up over time, we recognize a non-cash expense called *depreciation*.

SECURITY DEPOSITS—Money left with a landlord or equipment owner that will be returned at the end of a lease.

LIABILITIES

Things owed to others. The most obvious example is bank debt or accounts payable to creditors, but again, there are others:

ACCRUED EXPENSES—Expenses incurred or services received before payment has been made.

DEFERRED REVENUE—Money collected before a service is provided. A good example is tickets sold in advance. Until the performance takes place, you owe your patrons something. (As with inventory, we'll talk about *matching* and *revenue recognition* a little later.)

FUNDS HELD FOR OTHERS—Many not-for-profits receive funds that must be distributed to other people or organizations.

NET ASSETS

When you subtract total liabilities from total assets, *net assets* are left over. If you're a business, we call this *equity* and the owner gets to take it home. Not so coincidentally, an organization builds net assets over time by having more revenue than expense. Not-for-profits used to call this a *fund balance* or *accumulated surplus/deficit.* Now we call it *net assets.* If the revenues are more than the expenses, then net assets are positive. If not, then net assets are negative. This linkage between balances (assets and liabilities) and activity (revenue and expense) is what makes accounting work. Here's how:

THE ACCOUNTING EQUATIONS

There are two basic accounting statements: a *Balance Sheet* and a *Statement of Activities.* A balance sheet details assets and liabilities and provides a financial picture of an organization **at a particular point in time.** A statement of activities provides information on revenues and expense and shows financial activity **over time.** An accounting period (be it a day, month, year, or any other) starts and ends with a balance sheet and a statement of activities gets you from the beginning to the end.

These two statements often go by other names, but they do the same things. A balance sheet is often called a *statement of position.* Other names for an activities statement include *profit and loss, revenue and expense,* and *operating statement.*

Each of the two statements is based upon its own basic accounting equation:

BALANCE SHEET: ASSETS − LIABILITIES = NET ASSETS
This means that when you take what you have (assets), and subtract what you owe (liabilities) you have something left over.

STATEMENT OF ACTIVITIES:
REVENUES − EXPENSES = CHANGE IN NET ASSETS
Notice that you get the same number (net assets) when you subtract the total of what you spent from what you got, starting from the very beginning of time. The difference between revenues and expense in any given statement of activities will equal the change in net assets from that period's beginning to ending balance sheet.

If this is beginning to sound repetitive, then you're beginning to get the picture! These are all different ways of manipulating related information so that you can look at your finances in the way that will be the most useful.

If we string these two equations together, we get:

ASSETS − LIABILITIES = REVENUES − EXPENSES

A Venetian monk developed this basic equation in the 14th century. His name was Pacioli, and he invented what we call *double-entry bookkeeping*. It's called double-entry because in recording any event, **two** entries need be made to keep the equation in balance. If we increase assets by receiving some cash, we have to add the same amount to the other side of the equation (revenue) or subtract a similar amount from the same side by reducing a different asset or increasing a liability. If we don't, then the teeter-totter spills.

If we rearrange the basic equation to take away all of the minus signs (the only reason to rearrange it!), then we get:

ASSETS + EXPENSES = LIABILITIES + REVENUES

Pacioli himself decided to call the entries on the left side debits and on the right side credits, and the **only** reason for that is that in Italian at that time, debit meant left and credit meant right. The real beauty of this system is that because the debits and the credits must always equal, the system checks itself. No computer needed.

Now, in addition to these basic definitions, we have to get used to the ways these pieces fit together:

PRINCIPLES—ACCEPT THEM

Accountants are a principled bunch. In fact, they call the rules that they live by *generally accepted accounting principles,* or GAAP. Generally accepted, because the touchstone of accounting is consistency. This goes back to looking at accounting as a language. We're not going to understand one another if we don't use the same terms in the same way.

ACCRUAL-BASIS ACCOUNTING

This is the most important and most basic complication that accountants throw at their clients. Accrual-basis accounting tries to match income and expense with the *events that lead to them.*

There are other ways to recognize revenue and expense. The simplest, and the one that most of us use in running our households, is the cash basis. Cash-basis accounting means that you record income when you receive and expenses when you pay *money.* That's nice and simple and works very well for households and some simple organizations, but doesn't match up the movement of money with what's really happening and can lead to some really weird (and misleading) results.

Let's say you buy a computer system that you will use for five years. Cash basis says you have a large expense now, yet you get the benefit of this acquisition for five years. Accrual-basis accounting says that you've exchanged one kind of asset (cash) for another (equipment) and that the use of that asset will be recognized as it is used up over the five-year period. That non-cash expense that you recognize in each of the succeeding years is called depreciation.

Accounting is based for the most part on exchanges. I give you this, you give me that. We call these exchanges *transactions.* We recognize revenue and expense when transactions are completed. Now, completing a transaction sounds like a simple concept, but like many things, the time when a transaction is considered complete depends on your point of view. For accounting to have any meaning, we have to agree on when transactions are complete. For instance, do we recognize ticket revenue when a purchaser promises to buy a ticket, when she or he gives us the cash or credit card imprint, when the purchaser pays the credit card company the cash, or when the performance that has been paid for actually takes place? Do we recognize an expense when we buy the materials to make a house, when we finish building the house, at some point in between, or when we finally turn the house over to the people who will live in it?

In the first example, we recognize ticket revenue when the final part of the transaction is complete—when the performance takes place. Any money we receive from patrons in advance is a liability until the performance takes place. (Remember Pacioli's equation?) When we receive cash, we increase a liability, in this case *deferred revenue* to show that we owe our patrons something.

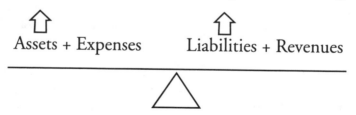

When the performance takes place, we increase revenue and decrease liabilities, and the teeter-totter stays stable.

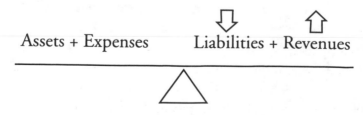

What about the house? When we buy the materials, we exchange one asset (cash) for another (inventory). We might create a special name for this kind of inventory, such as *construction-in-*

progress, but we're still exchanging one asset for another. (Got to keep Pacioli's teeter-totter flat!) When the new owners take possession, we reduce the asset that we've built up (the pun is absolutely deliberate) and recognize an expense. If we sell the house, we match that expense against the revenue that we earned by selling it. If we give the house to those who will live in it, we have only the program expense—there is no revenue.

We've gone over terminology and principles, and even the basic financial statements. This has been brief because it's a short book. There's a lot more we could address given more time, but there are many books out there that can help you with the next steps. Or talk to your accountants. As I said before, they are there so that you *can* ask questions—and you should—that's part of your job as a director. Let's wrap this up by talking about how the result of this process, financial statements, are used, and who uses them.

Whose are they and Who are they for?

The answer to the first question is very simple, but misunderstood by many. Financial statements belong to the organization. The organization should control what goes into them and how they look and, thereby, be responsible for the story they tell. If your organization has an audit or a review done (usually annually) by a certified public accountant, look at the package that comes out of that process. It should contain a set of financial statements, explanatory footnotes, and a report from the accountant to the reader. The ONLY thing in that package that belongs to the accountant is the report. Nothing else. Everything else is YOURS. The buck (again, the pun is deliberate) starts and stops with the board of directors. This is your story to tell.

The annual review or audit is only one of many financial reports that an organization might issue. The annual package is important because it's intended for people **outside** the organization—people who have no control over what goes into it. You give them what they get and a CPA adds her or his report, just so long as what you provide complies with GAAP. But the annual review or audit is not the only kind of financial report, and not necessarily the most important.

Most not-for-profits are exempt from federal (and state) tax because they are covered under section 501(c) of the Internal Revenue Code. These organizations must file an annual informational return (which includes a set of financial statements in a format prescribed by the Internal Revenue Service) with the IRS. It is called Form 990 or, if your organization qualifies, Form 990EZ. Unfortunately, these forms don't get the attention they deserve from the people who are filling them out. In 1993, the Connecticut Attorney General's office examined all 990s submitted to it and found that more than 80% had simple mathematical errors in them—the numbers just didn't add up! In addition, a similar proportion contained responses that simply didn't make sense. These forms were all signed by either the organization's chief staff person or board chair!

Once it is filed, the 990 is a public document. Many watchdog organizations, donors, and even members of the press scrutinize them, and they are now freely available on the Internet. (Check out www.guidestar.org.) By federal law, your organization's last three 990s must be available for public inspection at your offices, and you must make copies available to anyone who asks. (You may charge reasonable copying and mailing costs.) It's amazing that so many organizations pay so little attention to a document that says so much about what they are and how they do what they do!

Other financial statements can take different forms and be targeted at different populations. Financial statements can be used by managers within the organization to monitor different pieces of what's going on. For instance, if your organization runs a thrift shop, a homeless shelter, and a vocational education program, the board will probably (certainly it should) want to see how well each of those activities is working by itself. A separate plan and budget should be in place for each of them. Periodically, the plans should be compared to actual results, and those comparisons monitored (using financial statements developed for that purpose) so that changes can be made in their operations as needed. Your accounting system, whether computerized or not, should facilitate this.

There is no reason why such reports must stop with dollars and cents! They become even more meaningful if nonmonetary performance information is included. What if the financial statements on the homeless shelter I mentioned above also included statistics on how many clients had been served over the period compared to the previous year or month. For the education program, statistics on how many students were in each class would make the dollars and cents much more meaningful. Wouldn't those statements be more useful to management? To the board? These kind of mission-connected statistics can do a lot to put the dollars and cents in their proper perspective.

Donors who give money for specific projects often need (and, quite frankly, deserve) information about how their money is being used. This is another use for statements that look at only a portion of your organization's activities.

The bottom line (again—deliberate) is that understanding the tools and how they work makes them more useful. Understanding the tools makes it easier to ask the important questions and easier to get at the important answers. Understanding the tools means that you wind up spending less time worrying about the tools and more time worrying about what your organization is doing, and that worrying is worth doing.

Stanley L. Corfman, CPA

Stan's work combines two of his great loves: business and the arts. He is now Chief Operating Officer of the bicoastal American Academy of Dramatic Arts, the oldest acting school in the English-speaking world, and serves as Acting Executive Director of the Chamber Dance Project, a new contemporary ballet company he helped start two years ago.

He has worked with not-for-profit organizations for virtually all of his professional life. After graduating from Oberlin Conservatory, he began as a conductor and chorusmaster, but quickly segued from in front of the stage to behind it. After receiving his MBA from Columbia University's Graduate School of Business, he started as an auditor and business consultant at Price Waterhouse and has spent time working as Chief Financial or Chief Operating Officer of the YWCA of the USA, the New York State Theater at Lincoln Center, and the Museum of the City of New York.

Among other publications, he has authored articles for the New York State Society's CPA Journal and contributed chapters to the fifth and sixth editions of Price Waterhouse's Financial and Accounting Guide for Not-for-Profit Organizations. He also speaks regularly on issues affecting not-for-profits.

He has served on the Not-for-Profit and Exempt Organizations Committees of the New York State Society of CPAs, and the AICPA's Not-for-Profit Organizations Committee. He was Chair of that committee when it expired because of work he did on the AICPA's Restructuring Task Force. He now is a member of the AICPA's Expert Panel on Not-for-Profit and Governmental Organizations.

Stan lives with his wife Kim and daughter Abigail and son Danny where they enjoy everything the Big Apple has to offer.

Stanley L. Corfman, CPA – Chief Operating Officer
American Academy of Dramatic Arts
120 Madison Avenue, New York, NY 10016
212 686-9244
scorfman@speakeasy.org

CHAPTER 16

High End Strategic Alliances as Fundraising Opportunities

David Campbell

What kind of title is that? What kind of topic is this? What is a "high end strategic alliance"? Why does this topic matter? Before you turn the page, here my prediction that this issue is larger than most realize and will be critical in future nonprofit management, particularly for fund raisers.

A high end strategic alliance is any alliance involving two or more organizations in which substantial changes in governance are involved. Typical high end alliances are mergers, acquisitions, and parent/subsidiary relationships. They are important because they are increasingly a fact of life in the nonprofit sector. This topic is important, because these kinds of arrangements tend to strike fear in the hearts of board members and fund raising professionals. As strategic alliance consultant and author Tom McLaughlin has written, "fundraising professionals can easily get spooked at the prospect of a merger." (McLaughlin, p. 166). My informal polling of friends who serve on boards or who are development professionals reveals the same trepidation. I hear mergers are a sign of weakness; or, these kinds of arrangements threaten all the fund raising work that has come before. These things can happen, but they don't have to. Regardless, concern about fund raising outcomes is not going to stop the continuing movement toward high end alliances in the nonprofit sector. That's simply a reality, and an important reason why we need to look at these alliances as fund raising opportunities.

Indeed, if you are interested in the fund raising outcomes from these kinds of alliances, you should be ecstatic (all right, at least optimistic) about your organization's pursuit of them. High end alliances *are* fund raising opportunities. Foundation and corporate donors like them; they provide access to new donors and enable organizations to create new fund raising capacity. Read on, and you'll learn why and how.

In this chapter, I will provide an overview of the fund raising issues associated with high end strategic alliances. To consider this topic clearly, first we have to agree on definitions (there seem to be so many!). So, first, I will offer a definition for strategic alliances and identify different types of strategic alliances. Second, I will discuss why nonprofit organizations pursue strategic alliances, and why high end strategic alliances are a current and future trend in the nonprofit sector. I will present examples from several organizations, emphasizing the resource and fund raising issues associated with high end alliances. Third, I will provide a set of assessment questions that you can use in analyzing the potential fund raising impact on your organization of pursuing alliances. Finally, I will discuss strategies to maximize fund raising advantage from high end alliances. I will amplify these strategies with examples from organizations with which I have worked. When you're done reading, I'm hopeful that the connection between strategic alliances and fund raising will be clearer and, if you are involved in fund raising, that you will appreciate more the importance of strategic alliances, and view them as a fund raising opportunity.

I. What are strategic alliances?

As strategic alliances have become more and more popular in the nonprofit sector, there has been increasing confusion regarding the definition of strategic alliance, which means, of course, that I will offer my own. Let's begin with this definition:

A strategic alliance is the coming together of two or more organizations in which at least one partner gives up some independent decision making in order to accomplish an important organizational or community goal. Types of alliances exist along a continuum defined by the amount of independent decision making partners give up. High end alliances are those types at the right on the continuum in which at least one partner gives up significant independent decision making.

There are a couple of things that are important for people to notice in this definition of strategic alliances.

- *Organizations create alliance to accomplish something good for the community and for the organization* (despite persistent fears from some that no good is possible in alliances). There is no reason to pursue an alliance if it does not accomplish something good for the organization or the community. An alliance for the sake of an alliance (for reasons such as "everyone else is doing it") is boring and a waste of scarce nonprofit resources!

- *Strategic alliance is a category, a general, not specific term.* This is a place where a lot of people get stuck and confusion gets started. Strategic alliances represent any coming together that fits the first part of the definition above. There is no generic "strategic alliance." So, if someone tells you they are involved in a strategic alliance, you should be able to ask, "what type?" The answer can never be simply a strategic alliance; instead, it must be a merger, a consortium, a network or some other form of alliance.

- *There are many types of strategic alliances* (in fact creative organizations are developing new types of alliance every year). Alliances range from informal arrangements, such as co-sponsorships, in which two or more organizations work together on a small project, to consolidations, in which three or more organizations come together and form a completely new organization.

II. What are the types of Strategic Alliance?

As I have suggested above, there are many types of strategic alliances. The reason there are a lot of types of alliances is that organizations create alliances for a wide variety of reasons. When organizations come together, they do so to accomplish very specific goals. In each situation, the structure the partners need to accomplish the goals of their alliance differs. In effect, each type of alliance that exists is an answer to the question: What structure will best support the goals of my alliance? The answer to that question should be different for every alliance, although certain types of alliances are common because the goals of many alliances are similar. However, as the goals of alliance partners diversify, it's likely we'll see new types of alliance emerge from creative nonprofit professionals. As alliance expert David LaPiana pointed out in a recent report "variations [of alliance type] are constantly being invented and tested in the field." (LaPiana, p. 6)

As our definition notes, alliances types exist along a continuum. That continuum is defined by the amount of control or independent decision making each type requires partner organizations to give up. A co-sponsorship, at the far left end of the alliance continuum, requires organizations to give up very little, perhaps some decision making authority around a project, but little else. In contrast, mergers, and other high end alliances at the far right of the alliance continuum, require organizations to give up much more control, including as much as the organization's name, its independent status and its governing structure.

I have listed types of alliances below, in order from least control given up to most (essentially left to right on the continuum).

The Strategic Alliance Continuum: From Least to Greatest Control Given Up

- Co-Sponsorship
- Referral Agreement
- Coalition
- Consortium
- Federation
- Network
- Joint Venture
- Back Office Consolidation
- Parent/Subsidiary
- Acquisition
- Divestiture

- Merger
- Consolidation
- Conglomeration

III. Why Do Nonprofit Organizations Pursue Alliances?

When I first began talking with nonprofit professionals about strategic alliances ten years ago, the discussion was predictably reluctant. The suggestion that alliances with other organizations might prove a worthwhile way to accomplish their strategic plan goals was generally unwelcome. And why wouldn't it be? Who really wants to mess with all the control and governance issues associated with strategic alliances? Yet, in recent years that attitude has changed. Why? Perhaps the challenges facing nonprofit organizations have gotten more difficult and nonprofit leaders are recognizing that they may not be solvable without partners. What kinds of problems are driving organizations into alliances?

Lack of resources is the biggest reason organizations are pursuing strategic alliances. And, while resources may come in many different types: staff, buildings, equipment, etc., the bottom line is money. Organizations lack the money they need to accomplish mission. That lack of money is driving organizations to look to partners in alliances to gain the resources they need to accomplish mission.

But the issue is more complicated than simply money–money has never been in abundance in any nonprofit organization, at least not those with which I've worked. It's changes in the nonprofit sector in general that are making nonprofit resource needs all the more dramatic. What are some of those changes?

a. Increased Competition. Think about this fact: one recent nonprofit sector report indicated "as many as 30,000 new tax exempt organizations are created each year in the United States" (LaPiana, 1997, p. 9). Each of those 30,000 needs some money to operate and each of those will compete for its resources with all the other nonprofit organizations already in existence. For example, I know one mid-size urban area in which there are 30 mental health centers, all nonprofit, all seeking financial support from the local community. Ten of those mental health centers are less than twenty years old. Consider this question: How do fund raisers for those organizations raise money from the community when competition is so fierce? How does one organization distinguish itself among donors from the other 29 mental health centers? What would you do?

b. Growing Pressure from Funders. Increasingly, donors to nonprofit organizations have grown uncomfortable with the number of nonprofit organizations and the volume of requests for support they are receiving. As far back as 1981, the Greater New York Fund/United Way published a merger guide, suggesting at least their tacit interest in decreasing the number of nonprofit organizations (Greater New York Fund/United Way, 1981). That pressure has continued. In fact, the New York United Way has created a special fund to encourage alliances between organizations (United Way of New York City, 1997). In my conversations with nonprofit professionals throughout the country, almost all report that their United Way has encouraged organizations to look at alliances, usually high end alliances, like merger. Often, colleagues report United Way dissatisfaction with the number of organizations and concern that limited United Way resources are not being used as efficiently as they could be.

Foundations too are pressuring organizations to consider alliances. David LaPiana, the author of *Beyond Collaboration: Strategic Restructuring of Nonprofit Organizations,* a report commissioned by James Irvine Foundation and published by the National Center for Nonprofit Boards describes this phenomenon: "Frustrated by overlapping programs, service gaps, turf battles and a lack of coordination, funders have begun to encourage, and in some cases to demand, closer collaboration between nonprofit organizations in return for new or continued funding." (Lapiana, p. 3). The proliferation of comparable reports, articles and special issues of journals speaks to this trend[1]. This phenomenon is not new to us, but why is it hap-

---

[1] See also McCambridge & Weis, (1997). *The Rush to Merger,* Mangement Consulting Services, Boston; and Moyers, R. (Ed.). (1997). The Power of mergers: Finding new energy through mission based restructuring [special issue]. *Board Member, 6 (8).*

pening now? The increasing number of nonprofits and the serious limits of foundations to provide meaningful support throughout the sector has forced foundations to look at alternative ways of maximizing their grantmaking effectiveness.

A case example makes this issue even clearer. In 1997, the National Center for Nonprofit Board's journal Boardmember published a special issue on nonprofit mergers. In that issue they describe the merger between two San Francisco AIDS organizations serving different Asian ethnic groups. In an interview, the director of one of the two organizations describes the difficulty he encountered raising foundation dollars: "As we stepped up our efforts to build foundation support...we found that funders were reluctant to commit to one or the other because differences were not distinct enough." (NCNB, p. 11). From the foundation's perspective, there was no reason for the two organizations to exist separately, each with its own management costs. The services they provided were so similar to the foundation that they could not be distinguished. As they were organized, foundation support for either organization was viewed as inefficient, and as such, not a good use of the foundation's limited resources. Indeed, from the foundation's perspective, it was their role to encourage the creation of a new structure that would make it possible for the foundation to make a cost effective grant to support AIDS services in the Asian community in San Francisco.

c. Lack of Organizational Capacity. Many nonprofit organizations lack the administrative capacity to do the things they need to do to accomplish their missions. This is particularly true for newer, small nonprofit organizations. From a fund raiser's perspective, this limitation is often experienced as an organization's inability to hire any fund raising staff. Organizational size simply limits the number of administrative functions that are affordable. Fund raising capacity, even though it brings in money, is often viewed as a luxury that small organizations cannot afford. But, if you can't hire a fund raiser and you need more money to operate your organization, you're faced with a serious dilemma. In effect you can't pursue the strategies you need to pursue to address the financial resource problems you are facing.

It's no different with other kinds of important organizational needs. Small organizations often lack staff with expertise in finance, human resources, information systems or other administrative areas; those functions may be given to the executive director or to a program director to manage. But without staff expertise in these areas, organizations are limited in their ability to address those challenges that require that expertise. I know several small organizations that receive public funding for the services they provide. For that support, those organizations have to prepare complex data and financial reports about how the dollars they receive are used. An executive director whose expertise is in social work or health care or the arts is likely to be ill-equipped to prepare such data or financial reports. Yet, what can they do if they work for small organizations without the money to buy expertise in those areas? Unfortunately, too often those organizations fare poorly. Despite hard work and earnest effort, they are unable to meet the reporting needs of their funders, and as such, make their organization vulnerable to losing their public support.

Strategic Alliances: A Strategy for Addressing Resource Problems

Increased competition, pressure from funders and the lack of sufficient administrative capacity among most nonprofit organizations is really about resources, more precisely, money. Nonprofit organizations don't have the money to create the capacity they need to meet funders demands and accomplish their mission as effectively as they would like to. Pressure from foundations is about the limited dollars they have to create good things in the nonprofit sector. And, increased competition simply means there isn't enough money to go around. So what's a nonprofit organization to do?

Strategic alliances, particularly high end approaches, provide options for nonprofit organizations to generate the resources they need to operate effectively and accomplish their mission. Let's look at how, emphasizing enhanced fund raising opportunities.

Before we proceed, it is important here to distinguish why I believe high end alliances to create greater fund raising opportunities than low end alliances, and as a result, why high end alliances are emphasized in this chapter. (This is not a point on which there is unanimity of opinion.) The greatest sources of fund raising opportunity in alliance building is the pooling of resources and the coordination of strategy. Higher end alliances allow the accumulation of greater total resources than low end alliances because they bring organizations together under new governance structures. Those new governance structures centralize decision making in such a way that effort can be focused on a singular set of fund raising (and other) goals. Those goals are the priorities of the combined partners, and a single board or executive director is accountable for the accomplishment of those goals. Competing interests are eliminated or minimized. In low end alliances, resources are more loosely brought together in one specific area and partners retain significant independent decision making. Coordination of fund raising and other activities is difficult in such circumstances because partners retain their separate interests and make separate decisions on how to proceed in any situation.

High End Strategic Alliances Create and Enhance Fund Raising Capacity.

There are several important ways in which high end strategic alliances can help organizations to improve their ability to fund raise. Here are some of them:

- Increasing the total number of fund raising staff in an organization

- Providing access to donors from other organizations

- Broadening an organization's constituency (and potentially its donor base)

- Combining boards to create greater fund raising expertise and access to new donors

- Creating new, collaborative fund raising events that build on partner strengths

- Increasing community awareness through more wide reaching events

- Bringing new fund raising competencies to an organization, like planned giving or direct mail.

Let's look at some of these benefits in greater detail, along with case examples that demonstrate these advantages.

1. *Increasing the total number of fund raising staff in an organization.*

In many of the high end strategic alliances in which I have been involved (mergers, consolidations, etc), creating an increased capacity to raise funds has been a driving force. Organizations have pursued alliances as a strategy to improve their ability to conduct fund raising. That is, they have realized that in forming an alliance they would be able to build on the individual strengths of each partner and create a critical mass that enabled the whole to fund raise much more effectively than each could individually.

Consider this example involving four human service agencies that recently completed a merger. Each of the four agencies provided critical social services to the community in which they were located. Each had an annual budget under three million dollars. Each had prioritized fund raising in its strategic plan, but no one agency was able to fund a full time development position. One of the organizations had a part-time grant writer, another retained a consultant to help with special events. All other development activities conducted by the four agencies were done by the executive director (almost always doing double duty as the grant writer) or another program staffer. None of the agencies had met their fund raising targets. (Is that any surprise, given their lack of staff?)

How did that merger affect the fund raising capacity of the four organizations? In effect, the merger brought the resources of all four organizations together. It allowed them to reorganize their administration. The leaders of the four organizations asked the following two questions: What are the resources we have? How can we use those resources to create the best possible fund raising operation? The organizations combined the resources that were already being devoted to fund raising in the four separate organizations and enhanced that by applying additional money saved by eliminating duplication (for example, elimination of three of the four executive director positions).

What did the merger and reorganization create as fund raising capacity in the new organization? Because of the new resources available through the merger, the new organization created a development department with two full time staff members, a director and a grant writer, and they retained consultation assistance for special events. Think about the change that brings from what existed in the four predecessor organizations. Here are some of the things they are now able to do that they weren't able to do before the merger:

- prioritize *and accomplish* fund raising goals

- represent fund raising interests at the senior management level in the organization

- hire people with fund raising experise to conduct agency fund raising

The table below presents, dramatically, how the merger from four to one creates capacity and a effective fund raising effort.

Four Separate Independent Organizations	One New Organization
Limited, if any staff. No more than part-time fund raising staff in any one organization.	Two full time fund raising staff. Resources available to retain specialty consultation as needed.
Fund raising prioritized **without** the capacity to achieve stated goals.	Fund raising prioritized **with** capacity to meet established goals.
Fund raising responsibility spread throughout the organization without accountability.	Fund raising responsibility centralized, accountable and represented as part of organizational decision making.
Limited, if any, professional fund raising expertise.	An agency Department with experts.

2. *Introducing new board members with fund raising potential to the organization.*

As many experts in nonprofit governance will tell you (the editor of this book included), fund raising is not only a staff concern, it is also a critical (but assuredly not the only) board function. Trustees have varying capacities to give or generate fund raising dollars to support nonprofit organizations. In fact some organizations, often those that are newer, more grass roots or simply small, do not have trustees who are capable of giving or generating large sums of money in support of the organizations they represent (actually, there are many large nonprofit organizations that face this challenge as well). Yet nonprofit organizations need help from board members to raise money to operate. Strategic alliances are one way organizations can gain access to trustees with more fund raising muscle.

Consider this example. I recently talked with two organizations involved in a merger. Both were long established and respected in the community. One of the organizations faced serious financial challenges. The trustees and the staff shared a strong commitment to mission and the services provided, and pursued merger as a strategy to preserve the work of the agency. The trustees of that agency were among that community's highest profile leaders, including representatives from the communities largest businesses. Because of trustee connections their fund raising efforts had been surprisingly successful (despite the absence of a full time fund raising staff member). Every year they were the beneficiaries of an impressive fund raising event, put on by the auxiliary of the community's highest profile organization.

In search of a merger partner, they approached another social service agency in the community. That agency was financially strong, operated quality services and was considered very well run. Its board was very active and committed but they were not as high profile as the trustees of the other organization. It had a fund raising department that had achieved moderate success. A strategic alliance assessment process determined that the two organizations were compatible and that a merger was in both their interest.

What happened when the organizations merged? The new organization built on the strengths of the two predecessor organizations. Among other things, the merger brought together the committed, active trustees of the financially stronger organization with the equally committed higher profile trustees of the other organization. Those trustee connections ensured that the new organization remained the beneficiary of the high profile fund raising event; and indeed the event became the foundation of their development program. Because of the new organization's fund raising infrastructure, they were able to leverage the event to create other fund raising opportunities for the new organization. In effect, the new organization benefited from the access to high profile trustees and its capacity to take advantage of their trustees strengths with a functioning development department. Those benefits were not available to either organization prior to their merger.

3. *Providing access to donors from other organizations and broadening an organization's constituency (and potentially its donor base)*

Alliances are not only about creating capacity, such as the example above. Alliances are also about enhancing capacity. What's the difference? Enhanced capacity refers to an organization's ability to make improvements in its fund raising efforts. Enhancement is truly a concept for organizations that already have fund raising apparatus, but who see alliances as a way to improve them. There are a variety of ways in which alliances can improve organization's fund raising ability. First, they can provide access to a constituency that an organization wanted to reach but had been unable to. For example, an alliance could bring arts donors together with social service donors, or eastside donors together with westside donors. Second, they can provide access to a particular fund raising competency. An alliance could bring together organizations with different but complementary fund raising skills, one with direct mail, the other with planned giving.

Let's consider an example. I recently worked with two organizations involved in a strategic alliance in which one of the two organizations was essentially being merged into the other. In the for profit world such arrangements are generally considered acquisitions or takeovers. Here, a smaller organization was incorporated by a larger one; the smaller one lost its separate identity, name and independent status. The larger one experienced no material change in its status.

For purposes of this example, let's focus on how this alliance enhanced the fund raising capacity of the larger organization. In this case, the smaller organization was located in a community that was on the outskirts of an expanding metropolitan area. The community was growing and home to many young, affluent families. The larger organization had been working for a long time to raise funds from residents of that community but had been largely unsuccessful. The larger organization attributed its lack of success to not operating programs in that community; it had no constituency there to which donors could respond. Through this alliance, the larger organization acquired a service operation there and access to the smaller organization's donors. Now, as a service provider in the community, the larger organization could claim a constituency. In effect, its previously unsuccessful fund raising argument was strengthened by the acquisition of a service operation in that community. At the same time, the larger organization could conduct much more effective fund raising in that community than the smaller organization because it already had a development department with several staff, technology and expertise. In short, a clear win, win from a fund raising perspective: more charitable dollars raised to support important service activities.

IV. Assessing Fund Raising Needs and Building Alliances to Support Them

I have described why nonprofit organizations pursue strategic alliances and some of the fund raising benefits alliances provide. But, how can a strategic alliance benefit your nonprofit organization and strengthen your ability to generate the funds your organization needs? Of course, before you can answer that question you need to know what your organization's fund raising needs are. It would be best if those needs had already been identified through an organizational strategic planning or annual goal setting process. However, if you have not thought systematically about your fund raising needs, you need to assess and identify them. In this context, they can be considered in terms of how alliances as a strategy can be leveraged to meet those needs.

Improved fund raising capacity is rarely the driver in creating strategic alliances, particularly high end alliances like mergers; rather improved fund raising capacity is usually a desired outcome from strategic alliances. So, the focus in this assessment should not be to use your organization's fund raising needs to drive a strategic alliance, it should be instead what are the organization's most pressing fund raising needs and how can those needs inform and benefit from the creation of a strategic alliance. If we take one of our earlier examples, the need to get donors from a developing affluent community did not drive the creation of that strategic alliance, however it did inform the larger organization's selection of an alliance partner (it tipped the scales in favor of pursuing an alliance with one partner over another).

Fund Raising Needs Assessment

Indicator	Level of Importance (1-5, 1 is most important, 5 is least important)	Needs no Improvement	Needs Some Improvement	Needs Great Improvement
1. The organization consistently meets its annual fund raising targets.				
2. Foundation solicitation effort.				
3. Government grants/contracts effort.				
4. Corporate solicitation effort.				
5. Direct mail campaign.				
6. Major donor campaign.				
7. Planned giving program.				
8. Fund raising events.				
9. The fund raising function is sufficiently staffed to meet the organization's needs.				
10. The organization has the expertise it needs to do fund raising well.				
11. The Board takes an active role in agency fund raising.				
12. Board members have access to resources and donors that enable the organization to succeed at fund raising.				

This assessment tool reviews the major aspects of fund raising operations, from foundation giving to events to planned giving, etc. and the capacities that support those operations. It asks you to consider which of these areas are most important to the fund raising future of your organization and how you are doing in those areas. Those areas of fund raising operations that are high priorities and in need of great improvement are those areas, obviously, about which you need to be most concerned. Areas that are of low priority, that are in need of no improvement should be no concern. Those areas falling in-between need to be assessed by you for their relative importance. Regardless, the outcome of this kind of assessment is a list of priority areas. The identification of these priorities provide useful data that help your organization understand what its needs are as it embarks on alliance planning. In particular, it provides specific information about how the fund raising function can be improved through strategic alliances and what kind of fund raising capacities the organization could look for in that alliance.

A quick example. If you identify that trustee access to donors needs improvement, and that this area is a high priority for the organization, then your strategic alliance efforts need to focus on identifying a partner who can help you achieve that goal. At the same time, if your planned giving effort is low priority and does not need to be improved upon, then selection of an alliance partner with a strong planned giving effort should not be important in your alliance planning.

V. Maximizing Your Fund Raising Advantage in High End Strategic Alliances

Our path to this point has been deliberate and logical. In short, I've taken you up to where you are about to embark on a strategic alliance. All this preparation has been about this question: Now that you're involved in a strategic alliance, how can you use it to maximum fund raising advantage? And, you have to look at it that way. Strategic alliances are fund raising opportunities rich with possibility.

Fund raisers are notoriously ambivalent about alliances. I noted Tom McLaughlin's comment earlier that " fundraising professionals can easily get spooked at the prospect of a merger," but I left out the second part of that quotation. It goes like this, "interestingly, their donors do not always share that reaction." (McLaughlin, p. 166). Indeed, as discussed earlier, funders are demanding that organizations pursue alliances. Donors rarely reject those who follow their advice. If the funding community is concerned about competition and scarce resources and you embark on a strategy to address that concern, your request for support will not go unanswered. At least, more often than not it won't. But let's talk about how we make sure that request is realized.

Five Strategies for Creating Fund Raising Opportunities from High End Alliances

In this concluding section, I will identify five strategies that you can pursue to raise money as a result of your involvement in a high end strategic alliance. Each of the five strategies is predicated on the notion that high end alliances are fund raising opportunities. I believe that maxim because high end alliances are strategies that address the fundamental issues that nonprofit organization stakeholders increasingly articulate, issues that have been touched on in this chapter: the proliferation of nonprofit organizations, competition for scarce resources, organization's inability to meet the requirements of their funders. While the five strategies I discuss are not exhaustive, they are intended to take advantage of the potential synergy between you and your stakeholders in the creation of a high end strategic alliance. No doubt you will be able to develop other effective strategies as long as you view your involvement in a strategic alliance as an opportunity.

1. *Generate Stakeholder Buy-in for Your Alliance.*

Every successful high end alliance in which I have been involved has included early and regular conversation with all participants' key stakeholders. It is important to do this checking in with all types of stakeholders, but for purposes of this chapter, let's emphasize funders. As Peter Brinckerhoff reminds us, our funders, be they foundations, government sources or other major donors are customers of ours (Brinckerhoff, 1996). It would be unwise for an organization to pursue any significant course of action, particularly one which potentially changes an organization's governing structure or core activities without reviewing that possibility and its rationale with major donors. You need to know what they think of this action before you pursue it. For example, will your strategic alliance support the service direction of your government funder? Does it represent the kind of direction your key foundation funders are seeking in the local nonprofit community? If the answer to these questions is no, you need to know that and determine whether your course of action is wisest (you may determine that a strategic alliance is not worth the damage it could cause to important stakeholder relationships). If, however, your stakeholders indicate that they like the idea of the alliance and it represents the direction they wish to pursue, then you have an opportunity to seek financial support for the alliance or associated new directions.

Here's a case example. Imagine this scenario, two organizations consider merging. One provides services to the mentally retarded, the other provides services to the mentally ill. The directors of the two organizations meet with the two county funders for mental health services and services to the mentally retarded. Both embrace the idea, indicating the two county funders might pool their resources to develop integrated services to the mentally ill and mentally retarded. However, when the merger idea is presented to a local foundation that provides a substantial annual grant to the mental health agency (totaling ten percent of its annual budget), there is concern. The foundation indicates that it does not see the two services as compatible and will not support the merger. In fact, the foundation expresses doubt regarding whether it will continue to be able to support the mental health agency if it merges. With the county funders, they have bought in important stakeholders who may increase their support. With the foundation, they know that if they choose to merge they may lose an important ally. Regardless of whether the two organizations choose to pursue the alliance, they can go into it with their eyes open about its fund raising advantages and potential pitfalls.

A corollary to this strategy is *maintain or increase the donations you receive from donors you share in common.* It is not uncommon for organizations to fear that high end alliances could result in a loss of support from donors the allying organizations share. Usually, that means United Way, or it could mean a foundation, corporate or individual donor who supports each of the partners in the alliance.

One way to address that concern is to make sure that these donors shared in common are included as stakeholders you meet with prior to formalizing your alliance. In preparing for those meetings, make the case for maintaining or increasing the funding you receive for them. Among other things, you may identify for them the value added to the community by the alliance between the partners. You may also choose to indicate that the alliance is intended to do the work of the partner organizations more effectively, but that effectiveness does not mean reduced cost. Remind those funders that the success of the alliance requires community support and one measure of that support would be maintained or increased support for the work of the partner organizations. In effect, you should argue that the increased value the alliance brings to the community merits ongoing level or increased financial support for the work of the partners in the alliance. Often, organizations who identify up front the value added by the alliance and the importance of maintaining shared donor contributions are successful. Again, alliances generally reflect stakeholder interests; maintaining funding support should not be a hard sell.

2.   *Fund the Development of the Alliance and its Implementation.*

Here is an opportunity that too many nonprofit leaders don't take advantage of. It is rare to find the foundation experience described in the example above. More often than not all funders, government, foundations and corporations support high end alliances. And, once you've bought them into the idea, get their help in funding it. High end alliances cost money. Here are the kinds of one time costs associated with creating a high end strategic alliance:

- Senior staff time

- Professional consultation

- Legal counsel

- Auditors

- Benefits enhancements as staffs are equalized

- Severance arrangements, etc.

There are similar one time costs associated with alliance implementation:

- Staff and Board retreats

- Training and development

- Computer networking

- New phone systems

- Public Relations

- New stationary

- Planning activities, etc.

Generally, those funds are not budgeted, and generally, non-profit organizations don't try to raise money to defray them. Yet they are used in accomplishing a community good, a community good that helps out your donors. The alliance may reduce the number of organizations, reduce competition and streamline service delivery. There is no reason not to request support for those one time costs from your funders. I have seen more than a few successful high end alliances that have received outside support for the activities associated with the development and implementation of the alliance.

Here's an example. A recent merger in which I was involved began at the urging of a local funder. The two organizations followed a process that resulted in a decision to merge. In the course of that process, the two organizations incurred costs totaling nearly $100,000. Those costs included the professional consultation to facilitate the assessment process, the creation of legal documents associated with the merger, a rigorous financial due diligence by an accounting firm and benefits equalization costs. The two organizations appealed to several local foundations and the local United Way to pay the merger costs. They did. They did for two reasons. First they had all been involved with or made aware of the merger from the start (see strategy one). Second, each agreed the community benefited from the merger and that the benefit was worth the investment of one time costs.

3. Prioritize Fund Raising in the Alliance Formation Process.

Alliance formation always requires a process of some kind between partner organizations. While that process differs in each case, the process to create high end alliances generally includes some form of mutual assessment, due diligence and the development of plans for carrying out the alliance plan. Along the way, there is often a coordinating committee and a whole host of subcommittees. One way to ensure that high end alliances are fund raising opportunities, is to make sure that fund raising issues are talked about in the alliance formation process. What I've seen work, is to build fund raising into both the assessment and implementation parts of the process. Create a fund raising subcommittee that first conducts an assessment of each partner's fund raising efforts and then a plan for implementing fund raising in the alliance. The assessment should include, for both partners, the needs identification we looked at earlier. The implementation should specifically consider strategies for bringing the alliance partner organizations together in ways that build on partner strengths and maximize capacity. If fund raising is a priority in alliance formation, fund raising will be a priority in alliance implementation. You need to think about and prioritize fund raising from the start.

4. Find an Ongoing Role for Constituents.

One of the greatest dangers in high end alliances is losing the volunteers and donors who have been critical to the ongoing life of the alliance partners. I have been involved in several high end alliances involving small, grass roots organizations. These types of organizations are often successful because of the energy and dedication of a sometimes small number of community leaders. While they are often fearful of alliances, they embrace the financial security that comes with them. For them, often that security is assurance that, after the alliance has been completed, they won't have to run the organization any more, or be responsible for raising enough money to keep it afloat. The danger here, and the danger in general with high end alliances, is that once the alliance is consummated, there is no longer any connection to the activists or the whole host of constituents (including former board members and other volunteers) who have worked hard for merging or acquired organizations. Those constituents are a critical fund raising resource. Successful high end alliances develop strategies for keeping them involved.

This issue can be one of the topics addressed by the fund raising subcommittee discussed with the strategy above. One approach that has commonly been pursued has been to create advisory committees comprised of former volunteers. Advisory committees can be program specific or community specific. The advisory committees retain volunteer involvement, continue to focus involvement with the kinds of things that energized volunteers previously (specific services or a commitment to a community) and invests them in the new alliance. That investment in the new organization is critical if the alliance is to build its donor base through the alliance. Fund raisers often see advisory committees as places in which fund raising events can be organized; and these kinds of activities, with some staff support, can often be successful.

5. *Retain Brand Identity (if it's an asset).*

One of the biggest fights that takes place in high end alliances is identity. Everyone likes the idea of the alliance, but no can agree on the name. It's the same as the conversation between expectant parents' about the name for a new baby, but it takes place between boards and it often takes place without parents loving give and take. I will weigh in on only one aspect of that often bitter conversation: Keep brand names that sell with the public. Alliances are about creating a greater whole. Name debates often degenerate into posturing about winners and losers. What matters is what is best for the organizations involved in the alliance and their ability to accomplish mission. If a particular name has high community recognition and brings in money, figure out a way to use it and keep it.

A quick example. An acquisition in which I was involved brought a small organization into one much larger. There was no question throughout that the smaller organization would be subsumed into the larger. But, there was the question of the name. The smaller organization had a local identity, with a catchy name and was well known in its community. The partners in the alliance agreed to keep the small agency name but to identify it as a program of the larger organization. That decision was critical. The larger organization needed the smaller organization's name to have fund raising and service access in the smaller organization's community. A decision to eliminate the name would have rid the community of its most tangible connection to the acquired organization and made the gains strived for in the alliance that much harder to achieve.

VI. Conclusion

I've defined alliances, indicated types and reasons why they are and will be a trend in nonprofit management. I've described the ways in which fund raising efforts are changed by high end alliances and listed strategies you can use in the development of high end alliances in your organization. No doubt, you're convinced, high end alliances *are* fund raising opportunities. I hope you've found the case persuasive.

Bibliography

Brinckerhoff, P. (1996). <u>Financial empowerment: More money for more mission.</u> New York: John Wiley & Sons.

Greater New York Fund/United Way. (1981). <u>Merger: Another path ahead</u>. New York

LaPiana, D. (1997). <u>Beyond collaboration: Strategic restructuring of nonprofit organizations</u>. Washington D.C.: National Center for Nonprofit Boards.

McCambridge, R. & Weis, M. (1997). <u>The Rush to merger</u>. Management Consulting Services: Boston.

McLaughlin, T. (1998). <u>Nonprofit mergers and alliances: A strategic planning guide</u>. New York: John Wiley & Sons.

Moyers, R. (Ed.). (1997). The Power of mergers: Finding new energy through mission based restructuring [special issue]. <u>Board Member, 6</u> (8).

United Way of New York City. (1997). <u>The Strategic alliance fund: Lessons learned year one</u>. New York.

David Campbell

David Campbell is something of a geographic Gypsy. He received his B.A. from Bates College in bucolic Lewiston Maine, his Masters is from Yale in New Haven and his Ph.D. from Case Western Reserve in Cleveland. He now works in New York City at the Community Service Society of New York. When asked which he prefers, rural, urban or suburban, he is just not sure.

This ability to adapt and enjoy different surroundings has made David particularly well suited to his area of expertise: organizational planning for strategic alliances, particularly mergers, consolidations and those types of alliances which result in changed governance structures. He enjoys recommending adaptation techniques to people in organizations experiencing mergers!

David was featured on the Learning Institute for Nonprofit Organization-PBS series where he taught the program "Strategic Alliances: Extending Your Reach." He is also an adjunct faculty member at the School of International and Public Affairs at Columbia University where he teaches nonprofit management in the executive MPA program.

He has written numerous articles including "Managing Mergers and Consolidations," in Skills for Effective Management of Nonprofit Organizations, and has worked with many social service and funding organizations.

When not reforming and reshaping organizations, David enjoys distance running and reading fiction.

David Campbell
Community Service Society of New York
105 East 22nd Street, New York, NY 10010
212-614-5564 • 212 614-9441 Fax
dcampbell@cssny.org

CHAPTER 17

Donor Recognition

Cecile W. Garrett

P roviding recognition and stewardship to donors, first and foremost, is the right thing to do. Giving thanks and recognition for a generous gift keeps us humble, civil and gracious. At the same time, effective donor recognition accomplishes much, much more. For example:

- It allows donors to become more involved with your organization.

- It helps in securing future—and often upgraded—gifts from those same donors.

- It gives you an opportunity to "tell the world" about the gift and the donor.

- It helps reinforce within your organization the importance of positive, healthy donor relations.

- It allows you and the recipients of your organization's services to show appreciation to your benefactors.

- It puts your organization in a positive public light.

Defining terms: Cultivation, recognition and stewardship

This is a good time to make the distinction between cultivation and recognition. We'll define *cultivation* as the process of engaging donors as you seek their gifts. *Recognition* takes place after having received a gift. It's not easy to keep the terms cultivation and recognition separate because fundraising is not a linear process.

Though cultivation is a different stage in the donor development process than recognition, the two go hand-in-hand. There's no avoiding using the two terms together at times.

Be generous with cultivation—reaching out to both current donors and prospects—but reserve recognition for those who truly should be recognized. Perhaps the most common mistake development professionals make in mid-level and upper-level giving is this: They stop providing donor maintenance once a gift is made.

So, too, will we use the terms *stewardship* and *recognition* interchangeably at times. Arguably, stewardship is a much broader term. For an organization, responsible stewardship means keeping positive donor relations, maintaining accountability, providing appropriate recognition and benefits, and engaging in activities aimed at guarding the public trust and remaining true to your organization's mission.

Donor-Centered Recognition from the top down

There must be an understanding within your organization that the entire fund-raising process—of which recognition is part—is a long-term strategy. Everyone must believe in the value of getting to know donors and understanding what motivates them. If the only value placed on a donor is that of their next annual gift, establishing a truly donor-friendly cultivation and recognition program will be difficult. Donors must feel that making a gift to your organization, regardless of the size of their gift, is enjoyable.

This approach requires that you have a sense of your donor's hopes, wishes and dreams. In many cases you may rely on giving history, demographic data and survey results to learn this information. As a contributor becomes a major donor or a candidate for planned giving, this information can be gathered through personal meetings and targeted research.

As donors move up the giving continuum (or pyramid or ladder—whatever term you happen to use), the character of your communications with them should change. So must donor recognition.

Before determining how to give recognition to a *major* donor, remember that, to most donors, being a major donor means two things: It means caring a great deal about the organization they are supporting and it means giving an amount that to them is extraordinary. Most donors, therefore, define major donor by *how they feel when they give*. We need to revisit this truth to understand what type of recognition would be meaningful to them.

Fund-raisers, however, tend to define donors by dollar classes or thresholds relative to their own nonprofit sector's experience of conventional-level giving. Donor recognition is often compartmentalized the same way based on the dollar amount of the gift. If fund-raisers can step away from that mind-set somewhat, they will free up their minds to find creative ways to involve and recognize their donors one-on-one.

Internal readiness

It's neither necessary nor feasible for every person in your organization to be part of the donor *solicitation* process. In fact, not everyone is cut out for that type of interaction but everyone certainly can and should be expected to play a role with donor recognition. The very livelihood of your organization depends on your donors, and everyone must understand how important this constituency is.

As a starting point, make sure that members of your front-line staff recognize and acknowledge your major donors when they call. Similarly, whenever board or staff members enter a donor's place of business, they should acknowledge the donor's support of your organization.

The interesting thing is that once you involve others in the recognition process, they will come to enjoy the role they play. This can be a great strategy with a new board member or president who is not yet comfortable with fund-raising. Newcomers will see how rewarding it can be to personally thank special donors and later, as their confidence builds, they will move up to another step: making a solicitation visit or call.

Identify key players who will play a role in your donor-recognition program—for example, the development staff, board members, chief executive officer, chief financial officer, and Board chair. Remember to include program staff; they are the ones who can really bring the passion that will engage your donors. Select a committee, develop tasks that everyone agrees to, and continue to keep everyone motivated about the roles they play. Keep it top-of-mind for those involved. Send a fax or e-mail to your board weekly to inform them of gifts made and of successes so that they'll know which donors to call or write.

Take your organization's temperature: the big picture

What image do you project to the public and to your individual donors? Examine your program from the outside in—from the eyes of *potential* donors. How are staff or volunteers spending their time? Are their activities allowing donor relations to progress? We all have issues that we must attend to daily, such as reports and budgets, database glitches, or other administrative matters. Unfortunately, donor-related aspects of our daily work too often get the lowest priority.

Next, examine the attitudes of your volunteers and staff. How do they communicate on the phone or at events? How responsive are they to your donors' concerns? This also means taking a critical look at your own attitude. Are you projecting to your staff an attitude that's donor-centered?

You'll also want to have a handle on how your organization is perceived and supported in the community. Do you have a visible board? Are you reflected positively on news reports? Are you getting any feedback—positive or negative—from donors? Do your communication vehicles—fund-raising letters, thank-you letters, newsletters and news releases—reflect your organization in the most positive light? What do the clients who receive your services think of you?

Once you've taken a broad view and have made observations, consider which factors are within your control. Though you probably don't have the power to hand-pick your board or change some of the external or political factors that affect your organization, there are specific things you can do internally to steer your donor-recognition program in the right direction.

Map out every step in your donor-solicitation and -recognition program. Through the use of focus groups, surveys and face-to-face meetings, ask donors where you can improve the process and add value. Learn how easy, or difficult, it is for someone to make a gift to your organization. If your organization is not focusing on its donors and on the experience they have in offering philanthropic support, you can be sure that another organization will.

The thought process for donor recognition should actually begin somewhere in the cultivation process. Keep notes on what types of personal attention the donor would appreciate when a gift has been made. Identify areas where ties between the organization and the donor should be strengthened. Create a plan to provide donor recognition and determine who, specifically, will carry out the action. And, of course, examine what further interests and needs of the donor may be served by another gift.

How does your current recognition program measure up?

Janet Hedrick, CFRE, of the UMass Memorial Health Care Foundation in Worcester, Mass., has developed an acknowledgment and recognition program for numerous organizations in her development career. She believes that revisiting an organization's policy regularly and updating it as needed will help keep it vibrant. She offers the following inventory to help organizations assess their current acknowledgment and recognition program and to identify ways to enhance their programs:

Acknowledgment:

1) Have you handwritten a personal thank-you note to a donor in the past week?

2) Have you called a donor in the past week to say "thank you"?

3)   Has your CEO called a donor in the past week to say "thank you"?

4)   Has your board chairperson called a donor in the past week to say "thank you"?

5)   Does your CEO write personal notes on selected acknowledgment letters?

6)   Do you have a written acknowledgment plan that indicates which donor gets what letter, note, phone call, or newsletter, when and from whom?

7)   Do you review your acknowledgment letters every three to six months? Annually?

8)   Do you have special acknowledgments for the following: gifts of certain magnitudes, first-time donors, reactivated lapsed donors, increased gifts, multiple gifts, and gifts with matching gift forms? (Or do you send the same letter for every type of gift?)

Recognition:

1)   Do you provide gift club recognition for annual giving?

2)   Do you provide gift club recognition for lifetime giving?

3)   Do you provide gift club recognition for bequest intents?

4)   Do you provide gift club recognition for other planned gifts?

5)   Do you have a written policy on recognition?

6)   Does your policy on recognition indicate whether matching gifts, unrestricted or restricted gifts, support for special events, or memorial gifts are included in determining gift level for recognition?

7)   When a donor has given you multiple gifts, are you able to effectively acknowledge that in your initial letter? (Or do you send the same letter, regardless of the type of gift?)

If you think your organization's acknowledgment and recognition program has lost its luster, it's time to ask your donors what types of recognition they'd like to have. Conduct a simple survey or make some personal phone calls to get their input. Later, report back the findings of your survey. It will demonstrate that you took their suggestions to heart and have made changes based on their feedback—that the survey wasn't simply a superficial exercise.

Basic Ways to Thank your Donors

If you want your $50 donors to become $100 donors, then treat them like $100 donors. For the small amount of extra time and expense of a letter versus a postcard acknowledgment, you should send the letter. Develop a plan that will differentiate a multiple gift versus an upgrade gift versus a new gift. (I know of more than one organization that bothers to thank only donors who make gifts above a certain dollar level. Unfortunately, this practice is more common than you might think.)

Thank donors within days of receiving their gift. For certain levels of giving, a personal phone call is warranted. Thanking donors within the same day you receive their gifts is very powerful. The most important correspondence a donor will ever receive from your organization is the first thank-you after the first gift. That's often when donors decide whether to renew their support the next time. Make it count.

It's often said that you should thank donors seven times for each gift. That doesn't mean you need to send seven letters, but it does mean you should find seven opportunities to offer thanks. Before you say that just isn't possible for every single smaller-gift donor, look at the following example offered by Michael J. Rosen, CFRE. Rosen is executive vice president of marketing for The Development Center, a telemarketing consulting firm based in Philadelphia. The example is based on a small gift received as a result of a telephone fund-raising call.

1)   At the end of a phone appeal, the fund-raiser thanks the donor.

2) Before the phone is hung up, the phonathon coordinator thanks the donor.

3) The donor gets a pledge confirmation letter that includes a thank-you.

4) Once the gift is received, a thank-you letter is sent to the donor.

5) The donor is recognized in your annual report, donor honor roll, or other listings.

6) If you invite donors and nondonors to an event (such as a lecture or gala), donors can receive a tailored invitation. (For example, schools might give donors the chance to order basketball tickets before nondonors can order them.)

7) In your next appeal, thank the donor for past support before asking for another gift.

Here are a few recognition ideas to consider, if you're not offering them already:

Send a welcome package to your new contributors. This need not be an expensive mailing. Provide a friendly letter, along with some fact sheets about your organization, a contact name and phone number to call with more information, a low-cost logo item such as a refrigerator magnet or sticker, and some information about volunteering.

Personalize the "look" of the mailings to select donors. You may be saying the same things to your mid-level donor that you're saying to your annual fund donors but you do so in a more personal way: live stamps, letterhead instead of the typical direct-mail paper stock, personal signature instead of a laser-printed one—and with a personal note at the bottom, it's even better.

Segment your new and renewing members. Let your donors— and this includes your new annual fund donors—see that you know and appreciate how long they've been a part of your program.

Hold an annual donor-appreciation event. This doesn't need to be a lavish gala. Instead, it could be a simple meet-and-greet reception or picnic where the donors can meet staff and individuals who benefit directly from your organization's services.

Present or send a gift of appreciation. The gift should not be expensive. It should, however, be an item that will acknowledge the donor's support and identify the organization so that each time the donor uses the gift, it will serve as a reminder of this association.

Institute special donor clubs or destinations. (We'll discuss this idea more fully later in this chapter.)

Include a listing in your annual report. This is an easy and obvious way to recognize donors.

Honor certain donors publicly at a special event. First, be sure the donor is comfortable with this. The more specific you can be in expressing how the donor's contribution has made an impact on your organization, the better.

Send special cards on special occasions. This helps show donors they are thought of and appreciated throughout the year, not just when you want something or they are giving you a gift.

Have others send personalized letters or make phone calls. Depending on the size of the gift (and depending on your organization, anywhere from $50 to $50,000 could constitute a large gift), the director of development, the executive director or the president of the board should write a letter of thanks or make a phone call. This should be done in addition to your organization's initial thank-you letter.

Host a thank-a-thon. It's not feasible to send personal notes to each and every donor, but thank-a-thons that involve both volunteers and staff members at your organization provide a chance to make contact with your donors. Make an event out of it: order pizza one evening, and divvy up the donor calls. Later, you can compare notes on donor response to the calls.

Send a quick postcard. Some public television stations will send a "checking in" postcard a few months after the donor has joined the station to ensure that the member is receiving his monthly program guide, that the mailing label is addressed correctly (correct spelling, etc.), and that his thank-you gift (if one was sent) arrived.

Highlight a donor in your general communications. If you have a regular newsletter, you may already be "spotlighting" volunteers or staff members or even those who are benefiting from your program's services. These are all the right things to do, but how about spotlighting a donor each time, too? Not all donors will feel comfortable with this (so, of course, you would seek their permission first), but many will, and they'll be pleased by the recognition.

Put select donors on special mailing lists. Including donors on certain press release mailings can really give them a sense of getting "inside" information from your organization. If you're a medical-related nonprofit, send donors a medical "alert." If you're a social-service agency or an organization that is active in grass-roots advocacy, you may want to provide your contributors with legislative updates.

Include stewardship reports to appropriate donors. Evaluation is everything. The public and your donors expect more accountability and effectiveness than ever before. Donors expect your organization to produce better results for less cost over time, just like every other organization on the planet. Contributors expect your organization's services to empower your clients or recipients and expand their life control rather than enabling their dependency. Demonstrating how you provide services that are effective, efficient, and relevant will make your stewardship reports very powerful.

Due Diligence: the Basic Acknowledgment Letter

Though acknowledgment isn't considered donor recognition in terms of a "benefit," the way to acknowledge and thank your donors will have a lasting impact on how they feel about making their gift.

What should be included in your basic acknowledgment letter? Remember, you're not just thanking them; you're expressing gratitude for their making a choice to support your cause. Your letter should also convey the importance of your program and tell how you'll use their gift. Of course, every $20 gift isn't designated to a particular need, but you can certainly illustrate in general terms the impact their gift will make. Use facts and results.

A basic "housekeeping" tip: Remember to state the amount of the gift in an acknowledgment. We've all seen lovely, preprinted thank-you cards that organizations use as their standard acknowledgment letter—cards with a moving poem or appropriate quote from a visionary that speaks to the organization's mission. But often those cards fail to state the amount of the gift! Whatever their reasons for making charitable gifts, donors usually also want to deduct them on their tax return. To do so, they'll need to have their full name, gift amount and date listed on the acknowledgment. Don't make them have to call your organization to request it.

Another point to make here is the importance of noting benefits that are not tax-deductible to the donor. Your recognition program may include fabulous benefits, such as an annual appreciation dinner or an engraved silverplate letter opener, that are not tax-deductible. Organizations often wait until the end of the year, when they send donors the required tax substantiation letter, to spell out the value of the benefits they received that year. That certainly meets the requirement of the law, but from a donor stewardship point of view, it's not proactive. Some donors might have declined those benefits had they known the fair market value would be subtracted from the initial amount of their gift. By year-end, it's too late for the donor to decline them. At that point, the donor may be left with a bad taste about the gift that was made.

Have you ever received a call from donors at year-end who say: "But I didn't attend the event. Can I claim the full gift on my taxes?" Unfortunately, they cannot—unless they expressly declined the invitations or returned the tickets to your organization prior to the event.

To avoid this, state the value of any benefits in the initial gift acknowledgment letter and give donors the chance to decline the benefits. (This issue comes up frequently with public television stations, which have honed to a fine art the thank-you packages offered during their on-air pledge drives.) You could simply have a check-off box that says something like this: "I prefer to decline my thank-you gifts so that my full donation can go directly to serving those in need of food and shelter." (Rewrite as needed to reflect your organization's services.)

This may seem impersonal, but the initial acknowledgment needs to be an official document. In six weeks or so, look for another, more personal way to thank your donor. Involve others who have a stake in your organization, such as the chief executive officer, board chair, or volunteer solicitor. University groups have done a good job of involving parties other than staff—students, faculty, board members and scholarship recipients, for example—to thank donors. Think of individuals you serve who have a stake in your organization.

Donor Clubs

Most organizations have a significant group of donors who run the risk of "falling through the cracks" in a donor cultivation and recognition program. They don't give enough money to warrant personal contact, but they give enough to be treated with more personal attention than just receiving your standard appeal letters. A donor club can do many things: provide structure to increase donor involvement, provide a natural progression for upgrades, create a bridge to major giving, and provide your organization with predictable income.

Consultant Tom McCabe, a principal with KMA Companies in Dallas, has helped numerous nonprofit organizations establish donor club programs. He notes that, in annual giving, essentially there are three types of clubs: *annual dollar goal* clubs, *frequency-based* clubs, and those clubs that are *affinity-based*.

First, let's look at annual dollar goal clubs. Donors are asked to join at a certain dollar level, and whatever the entry point—whether it's $50 or $500—a certain set of benefits is usually given in exchange. Generally speaking (though there are exceptions to every rule in fundraising), donors who participate in this type of club are older.

Each threshold should have its own special name to set it apart from other levels and to heighten its visibility. Whatever name you choose—the Gold Circle or the Leadership Society, for example—should have some connection to your organization. What's significant about this type of club is that donors begin to realize that they are part of a like-minded group in their community, and most people fundamentally like to be connected to a group.

By analyzing your donor base, you'll find those who may be good candidates for a donor club. Perhaps their giving over the past twelve months is a step or two below your minimum level, they've been on your file for several years, or their record mentions some special affinity with your organization. You'll want to invite them to join this club. Not all of them will join—though about 8 to 12 percent will. You'll begin to see which donors want to be a part of this type of club and which don't.

You'll probably also find that you have many donors who already fall into this club level on their own. Let them know that, by virtue of their giving threshold, they qualify for this special club. McCabe refers to this as "knighting" them. As he puts it, "Don't just put people in a club by virtue of their giving level and start communicating to them with your special letterhead. Donors will get this mail and wonder what it is. Make sure they know where they are and why they're there." Many will say "no thanks" but, interestingly, 10 to 20 percent will give at that level again anyway. Once again, you've learned something important about whether these individuals want to be recognized in a club or not.

Once they're in a club, you'll want to communicate with them regularly, even monthly. This communication gives you opportunities to thank them and reinforce the commitments they have made. These communication pieces also are great places to ask for feedback. People want to give to institutions where they're really appreciated. This appreciation is exemplified when you ask them for feedback.

Any time you create a new program and you bring in a donor as a "charter member," maintain that recognition of their charter participation throughout that donor's lifetime.

If you're a one-person shop or have no staff, you may be wondering how you can possibly offer a multitiered club program. Keep in mind that your organization's benefits program doesn't need to be elaborate. If a gift club is part of your benefits program, identify four no-cost activities you could host for donors annually. Look at each and assess your organization's capabilities. How much lead time is required for each? Winnow your list down to two or three events. You'll be surprised to see that you can pull off a few activities that won't involve a great deal of time or effort. Then, identify two low-cost, mission-oriented items that may be used as thank-you gifts.

Not all organizations, though, are suited for this type of club program. Multiple donor clubs work very effectively for cultural institutions with a local facility that attracts visitors. Zoos, museums, and theaters, for example, are obvious candidates because these places can offer an array of meaningful benefits. And you'll need to offer different benefits to each level of club to set each level apart from the others.

Some examples of benefits that fit nicely in a club program are free, unlimited admission; discounted admission; guest coupons; newsletter subscriptions; advance notice of shows; free or reserved parking; private receptions, screenings, visits or other "insider" events; and donor listings in playbills or programs. Obviously, this isn't the approach you'd take if your organization is a homeless shelter or hospice program.

This brings us to the next type of club program—the *frequency-based* club. Virtually any nonprofit organization can benefit from instituting this type of giving club. This could be monthly, quarterly or whichever frequency makes the most sense for your organization, though usually these are monthly giving programs. Where do you find the prospects? Those who are already giving you more than one gift per year. Perhaps they're responding to your special appeals. Or if you typically send a reply envelope with your acknowledgment letter (as many organizations do), these are the donors who respond with another gift.

Organizations often find that with their lower-dollar donors, it's a challenge to renew them, as well as to upgrade them. Nonprofits are finding that frequency-based clubs help with these two issues because the best way to get lower-dollar club members to upgrade is to get them to give more gifts rather than a larger one-time gift. And it's not out of the realm of logic for a donor to contribute monthly. (They pay their bills that way; they're used to it.) Typically, younger donors are attracted to this type of program.

Here again, regular monthly communication is key. This communication should be a combination of a soft solicitation and regular information about your program. If you mail to them on a frequent basis, you'll dramatically increase your fulfillment rates (three to four times the normal rate of fulfillment). Often, donors don't fulfill what they had committed to; many actually give an average of seven to eight times a year. Still, it's a substantial upgrade from where they'd been, and they're remaining with your organization. Most important, you're beginning a relationship with them that can grow.

Special affinity-based clubs are often offshoots of a larger donor group. Individuals join around a theme or interest that resonates with them. Many public television stations offer program- or genre-related clubs for donors. They'll offer family memberships or kids club memberships that include program-related benefits, such as "Arthur" stickers or "Sesame Street" balloons, or, for the parents, educational materials to supplement the lessons taught in the broadcasts of certain programs. Another example is with WMVS, the public television station in Milwaukee, which broadcasts "Outdoor Wisconsin," a popular local television series. For several years, the organization has had in place the Outdoor Wisconsin Club, an offshoot of the regular membership "club" at the station. The Outdoor Wisconsin Club, which boasts 2,100 members, is not labor-intensive to administer by any means. Benefits include advance notice for ticket sales to the annual Outdoor Wisconsin banquet (a successful fund-raising event the station has been holding since before the club was initiated) and a quarterly newsletter about upcoming program episodes and related interests. (Most of the newsletter's content is written by the show's host.)

This same type of affinity club can be instituted with mid-level and major donors. Members of affinity groups share a common ethnic, cultural, age, professional, lifestyle or community interest. For example, when the University of Virginia Law School launched a capital campaign to renovate its new Law Grounds and Withers Hall Lobby, major gifts director Laurel Alexander saw a terrific opportunity to form an affinity group—female graduates of the law school.

This was a group that previously had not been identified and targeted for major gifts cultivation nearly to the degree that the male alumni had. With the renovation, there was a new opportunity for these individuals to be recognized publicly. A special plaque in the main lobby provided the perfect vehicle for giving new visibility to this group—as individuals and as a group. These 200 women donors, many of whom had never given anything to the University of Virginia Law School, made four- and five-figure gifts and paved the way for future giving from the law school's current 40 percent women student population. Significant inroads now have also been made with the law school's African-American alumni who had never been approached as major gifts prospects.

In the major gifts arena, the donor club concept also lends itself nicely to *legacy* and *campaign* donor clubs. These types of clubs, more specialized than the more common types we've described above, are often one time gift clubs that offer very special recognition to a select group of donors. More and more, these special clubs are being incorporated into institutions' fund-raising programs.

Matching gifts credit

Many employers see the value of financially supporting select nonprofit organizations in their communities and encourage their employees to do so. Often, these companies will provide a greater incentive by matching individual gifts. Nonprofits often debate whether or not to include the *employer's* portion of the gift toward the donor's qualifying for a certain club level. IRS regulations prohibit an organization from offering "hard" credit to the donor for the employer's share. A separate gift acknowledgment should be issued to both the donor and to the employer for the amounts each has contributed respectively.

There is nothing prohibiting an organization from offering "soft" credit to the donor, however, for the combined amount of the gift. Many organizations still prefer to give donors credit only for their individual portion, feeling that to do otherwise places those donors at an unfair advantage over donors who don't happen to work for an employer that offers a matching-gifts program.

Another way of looking at this, though, is that, had it not been for the donor's initiative, the nonprofit wouldn't have received the matching portion from the employer in the first place. From this point of view, why not give the donor credit? I am reminded of an alumnus from a prestigious northern university who, for years, enjoyed being a part of his alma mater's $1,000+ alumni club. This gentleman was in his early thirties, and his employer matched his $500 gift, which enabled him to qualify for this particular giving club. (This university's matching-gift policy was to give the donor full credit for the gift.) After three years, the alumnus switched employers and no longer had the benefit of an employer matching-gift program. He then had to increase his own giving to continue being recognized in that club, which is exactly what he did. The university had done such a good job with its recognition and benefits program that it had created a destination that he, frankly, didn't want to leave.

Another example involved a classmate of mine. Our own alma mater mistakenly "placed" her into the "Century Club" for $100+ annual alumni givers. She'd given only $40. She got lots of nice communication from the university, a lovely brass bookmark denoting her participation in the program, and an invitation to a special luncheon during homecoming weekend. It took her awhile to realize that she was actually in the club by mistake! But she liked being part of the group and has remained there since. Though we don't advocate giving recognition where it's not warranted, care should also be taken not to be unreasonably stingy when rewarding donors for their involvement with your organization.

As stated before, one of the goals of providing these types of clubs is to get donors to upgrade. But not all of them will move up. Some will remain comfortable with the level at which they've been giving for years. That's o.k. too. They've remained with your organization and are worthy of continued recognition. And, of course, with a well-defined donor club program, you have many other donors who are demonstrating potential for giving more substantial gifts!

Gender Sensitivity in your Recognition Efforts

Women have always made their mark in philanthropy. What's evolved somewhat over the years is their giving style and their feelings about recognition.

Women who are part of the generation influenced by the Great Depression and by World War II (birth years 1910 to 1930) often give anonymously or in another's name. The recognition they value often is simply a personal thanks. Many women born between the years 1931 and 1945 were part of another cultural phenomenon. These women were influenced by such things as Betty Friedan's revolutionary book, *The Feminine Mystique*. Many a woman of this era essentially "reinvented" herself. This type of woman was wary of money and power.

The baby-boom generation of women (born between 1946 and 1964) gives to causes that can serve as a catalyst for change. These women are more comfortable with money and power. They make their own decisions, including philanthropic ones. They are more comfortable with public recognition of their gifts.

This is just a brief illustration of how varied the groups within your donor base view donor recognition and philanthropy in general. The key is to recognize these differences and to continually evaluate your different donor bases to ensure that your recognition program remains vital and meaningful to both men and women of all ages and generations.

To ensure that you maintain gender sensitivity in your recognition program, review your record-keeping methods and gift coding. Make sure you know which partner in a marriage is the constituent. Who made the decision to give? How does that donor wish to be acknowledged? If need be, send a reply card that asks the donor how to credit and acknowledge the gift. Ensure that your database can code correctly and that spouses can be credited differently should they wish to be.

It's also good practice to research and publicize past gifts from women. This can help cultivate new donors by providing role models. It also reinforces the value your organization places on recognizing gifts from women and increases pride among more recent female donors for having made a recent gift to your institution.

Donor Motivations and the "Seven Faces of Philanthropy"

In examining what kind of recognition would be meaningful for your donor, it's helpful to know what motivated them to make the gift in the first place. It's often been said that for both donors and volunteers, the single greatest motivation is the perceived opportunity to make a difference. To demonstrate sincerely to the donor how their gift directly saves a life or enriches a person's quality of life (or whatever their gift enables your organization to do) is a form of recognition that's unmatched by anything else.

Having said that, there has certainly been a vast array of research conducted to further assess philanthropic trends and donor motivations. Among such research is an interesting theory based on research by Russ Alan Price and Karen Maru File (*The Seven Faces of Philanthropy: A New Approach to Cultivating Major Donors*, 1994, Jossey-Bass). Their research asserts that there are seven basic subcultures of donors, with respect to their motivations for giving.

First, there is the *communitarian*. This donor usually has roots in the community and believes that the stronger the overall community, the stronger their own personal and professional success will be. This individual has high trust in organizations and tends to serve on boards. This donor desires periodic feedback and appreciates attention and public recognition of gifts.

The *devout* donor feels that "doing good is God's will" and that the more you have, the more you should give. This donor does not particularly like public recognition and thinks donations should be recognized equally.

Next, there's the *investor*, who believes that "doing good is good business." This individual believes that philanthropy is a *business relationship*. This donor looks for a measurable return on investment and gives only after a careful investigation of chosen organizations. Tax avoidance is a high motivator for giving. The investor chooses charities that are run like a business; he demands accountability.

There is also the *repayer*, who gives as a response to a life-changing experience. The two primary groups to which repayers give are health and education. Their giving is for highly emotional reasons. The repayer wants to know how the gift is going to benefit the organization, although this type of donor tends to have low involvement and does not seek a lot of attention.

Next comes the *dynast*. This donor feels that "doing good is a family tradition." Dynasts won't necessarily give to the same causes as their parents; their giving is shaped by generational events that they're exposed to. The dynast seeks minimal recognition and attention. This donor will pay attention to the core mission of the institutions he or she considers supporting. Dynasts want to know that your organization truly is doing what it set out to do and that you aren't just "chasing the dollars." They're looking for new, creative ways to use their philanthropy and tend not to give to traditional organizations.

Then, there is the *socialite*, the donor who feels that "doing good is fun." The socialite donor is motivated by the creativity of event planning and sees philanthropy as a *social* exchange. Don't honor socialites by putting their name on a plaque in your building. They would rather be honored in front of their social network.

An *altruist*, by contrast, is a genuinely selfless donor who is very internally driven. Altruists often focus their giving on social issues. This donor type is closest to the devout, though has more of a humanistic philanthropic face. Altruists are not easily influenced by others. This donor seeks no formal recognition and, in fact, is often anonymous. Altruists give to a broad range of charities and, therefore, don't generally feel the need to get heavily involved with any.

This is an oversimplified description of the seven different philanthropic faces, of course, but yet another illustration of why it's important to understand the different motivations of donors before determining appropriate recognition for them. Price and File's book is worth the investment.

Remember the Four I's

A donor cultivation model to which development officers often refer states *Identification + Interest + Involvement = Investment*. For donor recognition, we continue that mind-set, but here we've changed the first *I* to *informed*.

Informed

Never underestimate how crucial it is to keep your donors informed. Information builds interest and commitment. Special events, newsletters, and other special, personal mailings that keep donors up-to-date on the good work of your organization are useful tools. Once you make it part of your plan, it'll become automatic. You'll also find it to be rewarding and fun when you get feedback from donors on the items you've communicated with them about.

Interested

Their questions, comments and suggestions are big signs of *interest*. Don't say to yourself, "We've already received their gift and now they want to run the organization." Their comments deserve to be heard and responded to. In fact, you could uncover information that can help you raise more money and communicate with other donors.

Involved

Find ways to remind donors that they are a part of your organization. Ask the donor who's particularly enthusiastic about your program to make a presentation on behalf of your causes. This is a powerful recognition tool in itself. It again allows you to tell the public about the donor's involvement. I recently served as a committee co-chair for a fundraising event, where we were seeking involvement from area retailers. We requested ten minutes time for a presentation at a monthly local merchants meeting. The development director and I agreed that, as the volunteer, I should be the one to make the presentation. Next time, once the event is more established, we'll have a participating retailer actually make the "ask" since peer solicitation is even more powerful. Here, our involving the donor gets them more invested.

Invite donors to visit your office to see the facilities or to join in a celebration. If you're manning a booth at a community event, write notes to tell donors where you'll be and invite them to stop by and say hello.

Public television stations often invite certain segments of donors to serve as on-air phone volunteers on a special night during televised pledge drives. Then, the on-air talent that evening will announce over the air: "This evening, some special supporters from our Leadership Circle are in the studio." This gives the station the chance to involve the donors and give them a "behind-the-scenes" experience, allows the station to honor the donors publicly over the air, and it promotes to the viewing public that there is this special club. Sometimes the donors themselves will serve as on-air talent.

If you keep them *informed*, *interested*, and *involved*, you'll find that they'll stay *invested* in your organization and your program.

Personal, One-on-One Recognition

If there's one truth about successful development officers, it's that they can be resourceful and creative when it comes to giving unique donor recognition. Fund-raisers realize the value of looking beyond the traditional ways of acknowledging and recognizing a donor's special contribution. Here are a few fun examples:

- As part of its capital campaign, a food bank in Oregon sold "bricks" but not in the conventional way. The organization had a colorful mural of a "Main Street" scene that showed indications of the food bank's many activities—from produce stands to food rescue to restaurants that donate food. The mural incorporates into its design actual building windows. The lead donor on the campaign was a single mother with two daughters. The three of them are regular volunteers in the food rescue kitchen. They were a bit shy about getting recognition of their gift, so the organization worked them into the mural by painting on the window "Marion, Kate and Cama's Kitchen."

- A philanthropist in Texas, whose surname was Seay (pronounced "see") gave a local high school the money for a new tennis center. When the team qualified for the state tournament, team members had shirts printed that read "Seay you in Austin," had their picture taken in them, sent the photo to the local weekly newspaper to be published, and sent the donor a copy.

- A gentleman in Missouri gave a significant gift to his alma mater's athletic center and had the building named for him. He was a distinguished sort who was rather famous for the bow ties he always wore. Before a big basketball game, all of the players came out wearing bow ties and lined up to "salute" him in the stands.

- An East Coast food bank got an outdoor advertising company to donate a billboard on a main highway to publicly thank a lead donor.

- The top donor to a local symphony orchestra in Oregon was greeted one Saturday morning with a concert serenade on his front lawn.

- One fund-raiser in Massachusetts likes to send a single red rose to her older women donors who are living alone. (Sometimes a quiet, simple gesture can mean a great deal.)

Perhaps these examples will inspire you to find special ways to give your donors the recognition they deserve. Special recognition can also inspire others to contribute in the future.

Ted R. Grossnickle, president of Johnson, Grossnickle and Associates in Franklin, Ind., has counseled numerous nonprofits on the nuances of building an effective major gifts program. He sums up the importance of donor stewardship and recognition in this way: "We deal on a daily basis with what I would call the technical aspects of good stewardship—prompt gift acknowledgment, appropriate donor recognition, and accurate and timely reporting on the use of gifts. But while we're busy following the letter of the law we often become too busy to consider the spirit of the law—that is, the philosophic underpinnings of good stewardship that must inform our practice as fund-raising professionals if our organizations are to grow and flourish in the long run."

Special thanks for their assistance with this chapter go to:

* My colleagues at the Public Broadcasting Service, Alexandria, Va., and member public television stations around the country.

* Women's Philanthropy Institute, Madison, Wis.

* Janet Hedrick, CFRE, UMass Memorial Health Care Foundation, Worcester, Mass.

* Michael J. Rosen, CFRE, The Development Center, Philadelphia, Pa.

* Tom McCabe, KMA Companies, Dallas, Texas.

* Ted R. Grossnickle, Johnson, Grossnickle and Associates, Franklin, Ind.

* Shelley Winship, University of Oregon, Eugene, Ore.

* Rhonda Talley McClung, Midwestern State University, Wichita Falls, Texas

Cecile W. Garrett (Cele)

Cele W. Garrett spent 10 years with the Public Broadcasting Service (PBS), where she served as Assistant Director of Individual Giving. She left PBS in 2001 to focus on her freelance copy writing business. (But she quickly realized that you can never really "leave" public broadcasting once it's in your blood, so she consults and writes for public television and radio stations much of the time!)

In recent years, Cele has served as a member of the DMA Nonprofit Federation's Postal Issues committee and has been coeditor of the Development Director's Letter, a monthly national newsletter for nonprofit development officers. She serves on the advisory board of the Klippel-Trenaunay Foundation and is an active volunteer with the Northern Virginia AIDS ministry.

Cele is a graduate of the University of North Carolina at Greensboro and has earned an Editing and Publications certificate from Georgetown University.

Some of Cele's favorite pastimes include tennis, antiquing, cooking and reading. Most days, though, you'll find her playing "Chutes and Ladders" with 5 year old Holly or chasing down two-year-old Cole. She lives in Arlington, Virginia with husband Scott and her two young kids.

Cecile W. Garrett
610 Melrose Street, Alexandria, VA 22302
phone: 703/931-7127 • fax: 707/516-2389
E-mail: celegarret@earthlink.net

Other Books from the Nonprofit Pros

by Peter Brinckerhoff:

Social Entrepreneurship, John Wiley & Sons, New York, 2000

Faith-Based Management, John Wiley & Sons, New York, 1999

Mission Based Marketing, John Wiley & Sons, New York, 1997

Financial Empowermen, John Wiley & Sons, New York, 1996
McAdam Award Winner

Mission-Based Management, John Wiley & Sons, New York, 1994
McAdam Award Winner

by Elaine Floyd:

Quick and Easy Newsletters, Newsletter Resources, 1998

Marketing With Newsletters, Newsletter Resources, 1997

Newsletter Editor's Handbook, Newsletter Resources, 1997

by Carol Weisman:

Build a Better Board in 30 Days: A Practical Guide for Busy Trustees, F.E. Robbins and Sons Press, 1998

Secrets of Successful Boards: The Best from the Nonprofit Pros, F.E. Robbins and Sons Press, 1998 (contains chapters by Steve Epner, David LaGreca, Mike Schroeder, Terrie Temkin, Ph.D., and Carol Weisman and others)

A Corporate Employers Guide to Nonprofit Board Service The National Center for Nonprofit Boards, 1996

Give the Gift of

MORE MONEY

For Your Mission

For Your Fellow Board Members,

Staff, Volunteers, Friends and Colleagues

**Check your
local bookstore**

**Contact any of the
nonprofit pros**

or order here

SECRETS OF
SUCCESSFUL
FUNDRAISING
The Best From The
Non-Profit Pros

	Qty	Each	Amount
Secrets of Successful Fundraising		$25.00	
Please add $4 shipping per book		S/H	
Allow 15 days for delivery.		**TOTAL**	
Canadian orders must be accompanied by a postal money order in U.S. funds.			

Name _____

Organization _____

Address _____

City _____ State _____ Zip _____

Phone _____ Email _____

■ Charge my credit card   ■ Payment enclosed

☐ **VISA** ☐ **MasterCard** | Card No. / / / / / / / / / / / / / / / /

☐ Check Money Order   Exp. date _____ Signature _____

Please make your check payable to BOARD BUILDERS

MAIL TO:
BOARD BUILDERS
48 GRANADA WAY
ST. LOUIS, MO 63124

Credit card orders...CALL:
888 500-1777

Fax order form to:
314 991-0202

Email us at:
Carol@boardbuilders.com

Visit us on the web at:
www.boardbuilders.com